AN ARCHAEOLOGICAL AUTOBIOGRAPHY

Frontispiece: The author addressing members of the Prehistoric Society at Belas Knap long barrow, Glos., September 1979. Photo: Alan Saville.

AN
ARCHAEOLOGICAL
AUTOBIOGRAPHY

L.V. GRINSELL

ALAN SUTTON
1989

ALAN SUTTON PUBLISHING
BRUNSWICK ROAD · GLOUCESTER · UK

ALAN SUTTON PUBLISHING INC
WOLFEBORO · NEW HAMPSHIRE · USA

First published 1989

Copyright © L.V. Grinsell 1989

British Library Cataloguing in Publication Data
Grinsell, L.V. (Leslie Valentine 1907–)
An archaeological autobiography.
1. Archaeology – Biographies
I. Title
930.1′092′4

ISBN 0–86299–658–9

Library of Congress Cataloging in Publication Data
Applied for

Typsetting and origination by
Alan Sutton Publishing Limited.
Printed in Great Britain.

CONTENTS

List of Illustrations   vii

Chapter 1
Childhood and Adolescence   1

Chapter 2
Barrow surveys in Sussex, Surrey and Wessex 1927–1941   4

Chapter 3
White Horse Hill and Surroundings   10

Chapter 4
An Egyptian Interlude   14

Chapter 5
Victoria County History of Wiltshire, I (i)   22

Chapter 6
The Museum Curator   26
    British Archaeology and Numismatics   26
    Egyptology   30
    Mediterranean Archaeology   32
    Ethnography   33

Chapter 7
Extra-mural Activities   35
    London   35
    Bristol   37
    Youth Hostel Archaeology Weekends   38
    Lectures at Universities, Public Schools and Elsewhere   41

Chapter 8
General studies on Wessex, Exmoor and the Cotswolds   44

Chapter 9
Regional Barrow Surveys Completed and Updated   46

Chapter 10
International Prehistoric Congresses   51

Chapter 11
Out with the Prehistorians   55

Chapter 12
Out with the Cambrians   65

Chapter 13
County and Local Archaeological Societies   70

Chapter 14
Folklore and the Folklore Society   74

Chapter 15
Mediterranean Holidays: 1   79

Chapter 16
Mediterranean and Other Holidays: 2   88

Chapter 17
Related topics   93
    Excavation   93
    The Kivik cairn, Scania   93
    The Cerne Giant and Other Hill-figures   94
    Archaeology in Literature and Fiction   94
    Christianization of Prehistoric Sites   95
    Preparation of Archaeological Reports   96
    The Lunatic Fringe and its Borders   96

Chapter 18
Music and Other Things   98
    Music   98
    Appreciation of the Countryside   100
    Running   100

Treasurerships and other posts   103

Honours and Tributes received   107

Excursus: Among my books   109

Glossary   111

Bibliography   115
  i   Books and papers   115
  ii Reviews   121
  iii Obituaries   123
  iv Ephemera   123

Indexes

Archaeological Sites   126

Personal names   131

List of Illustrations

Frontispiece: The author addressing members of the Prehistoric Society at Belas Knap long barrow, Glos., September 1979. Photo: Alan Saville.

1. The author with plasticine model, January 1919.

2. 'The barrow hunter's dream.' Sketch by Stuart Piggott to L.V.G., c.1931.

3. 'Grinsellbirds' to indicate the essential features of a rare type of round barrow, 1934.

4. L.V.G., 1938 and 1943.

5. Outing of Middle East (Photographic) Interpretation Unit to Saqqara, V.E. Day, 1945. Photo: L.V. Grinsell.

6. Styles of north point used in *The Archaeology of Wessex* (1958).

7. The author in stone-lined grave of round barrow in Langridge Wood, West Somerset (WITHYCOMBE 4). Photo: Anthony Locke.

8. Sketches by Peter Orlando Hutchinson (1810–97).

9. County barrow surveys 1932–1989 by L.V.G.

10. The author at porthole-entrance dolmen, Montplé, Minorca, spring 1980. Photo: José Mascaro Pasarius.

11. Plans of the giant of Cerne Abbas from 1764 onwards.

12. A Christianized dolmen at Carnac, Brittany.

13. The author receiving an Honorary M.A. degree from Bristol University, 1971. Photo: Bristol Evening Post.

14. The author receiving presentation to mark 50th anniversary of publication of *Ancient Burial-Mounds of England*, at Prehistoric Society conference April 1986. Photo: Clive Gamble.

15. The author receiving 80th birthday presentation of specially bound copy of *The Bristol Mint*, February 1987. Photo: Bristol United Press.

16. The author in front of Wayland's Smithy long barrow, Oxon.

Acknowledgement

The author is grateful to Mr Nicholas Thomas for reading an earlier draft and making suggestions some of which have been adopted.

Chapter 1

Childhood and Adolescence

'I like Mary, but I like chocolates better'.

When I was about six and before the First World War, I was taken to a party and somehow managed to find my way down to the kitchen where I met the domestic servant, named Mary. After a little while my father came down to fetch me and asked, 'Which do you like best: Mary or chocolates?'. I replied as quoted above. That is among my earliest recollections.

According to my birth certificate, I was born on 14 February 1907 at 47 Farrer Road, Hornsey, North London, and my father told me that this event occurred about 8.30 a.m. My father was Arthur John Grinsell, silversmiths' manager; and my mother Janet Christine Grinsell (née Tabor). My father was the only son of Thomas Bywater Grinsell, who died at The Haven, St Bernard's Road, Olton, Birmingham, about 1917. His father was John Grinsell, founder of John Grinsell & Sons Ltd., silver and cut glass merchants, of Birmingham.

In 1878 my paternal grandfather acquired 28 Linden Grove, Nunhead, south-east London, where my father was doubtless born on 1 March 1879. By 19 September 1894, when he entered Dulwich College as a day-boy, the family had moved to Holmehurst, Half Moon Lane, Southwark, within a few minutes' walk of the College. He left the College, where his record appears to have been undistinguished, in April 1898 (Dulwich College Register, 1926, student no. 4555). My father had two sisters both of whom died unmarried.

My mother was one of ten children most of whom married and produced their own families. I had an elder brother John, two years my senior, who died in 1986. A spaniel named Jockey and two cats, a black one and a tabby, completed our family.

About 1913 I was sent to my first school: Priory College in Priory Road, Hornsey, the headmaster of which was a Mr Bates. Soon afterwards the Great War started, and I have a clear recollection of the swarms of Belgian refugees who poured into North London as elsewhere. Inevitably some of our male teachers were called up and replaced by females.

As is well known, during Christmas 1914 there was a truce even at the Front. My parents were friendly with a German named Loeffler who was, I believe, the inventor of Sanatogen; and they invited him to spend Christmas Day with us. He brought with him a box of tin soldiers (or more probably two boxes of them) and gave them to my brother and me for Christmas. Without knowing that he was a German, after thanking him I remarked, 'Now we shall be able to beat the Germans!' I wondered why it was that my remark provoked a smile from those present.

I have one or two other recollections of the First World War. The loss of Lord

Kitchener on H.M.S. Hampshire on 5 June 1916 cast such a gloom over everybody that it almost seemed that the war was as good as lost. I was playing with a schoolfriend in the garden of our home in North London one Saturday morning when we saw some puffs in the sky, which my friend correctly interpreted as our anti-aircraft defences firing at enemy planes approaching London. After 71 years I cannot remember the date. According to *The Times Diary and Index of the War*, it should have been either 7 July or 29 September 1917.

Early in 1918, when the Zeppelin raids over London were becoming increasingly disturbing, my brother and I were sent to St John's College Hurstpierpoint, in Sussex, for greater safety. My brother went there in January and I followed a few weeks later. I was placed in the Shield House, presided over by Rev. P.R. Browne, a kindly and easy-going person whose style seemed to be reflected by the behaviour of the boys under his care. I was extremely happy there. The dormitory overlooked Wolstonbury Hill on the Sussex Downs, crowned with an undated earthwork. One Sunday Rev. Browne took a group of us up to Wolstonbury Hill (known to all the Hurst boys as Danny from the house beneath it), and during the walk he told us that it was crowned with a 'Roman camp'. His knowledge of archaeology was not in advance of his time. I found the dormitory rather too near the hill to inspire any enthusiasm for the Sussex Downs, my passion for which did not develop until several years later.

During September and October 1918 there was an epidemic of a very virulent type of influenza and I caught this and was put into the school sanatorium. After recovering and returning to school, I was given some baked beans which were 'off' by another boy and forthwith returned to the sanatorium for another few weeks. I was there when Armistice was declared on 11 November. I left Hurstpierpoint in July 1919.

From September 1919 I was sent to a small private school, Oakfield School, in Crouch End, North London, a few minutes' walk from my home. I remained there until January 1921 when I entered Highgate School and was put in the second form, then under Mr K.R.G. Hunt, an international footballer and therefore a good disciplinarian and also an excellent master. In due course I moved to higher forms including the Fourth form under Mr Corbishley, who had a remarkable gift for stopping boys from cheating, by trusting them and letting them know that he was doing so. He was also an excellent master. Soon after I left school in 1923 his health broke down and he committed suicide. From the Fourth form I moved up to a thing called, I believe, the Remove, under Mr S.P. Kipping, a scientist who was excellent but went a bit too fast for me.

An occasion which left on me the deepest impression was the Armistice sevice at Highgate School War Memorial (1914–1918) conducted by the Headmaster Dr J.A.H. Johnston, on 11 November 1921. The War Memorial, designed by Sir Reginald Blomfield, an Old Boy, had been unveiled the previous January. The service I attended was of course in the presence of a large gathering of parents of those killed in the War, many of them mothers weeping as the Headmaster led the singing of 'Oh God our Help in Ages Past'.

Because of a decline in my father's financial situation I was taken away from Highgate School in July 1923 and sent to Pitman's College in Southampton Row, London WC 1, where I studied for Matriculation (London University) intended as an end in itself rather than the first stage for a degree. At first try I failed in one subject and had to sit again some months later. I left Pitman's College and worked through a course with University Correspondence College, and passed Matriculation at my second attempt, about the end of 1924 or beginning of 1925.

My time at school and its extension at Pitman's College was undistinguished. I worked far too hard and was no good at organised games which at Highgate School were compulsory. I was in fact a 'swat', and might have had a better academic record had I led a more balanced life. At Highgate School I did however get the Junior prize for Drawing in 1922, and my proficiency in this subject has enabled me to produce the maps and line illustrations for almost all my publications.

My home life until I reached the age of 18 or 19 was by no means happy. I had an elder brother who tended to be jealous of my better progress at school and who remained at Oakfield School until the end of his schooldays. The decline in my father's financial position from about 1921 onwards was caused largely by his getting mixed up with a group of drinking friends – probably a legacy from his army friends of 1914–18, – and of course led to a lack of unity in our home life and eventually to my premature withdrawal from Highgate School. Throughout my school life I tended to be lonely and never felt able to invite any friends to our home. Small wonder that I became engrossed in escapist subjects. My aptitude for drawing caused me to develop an appreciation of the writings of John Ruskin and before I was 21 I had probably read most of his works including the five volumes of *Modern Painters*, and I developed a taste for the paintings of J.M.W. Turner.

With such a background it is not surprising that I lacked initiative when it came to seeking employment. My mother discouraged me from my wish to become an artist and my father seemed unwilling to take much interest in my future. Neither was attracted by my desire to become a museum curator. My decision to become a bank clerk was caused by an aunt who was friendly with one of the directors of Barclays Bank and gave me an introduction, but I should almost certainly have been accepted had I applied in the usual way.

Once on the staff of the bank, my colleagues soon discovered that I was the sort of person who could be 'put upon' through a certain lack of sufficient ability to defend myself: if only I had taken more interest in games while at school, this deficiency would have been remedied. However, the situation was monitored by a succession of wise Chief Clerks who kept matters under control. I was very shy at the bank until an old schoolfriend, Thomas G. Johnson, joined the staff and we became close friends and I overcame my shyness. Between 1925 and 1929 I worked assiduously for the Bankers' Institute examinations and passed Part I and part of Part II, in spite of the counter attraction of archaeological fieldwork which began soon after I moved to Brighton with my parents in December 1925. Within a few months I 'discovered' the Sussex Downs and began the fieldwork which forms the subject of the next chapter.

Chapter 2

Barrow Surveys in Sussex, Surrey and Wessex 1927–1941

You've seen our English barrows on the downs
  If you have walk'd from Hardy's Casterbridge
Through heather'd witchery of Egdon Heath . . . .
  So have I sprawled Lob-stretch'd on Maiden Hill . . .
and Counted the tumuli which, clogged to earth,
  Stand like a witch-struck sisterhood . . . .
Topping the swelling downs with grassy curves.
                – R. Campbell Thompson, *Digger's Fancy*, 1938, p. 13.

The Sussex Downs 1927–1932

On 1 May 1925 I joined the staff of the King's Cross branch of Barclays Bank Ltd as a junior clerk at a salary of £84 per annum. In December my parents moved to Brighton for business reasons. Being unable to support myself in any sort of accommodation in London on that salary, I moved to Brighton with them, and travelled up to London daily on a Southern Railway season ticket of nine guineas per quarter. The rises in salary were, if I remember correctly, £12 per annum until reaching the age of 21 when there was an increase to £170 per annum; with £20 annual rises thereafter making £250 at the age of 25.

It was probably in 1926 or 1927 that I began walking on the Sussex Downs, especially in the vicinity of Cissbury where waste flakes and occasional scrapers and other implements from the flint mines and their surroundings were abundant. I collected and kept a record of these almost useless finds, but eventually they came to occupy rather a lot of space, so I looked around for another archaeological outlet. The leading Sussex archaeologists of the day were Dr Eliot Curwen and his son Dr E. Cecil Curwen, both of Hove. The latter had already covered most of the known aspects of field archaeology, but he had avoided the barrows because his mother was very religious and had scruples about her son disturbing the graves of the prehistoric dead.

I therefore began to visit the barrows on the Sussex Downs. Having neither the skill nor the desire to dig into them, I limited my fieldwork to measuring them, classifying them according to their outward forms, and assembling the available early references and excavation records. That has been the pattern of my fieldwork ever since. I had already bought the 6″ to the mile Ordnance Survey quarter-sheet of the Cissbury area, and the first barrows I surveyed were those on that quarter-sheet. These quarter-sheets then cost two shillings each (the present 1988 price of a national gridded 6″ O.S. quarter-sheet, covering an area only slightly larger, is £12.25). By 1928–1930 I could afford to buy a quarter-sheet every two or three weeks in accordance with the needs of my fieldwork, which in principle continued throughout the year except during bad weather or when I was working for banking examinations. I soon found that quite a lot of the barrows were not then shown on the 6″ O.S. maps. After seeing 15 – 20 examples marked on the maps, I soon acquired the knack of finding 'new' ones, and plotting them on the maps with reasonable accuracy. The Sussex downs are the ideal training ground for recognising barrows. There are scarcely any other features with which they might be confused, except perhaps the occasional windmill mound. On one or two occasions I met a shepherd wearing a smock and carrying a Pyecombe crook: it was almost the end of an age. Among my early finds were the long barrow known as *Bevis's Thumb* (SU 788155) on the downs between Chichester and Petersfield, and the twin bell-barrow (SU 808107) on the south-western spur of Bow Hill north-west of Chichester, which although on the maps had not previously beeen identified as a rare type. By late summer 1931 my survey of the barrows on the Sussex Downs was nearing completion, and Dr Eliot Curwen persuaded me to give a lecture on 'Barrows, with particular reference to those of Sussex' at the AGM of the Brighton and Hove Archaeological Club on 13 October 1931. It was my first lecture to any archaeological society, and both the Curwens were present. On 21 July 1934 I addressed members of the Sussex Archaeological Society at *The Devil's Jumps*, the finest group of barrows in Sussex, at their summer meeting based on Treyford.

My fieldwork on the Sussex Downs was complemented by research on the literature in Brighton Central Library until 1931 when I moved to London and worked on Saturday afternoons in the British Museum library during the winters and on wet days. In 1932 I became a member of the London Library and have belonged to it ever since.

Surrey 1931–4

I moved to London in 1931 where I lived at the Bloomsbury House Club in Cartwright Gardens WC1, until it closed about 1947 (apart from the war years when I was in the R.A.F.). Gordon Childe lived there 1922–27 when he was appointed professor of prehistoric archaeology at Edinburgh University, and it was during his stay there that he wrote *The Dawn of European Civilisation* (1925). It was not long before I began my survey of the barrows in Surrey: after Sussex a comparatively light undertaking. Some of the fieldwork was done with Dr Wilfrid Hooper, a Reigate solicitor who was on the council of the Surrey Archaeological Society. My paper 'Some Surrey bell-barrows' (*Surrey Archaeol. Collect.* 40, 56 – 64, 1932) was to the best of my knowledge my only paper that any editor submitted to the local expert for 'vetting'. For this purpose it was submitted to Dr Eric Gardner, who advised that the references to the 'bell-barrow folk' be deleted. I have ever since been grateful for this advice. 'An analysis and list of Surrey barrows' followed two years later (*Surrey Archaeol. Collect.* 42, 26 – 60).

The surveys of the barrows in Sussex and Surrey showed that bell-barrows and other 'Wessex' round barrows occur only in the western parts of those counties. As it was well known that round barrows of bell and disc types tend to be concentrated around Stonehenge and on Salisbury Plain, my next task was to get at least a general idea of the types of round barrow in Hampshire. To this end I devoted a week's holiday probably in summer 1931. I went by coach to Alton in east Hampshire and proceeded on foot towards Stonehenge via whatever barrows were shown on the maps. In due course I reached Stonehenge. After visiting some of the barrow groups there I stayed the night in a little café which also did bed-and-breakfast, situated just north of the fork in the roads immediately east of the monument. This café was pulled down a year or two later. I rose very early next (Saturday) morning, had breakfast soon after 6 a.m. and was on my way before 7. The longest 'barrow-crawl' that I have ever done in one day followed. I do not remember the precise course, but it followed a north-eastward course via Haxton Down and possibly Snail Down and ended (as far as barrows were concerned) at Collingbourne Kingston, about 18 km (11½ miles) as the crow flies, but probably at least twice as long the way that I went visiting barrow after barrow. I tried to get accommodation at Collingbourne Kingston but there wasn't any. I then walked 2 km (1¼ miles) to the next village (Collingbourne Ducis) but was snubbed there as well. I then walked another 4 km (2½ miles) to Ludgershall, where I explained my predicament to the local policeman, who persuaded the proprietress of the Queen's Head inn to take me in for the night. It was then about 10.30 p.m. During that night I got very little sleep as my legs ached from the overstrain. In fact my left leg continued to ache for several months afterwards. The following day I returned to the Bloomsbury House Club, where my friends told me that I looked as thin as a rake, and enquired what on earth I had been doing.

During the period 1927–34 when I was devoting weekends to fieldwork in Sussex and Surrey, my holidays (a fortnight each year) were concerned with fieldwork elsewhere. The bank's 'holiday list' was compiled about February each year. The seniors picked August and the rest of the summer, leaving spring and autumn to the junior staff. That suited me fine, as fieldwork is preferably done either before the end of April (when the arable fields get under standing corn) or after the crops have been harvested. Some of these holidays were spent visiting other parts of England in preparation for my book *Ancient Burial-Mounds of England* (1936). *The Morning Post* for 6 February 1933 carried an article entitled 'Hunting the Tumuli: young bank clerk's hobby', written by a Mr Bond, one of their reporters who lived at my residential club.

During 1934 the main fruits of my previous several years' work were published:
'Sussex Barrows' (*Sussex Archaeol. Collect.* 75, 217–75;
'Surrey Barrows' (*Surrey Archaeol. Collect.* 42, 27–60;
'Bell-barrows' (*Proc. Prehist. Soc. of East Anglia.* 7, 203–30).

With these papers the first phase of my barrow surveys in southern England was completed.

From 1934 onwards the general pattern of my fieldwork comprised weekends visiting barrows in Berkshire and Hampshire.

Berkshire
Fieldwork on the Berkshire downs was facilitated by the fact that the railway stations between Didcot and Swindon (Wantage Road, Challow, Uffington, and Shrivenham) were still functioning, and likewise the Newbury and Lambourn lines, and the country bus services from Reading were excellent (I have never driven a car nor ridden a bicycle). On Good Fridays there was an excursion train from Paddington to Newbury and the Lambourn valley, of which I took full advantage. Some of my fieldwork in Berkshire was done with Wilfrid Seaby (then of Reading Museum) on foot, and some with F.M. Underhill (later Hon Secretary of the Berkshire Archaeological Society) by car. Work was greatly helped by making the fullest use of air-photographs taken by

Major G.W.G. Allen of Iffley near Oxford, several of whose air-photographs were included in my papers:

'Berkshire barrows'. *Berkshire Archaeol. J.* 39, 171–91 (1935)

"   "   40, 20–58 (1936)

"   "   42, 102–16 (1938)

"   "   43, 9–21 (1939)

'The Lambourn long barrow'. *Berkshire Archaeol. J.* 40, 59–62 (1936).

Hampshire and the Isle of Wight

This county provides the pleasant contrast of chalk downland in the north and the heathlands of the New Forest in the south-west. It contains more than a thousand barrows, compared with Berkshire which has around three hundred. For this reason I adopted the economical method of listing the bowl-barrows in tabulated form which I had done for Sussex which also has more than a thousand barrows. Most of the fieldwork was done during the two or three years before the 1939–45 War. At the time of the Munich Crisis (August–September 1938) I was on holiday based at Winchester, and had the pleasure of meeting Dr J.P. Williams Freeman, author of *Field Archaeology as Illustrated by Hampshire* (1915). It was at the conclusion of one of my weekends based on Winchester, while travelling from Winchester to Waterloo, that I noted an extremely flashy platinum-blonde woman passing through the corridor-type carriage in which I was travelling. On arrival at Waterloo she was met by (later Sir) Mortimer Wheeler who carried her bags for her. She was Mavis de Vere Cole, afterwards the second Mrs Mortimer Wheeler, who some years afterwards shot at and wounded Lord Vivian at Potterne near Devizes. On two or three occasions while doing fieldwork in the New Forest I had tea with Heywood Sumner at his house Cuckoo Hill, South Gorley near Fordingbridge, now a residential home for the elderly.

Of all the sites that I visited in Hampshire, that which gave me a particular thrill was *Meare Beorge* on the Warnford/West Meon boundary, at precisely the spot where it is indicated by a Saxon land charter although not at the time of my visit shown on the O.S. maps; although it had in fact already been noted by Dr G.B. Grundy in his fieldwork for his paper on the Saxon charters of Hampshire. It is at SU 633234.

At that time *Proc. Hampshire Fld Club Archaeol. Soc.* were printed by Frank Warren who was also the Hon. Secretary of the Field Club, and he evidently put his most reliable compositor to set the *Proceedings*. I found it almost exasperating to go through the proofs without finding so much as a single printer's error.

'Hampshire Barrows.' *Proc. Hampshire Fld Club Archaeol. Soc.* 14 (i), 9–40.

"   "   "   "   14 (ii), 195–229.

"   "   "   "   14 (iii), 346 – 65.

In the spring of 1940 I was fortunate enough to catch chicken-pox. After the disease had played itself out, my doctor gave me a week's convalescence, which was devoted to a survey of the barrows in the Isle of Wight. I travelled to Lymington and crossed over to Yarmouth, and followed the ridgeway from Headon Hill to Newport, and subsequently from Newport along the chalk ridge to Bembridge, and afterwards covered the Niton – Ventnor area to the south. The paper was done with G.A.

Sherwin, like myself a bank official, who was also Hon. Curator of Carisbrooke Castle Museum. He accompanied me on part of the fieldwork and provided all the references to material from barrows held in his museum. Being based in London I was able to provide the extensive references to Skinner's excavations, among the Journals of Rev. John Skinner in the British Library.

'Isle of Wight Barrows', by L.V.G. and G.A. Sherwin.
Proc. Isle Wight Natur. Hist. Archaeol. Soc. 3 (iii), 179–222. (1941)

Wessex
With Sussex, Surrey, Berkshire, Hampshire and the Isle of Wight completed to the best of my ability and nearly all published, I prepared 'The Bronze Age round barrows of Wessex' (*Proc. Prehist. Soc.*, 7, 73–113, 1941), which was published a week or so before I was posted to Egypt with the R.A.F. in early December 1941. The paper was by no means perfect, as I had not yet completed fieldwork in Wiltshire, Dorset and North-east Somerset. However, Piggott's paper 'The Early Bronze Age in Wessex' (*Proc. Prehist. Soc.* 4, 52–106) provided at least the 'Wessex culture' interments from the published excavation records. Fate decreed that I was destined to undertake a detailed survey of Wiltshire barrows as part of my work as assistant to Hawkes and Piggott for *V.C.H. Wiltshire* from 1949 to 1952. I had in fact nearly completed a paper on Dorset barrows, which was put into cold storage in the Dorset County Museum at Dorchester until after the war. On the advice of Col. Drew, I converted all the latitudes and longitudes (for nearly 2,000 sites) to national grid references: an extremely tedious job but which was however well worth while (*Dorset Barrows*, 1959; *Dorset Barrows supplement*, 1982).

At the end of a week or two of fieldwork in Dorset in the early or mid 1930s, I visited the Dorset County Museum in Dorchester, met its curator Lt. Col. Drew, and in my youthful enthusiasm told him that during my walking tour I thought that I had seen everything archaeological worth seeing in the county. He received my remark with kindly encouragement; but it took me another quarter century to fill in only those gaps necessary to bring *Dorset Barrows* up to a standard fit for publication, and to complete the fieldwork for the Dorset parts of my *Archaeology of Wessex* (1958).

Apart from 'Sussex barrows', in which the locations were given in measurements from the inner margins of the 6″ O.S. sheets (the margins of which have now all been changed), all my regional barrow surveys until 1941 gave the locations in latitudes and longitudes on the advice of O.G.S. Crawford, then Archaeology Officer, who told me that 'latitudes and longitudes will last as long as the earth lasts'. By about 1947 they were superseded by the national grid system which has since then been gradually introduced on all the O.S. maps as they have come up for revision and reprinting.

One evening in the late 1930s I was visited by L.F. Salzman who told me that he had just seen a sketch of the Hove barrow (in which the well-known amber cup was found in 1857) among the Journals of Rev. John Skinner in the British Library. This and other matters prompted me to prepare two short supplements to 'Sussex barrows', drawing attention to the references in the Skinner Journals, and to a recently located series of round barrows on the heaths of West Sussex (*Sussex Archaeol. Collect.* 81 (1940), 210–14; 82 (1942), 115–23).

Looking back in retrospect on my fieldwork done until 1941, it can be said that most of it was done while the going was good, and much of the downland was under either pasture or arable of the pre-1939 type, before the introduction of the more drastic agricultural machinery which followed soon afterwards. From about 1940 onwards a good deal of this pasture was converted to arable and many of the smaller (and some larger) barrows either reduced or levelled. The fieldwork was done more hurriedly than would have been the case if a world war had not been imminent. With 'The Bronze Age round barrows of Wessex' the second phase of my fieldwork in that region was concluded as I departed for Egypt.

My residential club in central London was in a very vulnerable area, being only a few mintues' walk from the main line rail termini of King's Cross, Euston and St Pancras, all of them targets for bombing. For this reason I got the final draft of that paper typed by an agency in Bath.

In early 1941 I was a spare time A.R.P. shelter warden in the air-raid shelter in the basement of the British Medical Association H.Q. near St Pancras Church. I was on duty in this shelter during the very severe air raids of the nights of 16 and 19 April and 10 May, during one of which a shower of incendiary bombs fell on the British Museum causing much damage. On quieter nights my shelter tended to be visited by torpedoed Norwegian sailors from the requisitioned hotel next door, who came not so much to get protection from the raids as to find a woman. I had recently bought a copy of *Danmarks Oldtid*, by Johannes Brondsted, and I used to bring this to the shelter and try to get these Norwegian sailors to help me to read it, as a diversion from their other interest.

Chapter 3

White Horse Hill and Surroundings

> Before the gods that made the gods
>   Had drunk their morning fill,
> The White Horse of the White Horse Vale
>   Was hoary on the hill!
>
> – G.K. Chesterton. *The Ballad of the White Horse* (1911)

Soon after moving to London in 1931 I became aware that the Great Western Railway ran a Sunday excursion once a month during the summer to Wantage Road, Challow, Uffington, Stratton Halt, and Swindon, the return fare being between 4/6d and 5/6d according to distance. After one or two preliminary visits I acquired the habit of alighting at Shrivenham, which the train reached about 12 noon, and walking to Ashbury for lunch at the Rose and Crown Inn, then a thatched building run by the Peoples' Refreshment House Association, which also ran the White Horse Inn at Woolstone and the Plough Inn at Kingston Lisle. At the Rose and Crown I used to have an excellent lunch including cold ham and salad for 2/-. I then walked up the hill to the Ridgeway and proceeded along it to Wayland's Smithy, then in its natural state before the restoration of 1964. Afterwards I continued along the Ridgeway to Uffington Castle Iron Age hillfort, the Uffington White Horse and the nearby Dragon Hill. From that group of sites I would continue along the Ridgeway past the ploughed-out earthwork on Ram's Hill to the top of Blowingstone Hill. I then descended Blowingstone Hill, sometimes blew through the Blowing Stone, but always had afternoon tea at the Plough Inn at Kingston Lisle. There was comfortable time to walk from Kingston Lisle through the hamlet of Fawler (so named from traces of a Roman pavement) and Uffington village back to Uffington station from which the return train departed about 7.10 or 7.20 p.m. and reached Paddington around 9p.m..

I would vary this route according to the mood of the moment. On one occasion in September 1935 I decided to alter it by visiting the Seven Barrows on Lambourn Downs. As I approached from the north I spotted an unrecorded disc-barrow on Sparsholt Down (SU 32838351), and looking westward to the plantation on Westcot Down I discovered the Lambourn long barrow, its western end protuding from the wood (SU 32328338). It was among the most exciting archaeological field days of my life. I got Major G.W.G. Allen to photograph it from the air which confirmed my identification, and a week or two later it was visited by H.J.E. Peake, Stuart Piggott, F.M. Underhill and myself. Some twenty years or so afterwards, Humphrey Case of the Ashmolean Museum (Oxford) was searching some Martin Atkins manuscripts in the Bodleian library which show that the long barrow had orginally been discovered by Edwin Martin Atkins who dug it and found in it 'more than one skeleton' between

1852 and 1858. Edwin Martin Atkins was Lord of the Manor of Kingston Lisle until his death in 1859.

When I informed Mr Murray, then Lord of the Manor of Kingston Lisle, of my discovery of the long barrow, he invited me to Sunday lunch at the manor house. I duly went, but for me it was a very 'posh' affair to which I was not accustomed. There were about a dozen of us including Sir John Siddeley of Armstrong-Siddeley, a friend of the Murrays. The waiter put a fresh bread roll on everybody's side-plate, and another waiter then brought in the soup. I immediately broke up my bread roll and put the bits in the soup, only to find that I was being looked at by the Murrays and the rest of the guests. Mrs Murray made some unnecessary remark about the weather, and my face turned the colour of a tomato or more probably a beetroot. For the first time in my life I learned that for some unknown reason it is not the done thing to put bread in one's soup when in polite society.

I became increasingly fond of the White Horse Hill area, and gradually acquired the relevant literature, including Francis Wise, *A Letter to Dr Mead concerning some Antiquities in Berkshire* (1738); Thomas Hughes, *The Scouring of the White Horse* (1858); Sir Walter Scott, *Kenilworth* (which mentions the Wayland Smith legend, told him by the wife of the rector of Uffington) and various other works. In the mid 1950s I purchased a copy of Wise's *Letter to Dr Mead*, bound together with the three other relevant pamphlets: *The Impertinence and Imposture of Modern ANTIQUARIES display'd* (1739) by 'Philalethes Rusticus' (Rev. W. Asplin, vicar of Banbury), *An Answer to a Scandalous Libel . . .*, (1741) by an anonymous author, believed to be Rev. George North, vicar of Codicote (Herts), and *Further Observations upon the White Horse . . .*, by Francis Wise, (1742): all of them now exceedingly rare.

My developing interest in folklore as well as archaeology was stimulated by continued visits to this region, and in 1938 I wrote a little book *White Horse Hill and Surrounding Country*, commission-published in early 1939 by the St Catherine Press. The printing comprised 250 clothbound and 750 paper-bound copies, selling respectively at 4/6d and 3/6d – a fair price in those days for a small book of 66 pages. The result was not entirely satisfactory. The cloth-bound edition has on the cover the White Horse in outline instead of solid, and the photograph of Wayland's Smithy was rather clumsily retouched. It was however favourably reviewed, notably by Leeds in *Oxoniensia* 4, 201 – 2; Peake in *Trans. Newbury Dist. Fld Club* 8, 215; Phillips in *Proc. Prehist. Soc.* 5, 204; and Piggott in *Berks Archaeol. J.* 43, 59–60. Because of the tradition of horses being left at Wayland's Smithy to be shod, as recorded in Scott's *Kenilworth* (chapters 9–11), I was particularly pleased at including a photograph (Plate 1) of Wayland's Smithy with two horses parked there.

At first I thought that it was not a good time to have a book published a short while before the start of a world war which was obviously coming. However, no sooner had the war started on 3 September 1939 than a considerable number of people were evacuated to the provinces and the villages in the White Horse vale received their share. This combined with the 'black-out' (which encouraged reading) to promote sales of my book, as those who move into a region generally take more interest in it than those who have always lived there. By the time of my return from the Middle East after the war had ended, the book had sold out. Sales were stimulated by the occupants of an American teaching establishment at Shrivenham, and I believe there are now more copies of *White Horse Hill and Surrounding Country* in the U.S.A. than in the U.K.

Within a few months of its publication, several of its readers sent me extra bits of information which were gathered together and published as 'Notes on the White Horse Hill region' (*Berkshire Archaeol. J.* 43 (1939), 135–9). The quality of these varied, from Sir Cyril Fox's demonstration that the 'currency bars' of pre-Roman Iron Age found by Reginald Smith at Wayland's Smithy in 1921 are not so, but more probably the hinges off a barn door, to Gerald B. Gardner's report of a witch's moon-dial found near Wayland's Smithy. It is curious that monuments with folklore attached to them sometimes attract more and not-so-reliable additional 'folklore'. Yet R.M. Holland Martin, a much more reliable person, also had a human skull marked 'Wayland's Smithy'.

It is opportune to reconsider the elements comprising the subject of my little book in the light of current knowledge. The Ridgeway is no longer as easy-going for the walker as it was before the 1939–45 war, partly because of the use of heavy agricultural vehicles along its course, and partly because of its use by motorcyclists, which in recent years the *Friends of the Ridgeway* have been trying to stop. It is no longer as certain as it once was that it has been a thoroughfare continuously since later prehistoric times, and there have been periods when parts of it have been under cultivation (Steane 1983).

Wayland's Smithy was excavated by Atkinson and Piggott in 1962–3, and shown to be a two-period monument: Wayland's Smithy I, an earthen mound covering a timber structure, and Wayland's Smithy II, a much longer wedge-shaped mound with a megalithic structure at its south-eastern end. Much has since been published about the Uffington White Horse. Mrs D. Woolner has done her best to show that it does not date from the pre-Roman Iron Age but was in her opinion more probably cut during the reign of King Alfred (Woolner 1965, 1967). However in the writer's opinion the consensus among current archaeological thought still favours a pre-Roman Iron Age origin for it. It is odd that nobody seems to have suggested that it represents an Iron Age racehorse, having regard not only to its thin body but also to the proximity of the racehorse training stables at Lambourn.

The scouring of the White Horse was the subject of a detailed study, commemorating the centenary of the Scouring and festivities of 1857, by G.W.B. Huntingford (1957, with full bibliography).

The transfer of the Uffington White Horse from Berkshire to Oxfordshire under the Local Government reorganisation of 1974 caused a great deal of bad feeling and rightly so. The Uffington White Horse was (and I believe still is) the emblem of the Berkshire Regiment and of the Berkshire Archaeological Society. The subject was comprehensively covered in *The Berkshire White Horse: a county saga*, by Michael Butler (1980). In the early 1970s I was approached by two pressure groups, one wanting me to sign a form requesting that the parish of Uffington be kept as it is and not split; the other asking me to sign a form requesting that the White Horse remain in Berkshire.

There has been little or no further progress in our knowledge of Uffington Castle hillfort, as no excavation has been done there in recent years. The almost ploughed-out hillfort on Rams Hill has been excavated but as it is virtually invisible the results will not here be considered.

Next comes the Blowing Stone. My short chapter on it in *White Horse Hill and Surrounding Country* was reprinted as a booklet and put on sale at one of the cottages adjoining the stone. When the stock ran out I did not get it reprinted but it would probably still sell. The secret of how to make the siren-like noise is simply to close the hole completely with the mouth and then blow; no great strength is needed; indeed I was first shown how to blow it by a boy of about 8, son of the family living in the cottage, who take the fees.

North of Kingston Lisle is a round barrow (SU 329882) which has been thought to be Roman, partly because it is off the downs, and partly because it is near Fawler whose name is derived from a Roman pavement, more than a dozen tesserae from which have recently been found by the present landowner (Hooke et al., 1988).

There has often been confusion, not only among the general public but even among some archaeologists, between the Ridgeway and the Icknield Way, especially the portion between Ashbury and Streatley. I have on three occasions issued correctives: on 9 June 1938 in a letter to *The Times*; on 1 July 1938 in a letter 'The Ridgeway and Icknield Way' in *The Autocar*; and in the January 1980 issue of *Popular Archaeology* (my letter on 'The course of the Ridgeway and Icknield Way west of R. Thames'). The Ridgeway is of course the unmetalled track along or very near the top of the downs, and the Icknield Way is the metalled road which runs along the foot of the downs.

The Lambourn long barrow was excavated by John Wymer in 1964. He showed that it comprised a long mound flanked by side-ditches. At the eastern end he found a crouched burial within a 'cist-like arrangement of small stones' but which could not be described as megalithic. The mound had been almost ploughed out.

I conclude this chapter with a description of my first flight in an aircraft. It was in the mid 1930s and my pilot was C.A.N. Bishop who lived at my club in London. We flew from a flying club at Woodley near Reading. Our aircraft was a Gipsy Moth which carried a passenger in front and the pilot behind. Our objective was the Berkshire Downs. As he circled around the Uffington White Horse and the Lambourn Seven Barrows, I began to be sick being unused to such movements, and held my head outside the cockpit for this purpose. He shouted, 'If you are going to be sick, please do it inside and not outside the aircraft, otherwise it will all blow in my face'. I then had the unusual experience of laughing and being sick at the same time. When we landed he asked, 'Do you want to lie down or anything funny?'

Bibliography since 1939
Atkinson, R.J.C. 1965. 'Wayland's Smithy'. *Antiquity* 39, 126–33.
Butler, Michael. 1980. *The Berkshire White Horse: a county saga.*
Case, H.J. 1957, 'The Lambourn Seven Barrows'. *Berkshire Archaeol. J.* 55, 15–31.
Hooke, Della et al. 1988. 'Anglo-Saxon estates in the Vale of White Horse'. *Oxoniensia*, 52 for 1987 (1988) 129–43.
Huntingford, G.W.B. 1957. 'The Scouring of the White Horse'. *Jour. Royal Anthrop. Inst.* 87(i), 105–14.
Steane, John. 1983 'How old is the Berkshire Ridgeway?' *Antiquity* 57, 103–8.
Woolner, Diana. 1965. 'The White Horse of Uffington'. *Trans. Newbury Dist. Field Club* 11(3), 27–44.
Woolner, Diana. 1967. 'New light on the White Horse.' *Folklore* 78, 90–111.
Wymer, John. 1966. 'Excavation of the Lambourn long barrow'. *Berkshire Archaeol. J.* 62, 1–16.

Chapter 4

An Egyptian Interlude

[Discovery of the robbers' hole in the pyramid of Khephren] 'gave me no little delight and hope returned to cherish my pyramidical brains'.
– Giovanni Belzoni, *Narrative of Operations and Recent Discoveries within the Pyramids . . .* 1820, 266.

When the discovery of the tomb of Tutankhamun was announced in November 1922, I was a boy at Highgate School. Sometime in 1923, after the tomb had been opened and relieved of almost all its contents except the mummy of the young king in its gold case, my form master, Mr Corbishley, set us to write an essay on the tomb of Tutankhamun. For this I received full marks : 20. This incident may or may not have played a small part in determining my eventual career; for I did not become a professional archaeologist until 1949.

It was a curious coincidence that I.E.S. Edwards, later Keeper of Egyptian antiquities at the British Museum, and I attended the same preparatory school – Oakfield School, Crouch End, North London, and each of us was destined to be stationed in the Cairo area during the 1939/45 war and to write a book on the pyramids.

I took no further interest in Egyptology until I was posted to the Middle East at the end of November 1941. Early in that year Grahame Clark, who was editing my paper on 'The Bronze Age round barrows of Wessex' for *Proc. Prehistoric Society*, told me that the R.A.F. were trying to get as many people as possible who were used to interpreting air photographs and suggested that I applied for a commission in air photographic intelligence. I did so and was called before the selection committee at the Air Ministry. To my surprise its chairman, a group captain I believe, commented, 'I see from your application that you are interested in archaeology'. I replied, 'Yes, sir'. He then handed me a flint implement which he had pulled out of his pocket and asked me to comment on it. I said that it was a flint scraper, found on the chalk downs as it had a white patina. He then gave a smile of approval to the rest of the selection committee and I was passed for the commission in air photographic intelligence.

The work of those engaged in air photographic interpretation has already been described in detail in two books: *Evidence in Camera* (1958) by Constance Babington Smith, and *The Eye of Intelligence* (1983) by Ursula Powys-Lybbe. Unfortunately both books are limited to what was done from the U.K. As to my own work, I spent five months at the R.A.F. unit at Medmenham between Marlow and Henley-on-Thames before being posted to the Middle East. I got used to stereoscopic examination of air photographs, and after a few weeks was put into a section devoted to the identification of camouflage and bomb-decoys. Before leaving England I also visited one of our own bomb-decoys which happened to be in an Iron Age hillfort within a few miles of an important industrial town.

After arriving at Heliopolis in Egypt, I was asked to start a section for camouflage and bomb decoys there. After a few months I got the impression that the enemy were making very little use of them in the Eastern Mediterranean. I found a possible dummy aerodrome at ATHENS/Menidi, but intelligence reports afterwards suggested that it was an emergency landing ground. (About 1972 Peter Warren, then of the British School in Athens, took me to see the fine tholos tomb at Menidi). Towards the end of the war however I located a magnificent dummy for the Ploesti oil refinery in Roumania. It was a few miles away from the real thing and in a situation which would have been 'on the way' from the likely direction of an intended attack. It was smaller than the real thing, in the hope of inducing an attacking pilot to lose height to get a closer view of his objective (thereby making himself an easier target for the defences). There was a snow cover, but the snow had melted above the control point 2 km or so away, which must therefore have been heated. This control point was connected with the dummy by a cable identified by a series of equidistant spots. Needless to say these bomb decoys were usually operated, by simulating a badly blacked-out town or factory, from a safe distance away.

Among my colleagues at our air photographic interpretation unit in Egypt were archaeologists including Charles McBurney (later a Cambridge professor) and R. Richmond Brown who had excavated under Flinders Petrie. For most of my service duties in Egypt I was occupied in bomb damage assessment (see chapter 16 under Rhodes).

It was natural that from the start of my almost four years in Egypt, based near Cairo, I should have taken a keen interest in visiting and studying the pyramids. Within a week or two of our arrival we were taken for a flight over the Pyramids of Giza to make us more familiar with the aerial view. I suspect that even before leaving England I had decided to devote my spare time to producing a book on the pyramids, parallel with my book, *The Ancient Burial-Mounds of England* (1936). Within a few days of my arrival in Egypt I paid my first visit to the Giza pyramids, with two colleagues, one of whom had been a schoolmaster in Cairo before the War. We were of course pestered by the native guides (dragomans) as though we were ordinary tourists which indeed we were. On my next or next-but-one visit, one of the same guides introduced himself to me as Ahmed Abdul Alim, son of the sheikh of Nazlet-es-Samman, beneath which is thought to be the valley temple of the pyramid of Kheops. He apologized for having treated me as a common tripper on my first visit. From then onwards I was often looked after by him on my subsequent visits to Giza and he protected me from being pestered by the other dragomans.

My first visit to the pyramid field of Abusir was made from Giza on a donkey (the first donkey-ride of my life) accompanied of course by a donkey-boy. After a while the donkey started to make an extraordinary noise. I suggested to my donkey-boy that perhaps we should rest awhile as the donkey was evidently a little tired. He replied, 'Donk no tired: donk want to fuck woman donk!'. In due course we arrived at the Abusir pyramids via the interesting sun temple of Abu Gurob. After I had completed my visit the native guardian and his wife offered me a cup of tea (or it may have been coffee). I accepted, and then they offered me a second, and then a third cup, all of which I accepted. It was indeed thirsty weather, and they followed by a fourth, fifth and sixth cup, after which I declined any further drinks. I afterwards read, I think in E.W. Lane's *Manners and Customs of the Modern Egyptians*, that it was considered polite to accept up to three cups of tea or coffee; but that it was considered abominably rude to accept more than three. By making such mistakes I gradually learned the manners and customs of the modern Egyptians, sufficiently to see me through my four years in Egypt.

By May 1942 there was still one pyramid not far from Giza which I had not visited: the unfinished pyramid of Djedefre at Abu Roash about five miles north of Giza. I had been on night duty which finished about 8 a.m. After breakfast I went by tram (as it then was) along the Giza road as far as the turning north to Abu Roash and proceeded to walk the rest of the way. However, the heat was increasing rapidly and before reaching the pyramid (on top of a hill, almost a mountain), I had to shelter in the shade of a small cave or crevice in the rock. By the time I had reached the pyramid I was near collapse and only just managed to take a few photogaphs before proceeding downhill southwards to a small military camp, I believe of the Polish army, where I was given a lift back to the road from Giza to Cairo. I spent the rest of the day having cold showers and cold baths at Music-for-All, a service institute in Cairo, before returning to my unit at Heliopolis.

Within a few weeks of arriving in Egypt I made myself known to the Library of the Egyptian Museum, whose librarian or acting librarian was Joseph Leibovitch, a Jew who was naturally very helpful to allied personnel. The Museum itself did not reopen until about the end of 1943. However, there was a tendency for the Museum library to be used as a social club by the Egyptian archaeologists, and it was not long before I discovered the library of L'Institut Français d'Archeologie Orientale, Sharia Munira, presided over by Arpag Mekhitarien, a charming Belgian who subsequently wrote an excellent book on Egyptian art. Conditions for study were much more peaceful there. I also had the run of Borchardt Institute despite the fact that it was really German, as it was being run during the war by Bernard Grdseloff, a brilliant young Polish Egyptologist, whose language in Cairo was normally French. I was also usually welcome at the library of Dr Louis Keimer (before 1939 Ludwig Keimer) of whose nationality I am a little uncertain. At all events, while I was working in his library it was his practice to pace up and down the passage way outside and hum or sing *God Save the King*, in order to leave me in no doubt as to his political sympathies. His native servant used to bring me a glass of iced lemon squash about every 15 minutes, which of course was not forthcoming in the other libraries.

It is time to explain how I managed to get opportunities for study. The *modus operandi* of the unit to which I belonged, in common with others based on or near Cairo, was to work between 8 a.m. and 1 p.m., and between 4 p.m. and 7 p.m. in winter and between 5 p.m. and 8 p.m. in summer. It was 'officially' considered too hot to work during the afternoon when we were supposed to rest or swim or indulge in some other form of relaxation. Ours was one of a group of units unofficially described by the desert squadrons as 'short-range desert squadrons' (the 'range' being between Groppi's tea shop in Cairo and the Mena House Hotel near the pyramids of Giza). I formed the habit of going into Cairo and studying in the libraries two or three afternoons a week.

At Heliopolis I got to know Dr Iskandar Badawy, a Coptic Egyptologist who for about three months gave me lessons in elementary Egyptian hieroglyphs. After he had to stop because of other commitments, I contacted H.W. Fairman of the British Embassy who continued my tuition in Egyptian hieroglyphic language where Badawy had left off. Fairman later became professor of Egyptology at Liverpool University.

Other Egyptologists whom I got to know included Dr Etienne Drioton (Director General of the Service des Antiquities), Rex Englebach (sometime Director of the Egyptian Museum), and Alfred Lucas, the government chemist responsible for the conservation of the objects from the tomb of Tutankhamun. My interest in the muslim architecture of Old Cairo brought me into touch with (Sir) K.A.C. Creswell, author of the standard book on *Early Muslim Architecture*, and Mme R.L. Devonshire, whose tours of the mosques and other Islamic buildings of Old Cairo were a feature of both 1914–18 and 1939–45 wars and I believe the years between, as also were her Sunday afternoon 'At Homes' between 3 and 6 p.m. at her house in Maadi, where all interested in muslim architecture were welcome. My interest in the pyramids and ancient Eygpt was best served by having a break about once a month and diverting my attention to Islamic studies.

In December 1942 I caught jaundice and was given a week (or perhaps a fortnight) convalescence which I spent at the Luxor Hotel. Staying at the same hotel was a group of Egyptologists and others, on an official investigation of the Theban private tombs with a view to their better conservation. This party included Dr Etienne Drioton and Alfred Lucas, his expert in conservation. There was also Prof. Alan Wace, whose special interest was in the pictures of Minoan offering bearers from Crete on the walls of several of the Theban private tombs.

It was on this occasion that I chose, from the large number of native guides wanting my custom, Ahmed Khalifa, a good looking young lad of 15 or 16. On my subsequent annual visits to Luxor I used to travel by the night train from Cairo arriving at Luxor about 6 a.m., where he would always be waiting to spot any of his previous clients, and I accordingly had him during my visits in 1943 and 1944, as well as for my retirement holiday in Luxor in 1972. From his collection of written testimonials I learned that he had also been the guide for I.E.S. Edwards of the British Museum. By 1972 I think he had become the owner of cars and perhaps coaches and I believe his children were donkey-boys.

It was also at this time that I first met Mohamed Aboudi, the well-known guide to the antiquities of Upper Egypt, who also had a shop in Luxor where he had antiquities and books for sale. Until I read his life by L.J. Craven (*Aboudi, Man of Luxor*, 1984), I was unaware that before the 1939–45 ar he had acted as guide to parties of Germans brought by Prof. Georg Steindorff and Prof. F.W. von Bissing; but Egyptology knows no political bounds.

About 1943 I got permission to visit the interior of the Step Pyramid of Zoser during a short period of leave when I was staying at the Mena House Hotel. I duly visited the Step Pyramid's interior in company with a Guide from the Service of Antiquities. However, an hour or two afterwards I devloped dysentery and was put into Abbassia Hospital, in a bed by a window with a fine view of the pyramids of Giza. I attributed the dysentery to having eaten grapes which had not been properly washed, rather than to the curse of the pharaoh Zoser.

At a later stage of my stay in Egypt, I believe in 1944, I suffered from overloading or overworking of the sweat-glands and was advised to consult a specialist in Cairo. He recommended *Pyramid Pomade* (though knowing nothing of my interest in the pyramids), and told me which chemist I could get it from. Unfortunately they were closed. The following day I was a good deal worse and reported to sick quarters. I was given wrong treatment by a doctor who had just come out from the U.K., and the following day I was sent to Heliopolis Hospital where I remained for several weeks. During that period my bedside reading was Sir Alan Gardiner's *Egyptian Grammar*.

During my four-year tour of duty in Egypt I had three memorable leaves of 48 hours: one to the rock tombs of Beni Hasan (with R. Richmond Brown) which included a visit to the Museum at el-Minya, another to the Faiyum where I stayed at the excellent hotel there and explored the pyramids and private tombs in the area: all except the seldom-visited pyramid of Seila as I was unable to find a taxi driver who knew where it was. The third was to two of the Coptic monasteries in the Wadi Natrun between Cairo and Alexandria.

Part of the preparation for writing my book *Egyptian Pyramids* comprised visits to the quarries from which the stone was obtained. The Egyptian Ministry of Mines and Quarries put me in touch with Fuad Henein, Inspector of Quarries, who took me to such of the Tura and neighbouring quarries on the east bank of the Nile as were accessible, and explained to me the methods of the quarrymen and the problems involved. It was from these quarries that the fine white limestone was obtained for the casing and other special parts of the pyramids; the local coarse limestone being used for the bulk of their interior. I also visited the granite quarry where lies the unfinished obelisk at Aswan, and a little known granite quarry at Abbasieh between Cairo and Heliopolis.

I made a detailed study of the builders' inscriptions in hieroglyphs on the exposed backing stones of the Giza and other pyramids, from which the casing had been removed in the middle ages to build some of the mosques of Old Cairo. The best time to see these inscriptions (all painted in red ochre which has faded with the passage of time) is in the very early morning. When staying at the Mena House Hotel I would go out at first light before breakfast with sunglasses and search the west face of each pyramid (then of course in shade) when these inscriptions can be clearly seen. They include phrases such as 'this side up' (important as sedimentary rock has to be used in a building the same way up as the position it occupied in its original stratum). Other inscriptions indicate the height of the masonry (in Egyptian cubits of around 20.61 inches) above the base-line at a given date. A typical example, on the pyramid of Queen Neit, a wife of Pepy II at South Saqqara, reads: 'Second month of winter, day 14 . . . work on the building, on the west side'. I found that the west side of each pyramid was where these inscriptions are the best preserved. The winds (Khamseens) from the Western Desert every spring bring sand which accumulates on this side of each pyramid and helps to preserve these inscriptions; but at intervals of every few years (or longer) this accumulation of sand is removed from the west face of each pyramid as part of the pyramid maintenance programme of the Service of Antiquities: and *then* is the time for studying these inscriptions. These and other relevant matters formed the subject of chapter 4 (construction) of my book *Egyptian Pyramids* (1947).

Being stationed at a photographic unit in the R.A.F., I was in an ideal position to get the best photographs from both the air and the ground. One of our flying officers took a series of excellent air photographs of the pyramids between Giza and the Faiyum during a camera test, but to my intense sorrow he was killed on an operational sortie a day or two later, before I had an opportunity to thank him. Among those who accompanied me on my visits to the pyramids were photographers of note including Tony Kersting and T. Herbert Jones. A selection of these photographs was included in my book.

Soon after the European part of the war ended in May 1945, M. Jean Philippe Lauer, whose work on the restoration and conservation of the Step Pyramid complex of Zoser had begun in the mid 1920s, returned to Cairo from France, and I had the pleasure of meeting him not only in Cairo before I left in December 1945, but also during my holiday in Egypt in December 1960. I visited Saqqara on Boxing Day and he showed me around his work at the Step Pyramid complex (he scared me stiff by persuading me to accompany him along the top of very narrow high walls to get a better view), and gave me an autographed copy of his little book *Sakkarah: the Monuments of Zoser*.

Egyptian Pyramids tried to achieve two objectives which are incompatible: to be a guide-book for use on the sites (for which 8vo format would be appropriate) and a 4to format book to do justice to the air-photographs. Despite its appearance a few weeks after the publication of *The Pyramids of Egypt* by I.E.S. Edwards, which appeared in the Penguin series, *Egyptian Pryamids* received several favourable reviews: by Herbert Chatley in *Journal of Egyptian Archaeology*; P. Gilbert in *Chronique d'Egypte*; Jean St Fare Garnot in *Revue des Etudes Anciennes*; G.A. Wainwright in *Antiquity*; Dows Dunham in *American Journal of Archaeology*, the most detailed and constructive of all the reviews. To the best of my knowledge it received only one review that was not so favourable: by S.R.K. Glanville in *Discovery*.

Another sequel to my sojourn in Egypt was my paper 'The folklore of Ancient Egyptian monuments' read to the Folklore Society on 12 February 1947 and afterwards published in their journal.

At that remarkable centre for the Forces in Cairo, Music for All, its literary director Dr Worth Howell arranged lectures by Miss Amice Calverley on the Temple of Sety I at Abydos, Mr H.W. Fairman on the Egyptian pyramids, Alfred Lucas on the Tomb of Tutankhamun and also on the Pharaoh of the Exodus, and Sir Ronald Storrs on Lawrence of Arabia, all of which I attended.

It is scarcely necessary to state that while in Egypt my interests in antiquity were by no means confined to the pyramids. Private tombs of unusual interest which I saw include at *Giza*, near the south-east corner of the pyramid of Kheops, the tomb of Seshemnefer, an Official of late dyn. V or early VI, which during the 1939–45 War was attributed to 'Kheops' Prime Minister' by the native touts conducting allied troops around the local sites. This tomb contained three guides – one for the outer chamber, one for the inner chamber, and one for the sarcophagus chamber, each of course expecting a tip. In addition to the three Guides there was a fourth Arab, wanting to tell your fortune in the sarcophagus chamber, the fortune doubtless varying according to the fee. It is of course centuries later than the reign of Kheops. The tomb of Debehen, south-west of the pyramid of Khephren, being locally considered as the sacred tomb of Sidi Hamed Samán, is the location of a religious gathering every

Friday. I once entered it on a Thursday afternoon (our half-day) only to find that the fleas left the previous Friday were ravenously hungry.

At *North Saqqara*, in addition to the famous tombs of Ty, Ptah-hotep/Akhethetep (joint tomb), and Mera, there is east of the last the tomb of Ankhmahor, a physician, shown on the wall reliefs performing various operations including that of circumcision. It was amusing listening to the native guides describing this scene in their own version of the English vernacular.

At *South Saqqara*, east of the pyramid of Pepy II, there are some fine shaft-tombs of the end of Dyn. VI, small but beautifully decorated and inscribed in the style confined (I believe) to that period. At *Lisht*, on the way from the Nile Valley to the pyramid of Sesostris I one passes the tomb of Senusret-ankh, probably early Dyn. XII, remarkable by reason of its walls being inscribed with the Pyramid Texts, normally reserved for the pharaohs in the pyramids of late Dyn. V. and VI.

In *Upper Egypt*, from Luxor I saw, usually with my excellent guide Ahmed Khalifa, the usual tombs in the Theban necropolis and some of the less visited ones. At Aswan I had the delightful experience of being rowed in a boat from Aswan to the granite island of Seheil, covered with hieroglyphic inscriptions many of which I photographed from the boat and others by going ashore.

This chapter may fittingly end in a lighter vein. After my early experience with a donkey, and finding that hiring a taxi or chauffeur-driven car to the pyramids south of the Giza group was very costly, I acquired the habit of travelling from Giza on the local bus to Badrashein within a mile or so of Saqqara. This was usually satisfactory, but on one occasion I got on a bus which was nearly empty, and asked the driver how long it would be before it started. He replied, 'one minute'. After waiting in the bus for about twenty minutes I asked him again and received the same reply. After about an hour the bus was still not quite full and it would still be 'one minute' before it could leave. Eventually all the seats were taken, but the bus driver was not ready to start until all the standing room was full. When that situation was reached, a man pushed his native wife, carrying a wicker basket full of chickens, through the window on to my lap, and I could visualise the probability that if I remained seated there my trousers would be at the receiving end of excreta from the chickens. I then went into a huff and got off the bus, the rest of whose occupants hooted with laughter, and the bus proceeded on its journey. I then hired a taxi to drive me to Saqqara.

I shared an office with a rather dreary officer who wished to marry a girl who lived in Cape Town. He paid about £200 for her fare from Cape Town to Cairo, and planned to propose to her at the Sphinx at full moon. To prepare for this event he took me to the Giza pyramids and Sphinx during one of our afternoon 'siesta' periods and got me to tell him all about the archaeology of the Sphinx, its approximate date, the fact that it was a representation of Khephren and surrounded by a quarry from which the stone for the interior of the Kheops pyramid had probably come, and so on. A day or two later he duly arrived at the Sphinx with his girlfriend shortly before midnight and regurgitated the archaeology and history of the monument to her, but she was by no means impressed and turned down his proposal. He then paid another £200 to transport her back to Cape Town. He was a somewhat disconsolate colleague for the next few weeks.

My activities in Egyptology after joining the staff of Bristol City Museum in 1952 will be dealt with in a later chapter.

Bibliography

1942 Review. C. Bachatly, *Bibliographie de la Préhistoire Egyptienne.* Antiquity XVI, 288.

1943 'The boat of the dead' [those adjoining the pyramids in Lower Egypt]. *Antiquity* XVII, 47–50.

Review. G. Jéquier, *Douze Ans de Fouilles dans la Nécropole Memphite. Antiquity* XVII, 108–9.

1944 Review. Selim Hassan, *Excavations at Giza*, I–IV. 1936–43. *Antiquity* XVIII, 104–5.

1947 *Egyptian Pyramids.* John Bellows Ltd., Gloucester. 4to. 194pp. 'Folklore of ancient Egyptian monuments'. *Folk-lore* 58, 345–60.

1949 Review. I.E.S. Edwards, *The Pyramids of Egypt. Antiquity* XXIII, 225.

Review. A. Lucas. *Ancient Egyptian Materials and Industries. Discovery.*

1950 Review. W.B. Emery. *Nubian Treasure. Archaeol. J.* 105, 95.

Review. H.E. Winlock. *Rise and Fall of the Middle Kingdom at Thebes. Archaeol. J.* 105, 94–5.

1957 Review. Z. Goneim. *The Buried Pyramid. Antiq. J.* 37, 75.

1957 'The ferryman and his fee'. *Folklore* 68, 257–69. (Egypt: 258–60).

1961 'The breaking of objects as a funerary rite'. *Folk-lore* 72, 475–91 (Egypt: 480–2); supplement, *Folk-lore* 84 (1973), 111–14.

1964 'The Pharaoh's Curse' (unsigned). *Mosaic*, no. 4 Jan 1964 (Bristol City Museum).

1972 *Guide Catalogue to Ancient Egyptian Collections*, 84pp. Bristol City Museum.

1975 *Barrow, Pyramid and Tomb.* Chap. 13 (Pyramids), 110–32; chap. 14 (Valley of the Kings), 133–43.

1978 *Pyramidi, Necropoli e Mondi Sepolti.* Italian translation of last.

1987 'The Christianization of prehistoric and other pagan sites'. *Landcape History*, 8 for 1986, 27–37. (Egypt and Nubia: pp. 27–8).

Chapter 5

Victoria County History of Wiltshire I(i)

'For this volume the committee . . . made provision for the full time employment of Mr L.V. Grinsell while he was compiling a large part of the Gazetteer'
V.C.H. Wiltshire I (i), Editorial Note.

It was quite by chance that Prof. Christopher Hawkes happened to mention to me that he and Prof. Stuart Piggott were involved in the preparation of volume 1 of the *V.C.H. Wiltshire*, covering the prehistoric, Roman and pagan Saxon periods, and that they were looking for an assistant to help to collect the material together. This was late in 1948, at a time when I was very dissatisfied with my progress in Barclays Bank. I asked him whether they might be prepared to consider me if I applied to be their assistant, and rather to my surprise they both expressed interest.

My resignation from Barclays Bank took effect on 23 April 1949, and I joined the staff of *V.C.H. Wiltshire* from 1 May. My mandate was to prepare the Archaeological Gazetteer of prehistoric, Roman and pagan Saxon remains.

The assignment had its problems. Of the 278 pages of the published gazetteer, 113 pages comprise lists of long and round barrows and tables relating to their contents. I had already published surveys of the long and round barrows of Sussex, Surrey, Berkshire, Hampshire and the Isle of Wight and had accumulated material for Wiltshire, and visited some years before the 1939–45 war some of the barrows in the military zone while the going was good. In other words my strongest suit was also among the strongest suits of Wiltshire archaeology. I had only an elementary knowledge of the archaeology of the periods from the Iron Age to the pagan Saxon, acquired largely through my extra-mural lecturing at the City Literary Institute in Bloomsbury between 1946 and 1949.

In 1913 the Wiltshire Archaeological and Natural History Society published Canon E.H. Goddard's 'List of prehistoric, Roman and pagan Saxon antiquities in the county of Wiltshire' (W.A.M. xxxviii, 153–378), originally prepared for a *V.C.H. Wiltshire* which was killed by the 1914–18 War. My task was to bring this up to date. My training as a bank official had developed in me a methodical mind and an understanding that if I were asked to produce an archaeological gazetteer in 250 pages or so, I should do my best to keep within the prescribed limits. They were exceeded only slightly, by the decision to include analyses of the contents of those barrows excavated with known result.

The 1939–45 war had largely put a stop to archaeological excavations in the county, and they did not resume on any appreciable scale until after I had completed my gazetteer. The archaeological scene was therefore fairly static. A major change was however proceeding at the Ordnance Survey. The national grid system had been introduced but the 6″ O.S. maps and other maps covering Wiltshire had not yet been published with the national grid superimposed. Charles Phillips arranged for me to be supplied with a set of 6″ O.S. sheets covering the county, and his chief assistant James Fox provided me with the tables necessary to apply the national gridding by hand. It was a laborious process to begin with but after the first few sheets I was able to grid them at the rate of about ten minutes per quarter sheet. The task took two or three days per week for several weeks, during which I learned a great deal about the set-up at the Ordnance Survey which was useful for the rest of my life.

My task was to bring Goddard's list up to date and this included allocating a national grid reference for each locatable site. There can be no doubt that my banking experience helped me to perform this task accurately. I felt obliged to accept Goddard's identifications of barrows and the parish numbers which he allocated to them, without question except in the few cases where he was clearly mistaken. Since publication of *V.C.H. Wiltshire* (I, i) in 1957, several of the round barrows have been re-excavated by Paul Ashbee, who has shown that some of Goddard's identifications of the barrows dug by Hoare and Cunnington need revision.

During the first few months with V.C.H. I was based partly in London from which it was convenient to visit the Ordnance Survey Office then at Chessington in Surrey, and on other days I worked on the Wiltshire material in the Department of Prehistoric and Romano-British Antiquities in the British Museum, where every facility was extended to me by (Sir) Thomas Kendrick and his assistant John Brailsford, who provided me with a House Key to facilitate my work on their reserve collections.

Before long however I moved to Devizes where I was allocated an office in the Museum of the Wiltshire Archaeological Society, whose Hon. Secretary was then C.W. Pugh, uncle of R.B. Pugh, general editor of the Victoria County Histories. I worked under the supervision of Stuart Piggott for the earlier periods (down to the end of the Bronze Age) but as those were the periods with which I was most familiar, and he was based on Edinburgh, I needed (and received) little supervision from him: perhaps up to half an hour every few months when he happened to visit Devizes for other purposes. For the periods from the Early Iron Age onwards I received every encouragement from Christopher Hawkes, who got me to stay with him at Keble College for two or three days every few months, when he gave me an immense amount of encouragement and guidance. The experience was extremely beneficial if somewhat exhausting, and the stimulus from each visit lasted until the next. The system worked very well.

My *modus operandi* was to do the research on wet or indifferent days and the fieldwork on fine days. I was determined to visit and measure every barrow both long and round and all these measurements are recorded in the V.C.H. I produced two (it may have been three) slip catalogues and I believe these included extra information, such as dates of visit and land usage at time of visit, which were not included in the published volume but are still available at Devizes and probably at either the R.C.H.M. or the Ordnance Survey office. Perhaps I should add that the O.S. archaeological field staff had only just been greatly increased and I do not believe that much of my fieldwork duplicated what they had already done. I also visited most of the other archaeological sites in the county, and examined the available air photographs stereoscopically. By the end of January 1952 when I had ceased to be on the payroll of

V.C.H., I believe about nine-tenths of my V.C.H. work had been completed; but I continued to type out the *Archaeological Gazetteer* for several weeks more, and to do a little fieldwork on outstanding sites well into that year. Due to circumstances beyond my control it was not published until 1957. It was fortunate that the proportion of wet and fine days was roughly equal to the amount of written work and fieldwork required.

The distribution maps were to have been done by the Archaeology Division of the Ordnance Survey. Unfortunately the arrangement with them broke down and the contract was transferred to George Philip & Son Ltd. The resulting nine period maps are fairly satisfactory except that in my opinion the blue-green geological base map used for each overlay is much too dark. For Map IV (Middle Bronze Age), the enlarged plans of the Avebury and Stonehenge areas were inadvertently omitted from vol. I Part i. The plan of the Stonehenge region appeared as Fig. 10 in vol. I Part ii, but the plan of the environs of Avebury was inadvertently omitted altogether. Volume I (ii) was not published until 1973 and the interval of sixteen years between the two parts of the volume made it difficult to relate the two parts and I was not kept in the picture.

Before taking up my V.C.H. appointment I went, on my next visit to Salisbury, to the cathedral and stood before the monument to Sir Richard Colt Hoare, realising that I was about to try to contribute to an updated version of his *Ancient Wiltshire*. I also took my extra-mural class from London to Stonehenge where we were but-tonholed by one of the uniformed attendants who tried to usurp my role as guide and explain the monument to my class. He explained that 'Professor Guy Underwood of the British Museum' had been there with his dowsing apparatus and discovered that there were intersecting streams beneath each stone, and provided us with a good deal of other nonsense that was then passing current in pseudo-scientific circles. I got rid of him by giving him a tip, after which my class secretary told me that I would have been wiser to have tipped him at the start of our visit than at the finish. This attendant very kindly offered to check whatever I wrote about Stonehenge for the V.C.H, but we did not avail ourselves of his services. Three incidents in the course of my fieldwork are perhaps worth recalling. While I was measuring a group of barrows near Everleigh (on or near Snail Down), a woman with a horse, accompanied by her husband also with a horse, said to me, 'I wonder if you would mind telling us *precisely* what you think you are supposed to be doing?' On another occasion when reaching near a disc-barrow a few miles north-east of Salisbury, I became aware that it was on the edge of a R.A.F. training school for police dogs, and on my approach a considerable number of alsatian dogs started barking. I made a strategic withdrawal and wrote the Adjutant of the School, who kindly measured the barrow and sent me the necessary details. Actually it was just outside the boundary of the school. During my work for the V.C.H. I was sometimes invited to lecture on Wiltshire archaeology to various local societies. I once lectured at Mere, following which a lady was asked to propose a vote of thanks to me. She started by saying that 'the lecturer has given us a most lucid account of the people who lived in the old barrows . . .'.

In the course of my work I consulted the records of the Inspectorate of Ancient Monuments (as it then was), and among them found an interesting 'triangle' of correspondence involving Sir Charles Peers (Chief Inspector of Ancient Mon-uments), B. Howard Cunnington, curator of Devizes Museum, and A.D. Passmore of

Wanborough. The last had applied for a 'Roman coffin' somewhere on the Marlborough Downs to be scheduled; but when the scheduling notice was served on the landowner, he replied that it was a horse-trough which he had seen his father make, or helped his father to make. B.H. Cunnington's letter said, 'I cannot think who could have put that object up for scheduling', or words to that effect.

During my fieldwork I received help and encouragement from members of the V.C.H. Wiltshire Committee and others, including H.C. Brentnall and E.G.H. Kempson both of Marlborough College, Owen Meyrick, Hugh Shortt of Salisbury Museum, and Dr T.R. Thomson of Cricklade, all of whom have now passed on.

The most interesting finds resulting from my fieldwork were perhaps the rediscovery of the little round barrow Mere 6a in May 1950 by the luxuriant growth of buttercups on it (*V.C.H.* 1(i), 182), and the recognition that the earthwork enclosure first noted by Hoare (*A.W.* 1, 42) on the north spur of Whitesheet Hill (Kilmington) is a neolithic causewayed enclosure, its southern margin being overlapped by a presumed Bronze Age round barrow (KILMINGTON 4). Contrary to Piggott (*W.A.M.* 54, 404), it was first identified from the ground and subsequently confirmed from air photographs.

To conclude, my mandate was to do the best in the time available and within the limits imposed: in fact to get a quart into a pint pot. I became so steeped in the subject that it did not occur to me that the Gazetteer would be difficult to use by those not so familiar with the material, unless it was accompanied by a better system of cross-referencing. Above all there should have been included a map showing the parishes. These criticisms were in fact made by John Musty in his review (*W.A.M.* 57, 413) and Nicholas Thomas in his (*Antiq. J.* 38, 132–3), and to some extent by C.A. Ralegh Radford (*Proc. Prehist. Soc.* 24, 234). A minor irritation was the insistence of the editors that disc-barrow should be spelled disk-barrow, contrary to the otherwise universal custom.

Chapter 6

The Museum Curator

'The attention of the curators will have to be drawn, not merely to the collection of useful specimens, but quite as much to the exclusion of objects which serve [no useful purpose].
– Lt Gen. A.H.L.F. Pitt-Rivers, *Address at the Opening of the Dorset County Museum*, 7 January 1884.

British Archaeology and Numismatics
As my work on *V.C.H. Wiltshire* volume I (i) was progressing, B. Howard Cunnington died in 1950 followed by his wife Maud E. Cunnington in 1951, and they bequeathed a sum which was, by the standards of the time, enough to provide a modest salary for a paid curator of Devizes Museum for the first time. It was however a year or two before their estates were wound up and an appointment became possible, and circumstances caused me to apply for the curatorship in archaeology and ethnography in the City Museum, Bristol, which had just become vacant. Of three candidates short-listed I was appointed, but it was some months before I was able to take up the appointment, which I did from 1 February 1952 when within a fortnight of my 45th birthday.

I arrived knowing nothing whatever of a museum curator's duties except what I had learned from being a customer of other museums. For this reason I was probably wise to enter a well-staffed and departmentalised museum. Having been Hon. Treasurer of the Prehistoric Society since 1947 I was personally known to many of the leading prehistorians and archaeologists of the day, and was in an ideal position to seek advice whenever I needed it, and I have never ceased to be grateful for the many kindnesses shown to me by fellow archaeologists whenever I sought their help. Within a year or so I was appointed Recorder of Section H (Archaeology and Anthropology) of the British Association for Advancement of Science, and this put me in a strong position to get similar help on ethnographical matters. There can be no doubt that I was doing too much in the way of extra-curatorial duties, but I managed by arriving at the Museum at 8.30 each morning and staying a good deal longer than the 'official' leaving time of 5.30 p.m. Between 8.30 and 9 a.m. I usually dealt with the Prehistoric Society treasurership, which included the chore of billing those in arrear as well as policy matters.

As barrows were among my strongest suits, one of my first tasks, having ascertained that the Marshfield barrows had been excavated between 1947 and 1949 but the report not yet published and not even written, was to borrow the excavator's notebook and draft the basis of a report for him. I sent it to him for correction and amplification, and submitted it to those who had assisted on the 'dig', and the result was 'The Marshfield Barrows' by G.L. Gettins, H. Taylor and L.V.G. (*Trans. Bristol Gloucestershire*

Archaeol. Soc. 72, 23–44, for 1953). The report is well below standard but the best that could be done in the circumstances.

There is no doubt that museum curators tend to attract the material in which they are specially interested. During 1953 (Sir) Thomas Kendrick, keeper of the department of prehistoric and Romano-British antiquities in the British Museum (of which he was later Director) passed to us on indefinite loan their excellent model of the Stoney Littleton long barrow, which we have had on display ever since. The same year we received, from a lad named P. Bush who then worked in a fried fish shop but assisted Guy Underwood of Bradford-on-Avon to excavate a round barrow called Jug's Grave at Monkton Farleigh, the sherds of a bell beaker which he had found there apparently in his own excavations. On 9 May 1956 I identified the foot-carvings on the cist-slab in the Pool Farm (Mendip) round barrow which had been excavated in 1930, and the slab was presented to Bristol City Museum and replaced on the site by a replica made by students of the West of England College of Art. During 1958 Mr James Deans, farmer of Marshfield, presented the bronze dagger and part of a second dagger ploughed out of the round barrow known as St. Oswald's Tump. The Museum also received from W.J. Wedlake the material found in Barrows II and III, Wall Mead, Timsbury, excavated by him 1965–7. Dr Herbert Taylor presented his excellent casts of the grave-goods from the Tynings (Cheddar) round barrows and the Corston (near Bath) beaker cists, the originals of which are in the Museum of the University of Bristol Spelaeological Society.

A high priority task was to improve the relations between the U.B.S.S. and the department of Archaeology in the City Museum. The basis of this should clearly be to accept the entitlement of the U.B.S.S. to the finds from their own excavations and research, but to assert the duty of the City Museum to attract finds from other sources. The situation was complicated by a tendency of some of those who made archaeological finds to report them to the University rather than the City Museum, under the impression that they were one and the same thing: especially as the main University building is next to the City Museum. A detailed account of my relations with the President of the U.B.S.S. (Dr E.K. Tratman) during this period would be out of place; it is enough to state that they were characterized by a veneer of urbanity.

A systematic record of routine matters would here be out of place and my observations are confined to certain occurrences of particular note. One of my first distinguished visitors was Hans Helbaek who came in Spring 1952 from Denmark to examine our Neolithic and Bronze Age pottery for taking casts of grain impressions for his study of prehistoric cereals. Unfortunately he called on the one day of the week when the Director called a staff meeting at which the attendance of all curators was obligatory. As Helbaek was an authority of international standing I was very upset when my Director insisted that I attend the weekly staff meeting, thereby having to neglect my distinguished visitor.

In my early enthusiasm I came to the Museum one Boxing Day (probably in 1954) although the staff were supposed to be off duty. The only other member of the staff of the Museum and Art Gallery present was my Director Dr Wallis. Sir Leonard Woolley came to see the Art Gallery director about some pictures but of course he was away, so Dr Wallis brought him in to see me. He stayed most of the day regaling me with his delightful anecdotal conversation which all may read in his little book *As I Seem to Remember* (1962).

Another distinguished visitor was Sir Cyril Fox, who came to examine our Celtic metalwork for his book *Pattern and Purpose: Early Celtic Art in Britain* (1958), I believe some years before the book was published. In my ignorance I had allowed the display technician to fix our magnificent bronze collar from Wraxall on a display panel with bits of wire which broke the continuity of the curvilinear decoration of the object. Sir Cyril drew my attention to this and it was not long before I had the object re-displayed. Sir Cyril had the gift of infecting others with his enthusiasm.

In 1956 I visited the Museum of the Bristol Waterworks Company and was particularly interested in their 'Bronze Age anvil' which had supposedly been found in the course of reservoir excavations, and was such an unusual item that an illustration of it was used on the dust-jacket of Dr Dobson's *The Archaeology of Somerset* (1931). I borrowed it and took it to the British Museum laboratory where it was examined by Herbert Maryon and Dr R.M. Organ, who after various tests concluded that it is a modern forgery. Their examination of a 'Bronze Age palstave' from the same source gave the same answer. These 'discoveries' resulted from the offer of over-generous rewards for archaeological finds.

I very soon learned that the commonest enquiries from the public involved the identification of George III 'cartwheel' pennies dated 1797, and much less frequently of Bristol farthing trade tokens, as these items were still being found in peoples' gardens and on allotments etc. It was during that period when one of the weekly or monthly magazines periodically carried an article on pennies of 1920 implying that not many were minted that year and they were worth £8 (i.e. 1,920 pennies at 240 to the pound equals £8). People would ring the museum curator and ask how they could get their £8, as they understood not many were minted that year. It was a pleasure to give them the answer recommended by the Department of Coins and Medals in the British Museum: 'the number of pennies and other coins minted each year can be ascertained by consulting the Annual Reports of the Royal Mint, available in your local reference library'.

At intervals during my curatorship pre-Roman coins were submitted which had been found locally. Each occasion constituted a 'red letter day':

1952:   pre-Roman gold stater of EISV found at Hardwicke near Gloucester; original retained by finder; electrotype made for Museum.

1955:   pre-Roman gold stater inscribed ANTED RIG found at Kings Weston near Bristol and purchased from the finder.

1958:   silver coin of the Coriosolites, from the Grouville hoard (Jersey) given by R.G. Fardon, cousin of the finder.

1964:   pre-Roman gold stater, 'British Remic' type, found at Kingswood near Bristol, acquired.

1965:   pre-Roman gold stater, Chute type, found at Pensford near Bristol, and acquired.

1968:   Two pre-Roman uninscribed silver coins of the Dobunni, found at Naunton on the Cotswolds before 1928, acquired.

In 1969 I had occasion to arrange the display in the prehistoric room of the new Gough's Cave Museum at Cheddar. For this purpose I had made electrotypes of the *obverse* and *reverse* of a pre-Roman gold stater found at Cheddar and in the British Museum. I had two pairs made – one for Gough's Cave Museum and the other for the reserve collections in Bristol City Museum. A few months later, on returning from lunch one afternoon I was handed a 'coin' for identification, brought in by a lad who gave his address as a naval training college at Portishead. I recognised it at once as one of these electrotypes. I rang the manager of Gough's Cave, Cheddar, to ask if he would check their museum display for this item, and he informed me that it was missing. The lad had stolen it from the showcase of Gough's Cave Museum and submitted it to the very person who had caused it to be made. The lad was stationed at a school of correction.

It was not long before I became aware that Bristol at one time had its own coin mint, but the fact was forcefully brought home to me when A.H. Baldwin & Sons sent us their catalogue of the first part of the R.C. Lockett sale in 1955. I quickly re-catalogued all our Bristol mint coins to ascertain exactly what we already held and from then onwards we got our agents to bid for whatever coins would fill the gaps in our series. In 1962 the Museum published my *Brief Numismatic History of Bristol* which increased public awareness of our mint and made it easier to strengthen our collection. From this time onwards I spent most of the annual purchase money of my Department on adding to our holding of coins minted in Bristol. Much of the last three years of my curatorship was devoted to the preparation of the Bristol portion of the British Academy *Sylloge of Coins of the British Isles: Bristol and Gloucester Museums* (1973), edited with great ability and charm by Christopher Blunt.

The millennium of the crowning of King Edgar in the forerunner of Bath Abbey also occurred in 1973, and I prepared a monograph on *The Bath Mint* which was published that year by Spink and Son. I was careful to state that King Edgar's four predecessors from Athelstan onwards were kings of all England for parts of their reigns, but my zeal for historical accuracy did not please those in authority in Bath, where it has for long been part of the 'tourist history' of Bath that King Edgar was the first king of all England (as stated on the bronze plaque on the wall of the east end of the Abbey). They refused to put my monograph on sale in the Mementos bookshop in the Pump Room, with the result that the book did not sell as well as it would otherwise have done. None the less it sold out after ten years or so and is now out of print.

On 15–17 April 1983 the British Association of Numismatic Societies held their Annual Congress at the Hawthorns Hotel in Bristol, when I took the opportunity to update my accounts of the mints of Bath and Bristol in a lecture on the mints of both cities and their interrelationship.

From the late 1950s I had a Conservation assistant, the first being Kenneth Barton (later Director of the Hampshire Museums Service) who was also an extremely keen excavator especially in medieval Bristol and its surroundings. From 1 January 1965 I had an Assistant Curator in the person of Max Hebditch (now Director of the Museum of London). We got on extremely well together. He tended to deal with Roman and later matters, my own provinces being prehistoric material and numismatics; but we were interchangeable when one was away.

During most of 1965–68 we were involved in planning and developing a new Gallery of South-Western British Prehistory, our deadline being to have it ready for the Summer Conference of the Prehistoric Society, held in the City Museum 1–7

September 1968 under the presidency of J.D. Cowen. The arrangement of this gallery was the only subject on which I had a major policy disagreement with both my Director and my assistant, who insisted that the material from the Bristol region be shown separately, presumably for the benefit of the Bristol ratepayers. My own view was (and remains) that this policy caused duplication by having a period sequence in both local and regional sections, and reduced the impact of the period displays by splitting the material in this way. The development of this gallery was somewhat retarded by my absence in hospital followed by convalescence for some weeks having a stomach ulcer dealt with.

By the skin of our teeth we not only managed to have the gallery virtually complete by 1 September, but also had the *Guide Catalogue to the South-Western British Prehistoric Collections* ready by the date, albeit bound in such a way that the pages fell apart as soon as it was handled, on account of some lack of liaison between designer and printer. This detail was subsequently put right. After almost twenty years this display continues almost unchanged, and has 'dated' very little: just some slight changes in dates due to C14 calibration, and perhaps a revision of the chronological sequence of chambered long barrows. The display does however lack the flexibility which might enable recent acquisitions to be absorbed in it.

Egyptology
When I was given a guided tour of the interior of the Step Pyramid of King Zoser at Saqqara c.1944, I asked my guide if I could pick up and keep one or two of the faience tiles which had fallen off the walls of the interior galleries. He told me that I could keep one or two of the broken tiles. When I assumed my curatorial duties in February 1952 I presented these to the City Museum (H 4967-8).

In 1956 Mr C.R. Mapp, a Cheltenham schoolmaster, died and bequeathed his collection of Egyptian antiquities and his books on Egyptology to Bristol City Museum. I visited his house to collect the material. At that time my storeroom was already full to overflowing and there were no foreseeable prospects of my getting more room. With much reluctance I found it necessary to decline one or two exceptionally large items from the Mapp collection. I only hope these items were comparatively unimportant. For this reason some of the items in the Mapp Catalogue are missing. My recollection is that the assemblage contained a fair proportion of modern fakes such as any collector without special knowledge would be likely to accumulate.

Among my visitors until c.1960 was Labib Habachi, sometime Inspector of Antiquities at Aswan, whom I had known in Egypt during the 1939–45 war. He came to inspect our pink granite statue of the Syrian goddess Anta. He was to guide me around the Tombs of the Nobles at Aswan during my retirement holiday in March 1972. Another distinguished visitor was Dr Dieter Arnold who was making a study of the reliefs from the funerary temple of Nebhepet-Re Mentuhotep, about which he wrote a book published in 1979.

One of the most colourful personalities in Egyptology was Giovanni Battista Belzoni, whose collection of drawings of the tomb of Sety I at Thebes was presented to the Museum in 1900, by Mr C.E. Wilson, a master at King Edward's School, London. The circumstances of this gift were not recorded and I never discovered how he came by the drawings. Unfortunately some of the drawings of the most interesting reliefs, including that of the snake of 24 coils, are missing, so that the collection is far from complete although it comprises more than 300 items nearly all of the tomb of Sety I. In 1959–60 I had the Belzoni drawings mounted by David Bull, then on the conservation staff of the City Art Gallery. In June 1959 a small selection of them formed the Museum's 'Feature of the Month'. In August/September 1961 I put on a much larger display which included a reconstruction of the astronomical ceiling from the tomb, and gave a public lecture on the tomb of Sety I and the Belzoni drawings on 5 September. Sometime afterwards it was a pleasure to welcome Stanley Mayes who came to see the Belzoni drawings when preparing his excellent book *The Great Belzoni* (1959), in which he speaks well of our interest in the Belzoni drawings.

In 1822 Mrs Belzoni put on an exhibition of Egyptian antiquities in Bath while her husband was on his way to Timbuctoo (where he died in December 1823). Some of the objects were for sale and were purchased by a member of the Paget family of Cranmore in East Somerset. One of their descendants gave them to Wells Museum during the curatorship of its founder H.E. Balch who tended to be omniverous in his collecting policy. When Dr F.S. Wallis became curator of Wells Museum he passed these items to my department. They contain nothing particularly outstanding but are of interest by reason of their association with Belzoni.

During my curatorship 1952–72 it was necessary to give priority to developing our collections of material from the Mendips, Cotswolds and the Bristol region, and to rely mainly on gifts for Egyptology. We had some pieces of good fortune. In 1964 we received from a lady in Bath, who had been using them as door stoppers, two royal heads: one a quartzite head of Nebhepet-Re Mentuhotep (H 5038) and a black granite head of Tuthmosis IV (H 5037). In the early 1960s I had occasion to visit Mere in Wiltshire and happened to notice, in the conservatory of the house next to the vicarage, a granite head later identified as of Horemheb, who commanded the Egyptian army in the reign of Tutankhamun. We eventually acquired this for a nominal sum.

In 1962 Dr John Harris, an Oxford Egyptologist (a former pupil of my Egyptology class at the City Literary Institute in London) went through our reserve collections at my request and picked out all the forgeries, which we then put in separate storage units. Eventually he came across a forgery of a forgery. We decided that this could safely be thrown away and acted accordingly. Some months later my Director invited Dr Glyn Daniel to deliver one of our winter lectures. He chose as his subject 'Fakes, frauds and forgeries in archaeology' and it was given on 12 December 1962. I was asked to arrange a small display to illustrate his lecture. The 'forgery of a forgery' would have been the centre-piece of this exhibit: but I had already thrown it away!

In 1964 I had published in the Museum news sheet *Mosaic* (no. 4) a note entitled 'The Pharaoh's Curse' in which I recalled that some years previously (almost certainly in 1954), a lady came into my office with a small collection of miscellaneous Egyptian antiquities, saying that ever since she got them she had been having bad luck, and was sure that they were possessed of the 'pharaoh's curse'. She therefore wished to give them to the Museum. She would not sell them because she thought that the bad luck would not then be transferred to the new owners. Accordingly we gratefully received her generous gift. Following publication of this note, one or two other people donated their Egyptian antiquities (including some modern forgeries!). This note resulted in my giving a talk on Radio Bristol at their invitation about the Pharaoh's Curse.

In 1966 we received on long loan from Bath Municipal Library some Egyptian antiquities formerly in the Museum of the Bath Royal Literary and Scientific Institution, which had become defunct some years previously. These included the coronation relief of Ramesses II, the inscribed upper part of a kneeling statue of Kha-em-waset (a son of Ramesses II who acted as an Inspector of Antiquities) and an Anubis figure of wood covered with pitch.

One of my last tasks as Curator of Archaeology before retiring was to prepare the *Guide Catalogue to the Collections from Ancient Egypt*, an 84 page book with which I was well pleased, although it suffered from unsympathetic handling by the Museum's Design Department (e.g. Fig. 1 out of its chronological place; figs 37 and 38 should have been placed on the same page, the head above, the feet below, and the latter is grossly over-enlarged; fig. 13 is over-reduced). Its publication in 1972 coincided with the 50th anniversary of the opening of the tomb of Tutankhamun. Egyptology was then all the rage, and on 23 November I gave the Museum lecture on the Egyptian pyramids as one of a series devoted to Egyptology. A stickler for correctness, one of my last acts before retiring was to paint out the left eye of the cast of the bust of Nefertiti to show it as in the original (she was blind in her left eye). I spent my retirement holiday in Egypt in February/March 1972.

There is a tendency for some of those submitting Egyptian antiquities for identification to say that they are said to have come from the tomb of Tutankhamun. Such a person came to me in the summer of 1968 with some odd Egyptian items, stating that his wife had received them from the Countess of Carnarvon, widow of the discoverer of Tutankhamun's tomb. I was then infernally busy preparing for the Prehistoric Society's Summer Conference in Bristol that year, and told him I could not spare him more than 5 minutes. He was annoyed and claimed that as a Bristol ratepayer he was entitled to more of my time. The matter was smoothed over; but some months later the *Bristol Evening Post* for 9 May 1969 announced the death of Lady Carnarvon on 8th at the age of 92, and her funeral a few days later which took place in Clifton Pro-Cathedral. She had been living for some years at 19 Hampton Road, Bristol 6, less than a km from my flat in Clifton.

Mediterranean Archaeology
One of my first acts after assuming my curatorial duties in 1952 was to remove from display the small but excellent collection of Attic black figure and red figure vases which were then shown in a wall case (in conformity with the testator's request that they always be shown in the case where they were then displayed). As I replaced these vases by palaeolithic hand-axes found within reasonable distance of Bristol, my conscience somehow told me that palaeolithic hand-axes do not have an aesthetic appeal equal to that of the Greek vases which they were replacing.

Two or three years later Prof. Brian Shefton, an acknowledged authority on Greek vases, came to examine such vases as we have. I picked up a vase by the handle to show him, and he forthwith gave me a mini-lecture on how to handle a Greek vase: *never* pick it up by its handle because many of them have had their handles broken off and stuck on again (not always very securely); *always* handle a Greek vase by its body and with both hands. After he had infected me with his enthusiasm, I again put our Greek vases on show, but in an 'island' case so that each vase could then be seen (more or less) through 360 degrees. As a matter of interest, most of our Greek vases were collected by Samuel Rogers (1763–1855), author of *Poems in Italy* and other works. From his collection they passed eventually to that of E. Sidney Hartland, sometime Recorder for Gloucester and an eminent authority on the disposal of the dead, who wrote several articles on that subject in Hastings' *Encyclopaedia of Religion and Ethics*. After his death his widow presented them to Bristol City Museum.

From 1957 onwards I began taking most of my annual holidays in the Mediterranean and my interest in Mediterranean archaeology rapidly increased. On each visit I tried to acquire a small item to add to the museum collection.

Ehtnography
My appointment in 1952 was as 'Curator of archaeology and ethnography' but I quickly discovered that it would be impossible to cover both subjects effectively. My predecessor had done so but only by not publishing anything except a couple of short notes. I must frankly admit that I had little interest in the ethnographical material, with the exception of the West African sculpture for which I had some affinity as I had spent a week in Lagos on the way to Egypt in December 1941.

In 1955 the British Association for the Advancement of Science met in Bristol and I was Recorder for section H (Archaeology and Anthropology). We decided on a theme, Death and the Disposal of the Dead, which encouraged both archaeologists and anthropologists to work together, and for this purpose I arranged a display which included ethnographical material selected with the help of Adrian Digby of the Department of Ethnography in the British Museum, and G.W.B. Huntingford who had much experience in East Africa. In going through the material in store for this display, Adrian Digby noticed a West African dish which had been ritually 'killed' at a funeral, by having a hole punctured in its base. My predecessor, not knowing the significance of this, had mended this hole, and I spent some time re-making the hole to enable the dish to be used in our display as a ritually 'killed' object. Our programme did have the effect of drawing together the two parts of section H which had been tending to drift apart.

In 1957 I had a visit from K.C. Murray, retired director of the Lagos Museum, who helped me to rearrange and re-label our West African material.

When Alan Warhurst became Museum Director in June 1960 he quickly realized that it was impossible for one curator to cover both archaeology and ethnography and arranged for another curator to assist with the ethnography. During the time that I tried to cover both, I put on a display of primitive currency and my article 'Primitive currency in a provincial museum' appeared in *Cunobelin* II, 55–57 (the Year Book of the British Association of Numismatic Societies).

The Report of Bristol Museum and Art Gallery for 1961 states that a Bristolian's drawing of one of the Museum's Mende masks was used as the design on two denominations of the stamps of Sierra Leone.

Those wishing to get a view of my Curator's Office in Bristol City Museum may like to know that its walls were adorned with:
   i)   an air photograph of the Belas Knap long barrow;
   ii) a photograph of myself lying extended in the stone-lined grave of a round

barrow in Langridge Wood, Withycombe, West Somerset, demonstrating that it is long enough to receive an adult male in the extended posture;

iii) a quotation from Lt. Gen Pitt-Rivers:
'As a rule I have been well served by my clerks'
— Pitt-Rivers, *Excavations on Cranborne Chase* IV (1898), 27–28.

I was awarded, by examination, the Diploma of the Museums Association on 11 February 1959 and was elected a Fellow of the Museums Association some years later. I resigned from the Museums Association on my retirement in 1972.

1. The author with plasticine model, January 1919.

2.   'The barrow hunter's dream.' Sketch by Stuart Piggott to L.V.G., c.1931.

7. BARROW EAST OF BEAULIEU HILL-TOP

Mound.

Berm.

Ditch.

Outer bank.

3. The use of 'Grinsellbirds' to indicate the essential features of a rare type of round barrow; first used in paper on 'Bell-barrows', 1933. *Proc. Prehist. Soc. East Anglia, VII.*

4. L.V.G., 1938 and 1943.

5. Outing of Middle East (Photographic) Interpretation Unit to Saqqara, V.E. Day, 1945. The group surrounds the reassembled casing-slabs of the south face of the pyramid of Unis, commemorating its restoration by Khaemwese, a son of Ramesses II. Photo: L. V. Grinsell.

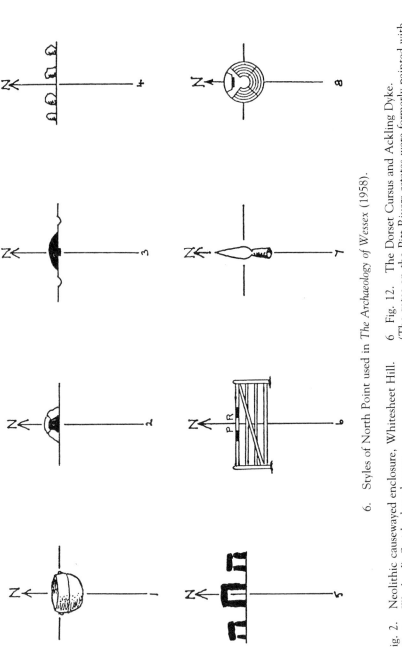

6. Styles of North Point used in *The Archaeology of Wessex* (1958).

1 Fig. 2.   Neolithic causewayed enclosure, Whitesheet Hill.
2 Fig. 4.   Wayland's Smithy long barrow.
3 Fig. 7.   Avebury and its environs.
4 Fig. 8.   Avebury circles and Kennet Avenue.
5 Fig. 9.   Stonehenge: general plan.

6 Fig. 12.   The Dorset Cursus and Ackling Dyke.
    (The gates on the Pitt-Rivers estates were formerly painted with
    a yellow band between two blue bands).
7 Fig. 15.   Late Bronze Age enclosures on the Marlborough Downs.
8 Fig. 18.   *Durnovaria* (Roman Dorchester).

7. The author in stone-lined grave of round barrow in Langridge Wood, West Somerset (WITHYCOMBE 4). Photo: Anthony Locke.

"There now! Driven off again, and my men scattered. I am tired of this. I am black and blue all over with hard thumps.

"Hangman's Stone," near Bovey House, about five miles east of Sidmouth. Sketched May 1857. There is a tradition, that a man once stole a sheep near this spot. In order to carry it away, he tied the legs together, placing them round his forehead, with the body on his back. When he came to this stone, he sat down, with his back against it, placing the animal on the top of it: but the sheep struggled, and accidentally slipped its legs round the man's neck. He was strangled, being unable to extricate himself. There is a separate sketch of the stone, in order to shew its shape.

8.   Sketches by Peter Orlando Hutchinson (1810–97).

Chapter 7

Extra-mural Activities

'Please Mr Grinsell, we keep on getting messed up with our PERIODS.' 'It depends what sort of periods you mean.' 'We are not sure whether the Bronze Age came before or after the Stone Age; and when was the Iron Age?'
– Q & A with two female students, at an extra-mural class on Prehistoric Britain, held at the City Literary Institute, London. *c.*1948.

London 1946–51
My first experience of exta-mural classes in archaeology was early in 1936 when I attended, as a student, a class at the City Literary Institute, London WC1, on British archaeology, run by someone with M.A. (Oxon) after his name. He was hopelessly incompetent, and in his first two or three lectures made such glaring errors as to describe the Coldrum (Kent) chambered long barrow as a stone circle, and to display his ignorance of the Alfred Jewel which he was unaware was in the Ashmolean Museum.

After returning from the 1939–45 war I was allocated to the British Museum branch of Barclays Bank Ltd from 1 February 1946, and very soon I renewed my link with the City Literary Institute whose Principal was then Mr T.G. Williams, who invited me to lecture there. Between 1946 and 1949 I lectured on both Egyptology and British prehistory. Among my Egyptology students was a boy of about 15 named John Harris, son of the Principal of Pitman's College in Southampton Row round the corner. This lad later went on to Oxford University where he took a degree in Egyptology and eventually became Professor of Egyptology at Copenhagen University and is now Director of the Gulbenkian Foundation at Durham University. Another of my students was Miss Barbara Sewell, who afterwards became personal typist to Sir Alan Gardiner and typed and indexed his book *Egypt of the Pharaohs* (1961).

As far as British prehistory was concerned I knew a lot about the Neolithic and Bronze Ages, especially long and round barrows, but very little else, and I usually had to 'mug up' each lecture in order to be at least one point in front of my class. Among my 'students' at the City Lit. were Miss Florence Patchett (an expert on Cornish archaeology) and Mrs Helen O'Neil (an expert on Cotswold archaeology and wife of the Chief Inspector of Ancient Monuments for England), who knew a lot more than I did about the pre-Roman Iron Age and once caught me out for confusing Iron Age 'A' and 'B'.

Among my other students was Miss June Morey, an expert on the petrological identification of prehistoric stone implements, and Miss J. Mollie Bull, who became Assistant Secretary of the Prehistoric Society for more than twenty years, and no society has ever had a more conscientious, devoted and reliable officer. Another was

Donald Bailey, then a lad of about 18 who was an assistant in the Marylebone Public Library, and spent his spare cash on collecting Greek, Roman and other ancient lamps – the cheapest antiquities available in the junk shops. He is now on the staff of the British Museum Department of Greek and Roman Antiquities, a leading authority on ancient lamps, and author of *A Catalogue of the Lamps in the British Museum* (1975 onwards), three volumes published so far.

Although the Goldsmiths' College in South London was a tedious journey, their Principal, Ian Gulland, was such an inspiring personality that it was a special pleasure to lecture there. My first lecture attracted only four people and he asked me if I was willing to continue. I replied, Yes – of course! The numbers slowly increased to ten by the end of the term. He suggested that the class continue after Easter but that the title be amended to 'Holidays with an Archaeologist'. The numbers at the start of the new term rose to 17 and afterwards we had no problem about maintaining the numbers. Ian Gulland and his wife almost always came on the Sunday excursions that I ran in conjunction with this class. On one occasion my Egyptology class was visited by an L.C.C. Education Inspector who usually looked into each class for ten minutes or so and covered six or more classes each evening. He came to my class when I was describing how the pyramids were built and he stayed the whole period of two hours and afterwards gave a favourable report to the Principal.

It was my practice to have a word with new students and ask them how they became interested in the subject. Once a lady told me that she had been enthralled by reading *The Riddle of Prehistoric Britain*, by Comyns Beaumont (a 'lunatic fringe' book). There is no doubt that books of that kind sometimes awaken an interest which can be guided into more appropriate channels.

When I ended my courses at the City Literary Institute in December 1951, my class members presented me with a Certificate worded as under:

'We the undersigned, all fully over-tumulised in the City Literary Institute Prehistory class, do hereby grant and devise to Leslie Valentine Grinsell FSA the following titles to use at his discretion and personal risk at all times and in sundry places, to wit:

C.C.   Critic of the Carvings
D.D.   Dragoman of the Dolmens
K.C.   King of the Cromlechs
LL.B.   Lord of the Long Barrows
L.R.B.   Lister of the Round Barrows

Dated this 11th Day of December 1951 A.D.
(Signed):   V. Leleux; J. Mollie Bull; E. Livens; R.U. Rowley; A. Halcrow Verstage;
              G. Cooper; F.S. Clarke; Gladys Best; A.M. Truman. [Other signatures
              have faded and are now illegible].

My first lectures at country houses adapted to weekend courses were at Pendley Manor (Herts) between 1946 and 1949, where Dr Margaret Murray and I and others ran a weekend on Ancient Egypt, and (Sir) Albert Richardson and I took part in a course on the Chilterns. During my lecture on barrows, I mentioned the story of the

Six Hills near Stevenage, quoting the local query 'which two are the farthest apart?', the answer being the ones at each end. Sir Albert, who followed me but did not hear my lecture, spoke on the local inns, and mentioned the same story in connection with the Six Hills Inn near the barrows, to everyone's amusement. I lectured at weekend courses at Urchfont (Wiltshire) at least three times: on V.C.H. Wiltshire, on the folklore of prehistoric sites, and (1–3 May 1981, with Richard Bradley and Alasdair Whittle) on the Bronze Age round barrows of Wessex. On another occasion I lectured at Dillington (Somerset) in a symposium on Wessex archaeology.

Bristol 1952–81

Soon after moving to Bristol early in 1952 I gave a term of evening lectures on archaeology at the Folk House, but ran into problems. In London it was obligatory to set 'homework' which had the effect of driving away the 'wallflowers' who would otherwise look passively at the slides without really taking an active interest in the subject or following it up with any practical work. Assuming that a similar situation existed in Bristol, I applied the same technique and set my class members 'homework'. The Warden's wife was among my class members and told her husband and various other class members were reluctant to do their 'homework'. Because of this I was not reappointed after this term. It was, I believe, three or four years before I was able to resume lecturing at the Folk House after another Warden had been appointed. I did not again try setting 'homework' but understood that members were expected to have an interest in archaeology outside the class: it might be digging on an excavation, or reading, or studying a particular aspect, or visiting sites at weekends or on holidays.

In Bristol my courses until 1958 were concerned with Egyptology and British archaeology (mainly prehistoric). From Christmas 1957 onwards I acquired the habit of spending Christmas and the New Year on archaeological visits to the Mediterranean, and my courses of lectures henceforth included an increasing proportion of Mediterranean material.

It was during this earlier period that a curious incident occurred. During my period as chief cashier at the British Museum branch of Barclays Bank Ltd 1946–49, a young Swede came to cash a cheque drawn on Svenska Handelsbanken, Stockholm, payable at Barclays Bank Ltd Foreign branch in Fenchurch Street E.C. I told him that I could not cash it because it was drawn payable only at our Fenchurch Street branch a couple of stations away on the tube. The cheque was signed Bertil Almgren. I asked him if he was by any chance related to Oscar Almgren, whose book on (Swedish) rock-carvings and folklore I had read (at least the French summary at the end!) He replied that Oscar Almgren was his father, and that he (Bertil) was in London studying the Viking antiquities in the British Museum. I then told him that I would be delighted to cash his cheque to save him the bother of going to Fenchurch Street.

Some ten years or more later, I was lecturing to my Folk House class on Saxon and Viking antiquities, and happened to mention my encounter with Bertil Almgren in the late 1940s. A member of my class, Mr G.L. Proctor, author of *The Young Traveller in Sweden* (1953), then said he could tell me the 'other half' of that story. When he was in Stockholm Museum being shown their Viking antiquities by Bertil Almgren, the latter told him: 'It is astonishing what a lot you British people know about Swedish archaeology. I went into a bank in the middle of London some years ago to cash a cheque, and the cashier who paid me my money told me that he had read my father's books on Swedish archaeology!'

Regrettably I have destroyed most of the programmes of my courses at the Folk House and elsewhere. It must suffice to state that each term the course included at least one or two field trips. There was a memorable one to the Wansdyke, by hired coach which dropped us at Shepherd's Shore on the road between Devizes and Beckhampton, and we walked on a magnificent day (I believe 21 March) all along its course as far as Shaw House (about 8 km as the crow flies) where the coach picked us up and took us into Marlborough for tea; then back via Avebury to Bristol.

My course at the Folk House October–December 1979 covered a little of Egypt, Byblos and the Lebanon, Cyprus, Minoan Crete, Mycenaean Greece, Sicily, Malta, Sardinia and Corsica, Majorca and Minorca, all from my trips between 1958 and 1978, and it included a visit to Bristol City Museum on a Saturday to see their Mediterranean material. My last course at the Folk House was October/December 1981, on 'Monuments of Ancient Egypt', and this likewise included a Saturday afternoon visit to the City Museum.

Several of my Bristol students have since attained archaeological distinction. These include Dr Ann Hamlin (now Chief Inspector of Ancient Monuments and Historic Buildings in Northern Ireland); Dr H. Stephen Green (now Keeper of Archaeology in the National Museum of Wales, Cardiff); Mrs Nancy Langmaid (sometime assistant at Norwich Castle Museum); and Dr Alan Vince, now on the staff of the Museum of London and a leading authority on medieval and post-medieval pottery.

Youth Hostel 'Countryside Archaeology' Weekends
Sometime between 1949 and 1951 I took my London archaeology classes on a weekend based on the Youth Hostel then at Plough Cottage, on the Bath road two miles west of Marlborough. I had already done a good deal of my own fieldwork from Youth Hostels since 1946 and was to some extent in tune with the average Youth Hosteller. I was therefore well placed to experiment with a weekend on 25/26 April 1953 entitled 'Wessex Prehistory', based on the Marlborough Youth Hostel. I had as co-director Nicholas Thomas, then curator of Devizes Museum. The emphasis in both the lectures on Saturday evening and the field trip on the Sunday was of course on Avebury and its surroundings. On Sunday morning we first visited the Manton round barrow just north of the Hostel: a barrow which yielded a rich grave-group now in Devizes Museum. We next proceeded towards the Manton chambered long barrow, but as we approached it I realised that it had been bulldozed, most probably during the previous winter, although it was a scheduled ancient monument. Our party of more than 60 people included a reporter with the Swindon newspapers, and of course he communicated the information to them on his return home on the Sunday evening. It was not long before the news had reached the national press, and when I came down to breakfast on Tuesday morning and opened my *Daily Telegraph* I was greeted with the headline, '4,000 YEAR OLD BURIAL GROUND DESTROYED: Long Barrow on Wiltshire Downs'. The same day *The Times* carried an article headed 'Manton Down barrow destroyed: discovery by Youth Hostel party'. *Punch* for 6 May 1953 followed with a humorous article entitled 'No Laughter at Manton'. During the following weeks my work at the Museum was hindered by my being pestered by 'phone calls from

importunate newspaper people and the media wanting to know more about the destruction of the long barrow.

Between 1953 and 1967 I arranged more than a dozen of these weekends, always in either spring or autumn, either before the fields get under standing corn or after the crops have been harvested: the best times of the year for fieldwork. Each normally took the form of supper on the Saturday evening with an appropriate menu written with a touch of humour (specimen: Fig. 1).

Countryside Archaeology Weekend
MARLBOROUGH YOUTH HOSTEL
25/26 Oct., 1958

Supper Menu, Saturday 25 October.

Creme du Tumulus Longue de Ouest Kennet
(Cream of the West Kennet long barrow)

Coupe d'Avebury
Maitre de l'Auberge de la Jeunesse
(Avebury Pie Warden of the Youth Hostel)

Jardiniere Wessex
(Wessex vegetables)

Le Mont de Silbury
(Silbury Hill)

Thé, tirée de la Chaudron de Marlborough
(Tea, drawn from the Marlborough bucket)

Evening Dress Optional

N.B. The Management reserve the right to exclude the admission of anyone they consider proper

The supper would be followed (after washing-up) by one or more usually two lectures dealing more particularly with the visible archaeological sites in the region.

I covered most of the best archaeological regions within striking distance of Bristol in this way. From the Cranborne Y.H. we covered Cranborne Chase (26–27 Sept 1953 with Nicholas Thomas; 25–27 April 1958). These included visits to the Oakley

Down group of barrows, Wor Barrow, the Roman Ackling Dyke, the Knowlton Circles (or a selection thereof), and the Pitt Rivers Museum at Farnham, then still open to the public and under the curatorship of Major Joyce and afterwards Mrs Joyce, who admitted Youth Hostellers at reduced fees and provided excellent teas with home-made cakes. On one of these weekends we had six or eight boys from Bryanston School including Nicholas Hawkes, son of Professor Christopher Hawkes.

The South Dorset Ridgeway was covered by a weekend at the Bridport Y.H. (9–10 May 1959). On the Sunday morning we were joined by Roger Peers (Curator of Dorset County Museum, Dorchester) and our route was via Martin's Down and Black Down to the Hardy Monument and then along the ridge via Maiden Castle and Maumbury Rings to Dorchester for tea.

I was particularly keen on the Cotswolds for the ten years 1954–63. The Cleeve Hill Y.H. near Cheltenham is well sited for the promontory earthwork and other earthworks on Cleeve Hill and for the Belas Knap chambered long barrow, and combines well with Sudeley Castle, which at that time included a small museum of local finds (since dispersed) and tea could be obtained either at Sudeley Castle or at Winchcombe, a little town of great historic interest dating from Saxon times. I ran weekends at Cleeve Hill 9–10 October 1954 and 17–18 October 1959, the latter with Nicholas Thomas.

From the Y.H. at Duntisbourne Abbots it is possible to explore the minor antiquities in the Duntisbourne valley including the Jack Barrow monument in Duntisbourne Abbots churchyard, Duntisbourne Rous church dating probably from late Saxon times, and Daglingworth church with its various Saxon features, ending at Cirencester, the Roman CORINIUM DOBUNNORUM and the most important Roman town after London. I ran two weekends at this hostel. The first was on 20/21 October 1956 when Mrs Elsie Clifford lectured on the Cotswolds in the Early Iron Age, with emphasis on the Bagendon earthworks which she had recently excavated, and which we visited the following day on our way to CORINIUM. The cyclists were led to the Roman villa at Chedworth by Miss Gillian Chapman, then at Bristol City Museum. The second was run with Richard Reece on 24–25 September 1960. On both occasions we were received at the Corinium Museum by its curator Prof. Donald Atkinson.

Stow-on-the-Wold Y.H. is an excellent base for exploring the North-East Cotswolds. The prehistoric sites in its vicinity are unspectacular but in a beautiful setting. On my weekends there 14–15 May 1955 and 19–20 October 1963 we visited long and round barrows near Upper and Lower Swell, part of the Ryknild Street (Condicote Lane) Roman road, and Salmonsbury Iron Age camp at Bourton-on-the-Water, the latter with Mrs Helen O'Neil as our Guide, who also provided us with tea at her house nearby. On our visit of 1963 our lectures were held in St Edward's Hall, whose Museum of antiquities formed by Rev. David Royce, vicar of Lower Swell 1850–1902, I had just previously rearranged.

From about 1956 my interests were extending westward to the Quantock Hills and Exmoor. On 19–20 October 1957, A.L. Wedlake and I arranged a Countryside Archaeology weekend based on the Crowcombe Y.H. Mr Wedlake lecutred on his finds of prehistoric flint implements in the area, and I covered the field monuments. Miss Gillian Chapman and I led the walk over much of the Quantocks including round barrows on Wills Neck, the linear earthwork of Dead Woman's Ditch, and Dowsborough Iron Age hillfort. We all had lunch at the Plough Inn at Holford, and a few days afterwards I was delighted to receive a letter from the proprietor of the Plough Inn, thanking me for bringing such a nice group for lunch: the only time that I have ever received such a letter!

On 13/15 May 1960 Mr Wedlake and I ran a similar weekend based on the Y.H. at Alcombe near Minehead. Most of the participants arrived on the Friday evening, enabling us to have a field trip on the Saturday which was devoted to the barrows near Selworthy Beacon, the hill-slope enclosure on Furzebury Brake, and Bury Castle hill-fort, finishing with tea at Selworthy. On the Sunday we walked over Grabbist with its linear earthwork to Dunster, where we visited the earthworks of Bat's Castle and Black Ball. We made our way to Williton for a memorable tea.

On 1/3 May 1964 Frank Noble (founder of the Offa's Dyke Society) and I ran an archaeology weekend at Shrewsbury and Bridges Youth Hostels. I have mislaid the programme; but my recollection is that Frank Noble must have conducted us along part of Offa's Dyke, and I certainly led a visit to Mitchell's Fold stone circle and to Middleton-in-Chirbury church nearby with its carved capital illustrating the Mitchell's Fold 'dun cow' legend; and probably to some of the barrows on the Long Mynd.

To conclude: for all these YHA weekends the lecturers always gave their services, and the charge to the Youth Hostellers was no more than the normal booking fee.

Lectures to University Archaeological Societies
My first experience of this type of lecturing was on 21 November 1936 at Cambridge. Glyn Daniel, who had just taken his degree there, invited me to lecture to their undergraduate society on Barrows, about which my book *The Ancient Burial-Mounds of England* had just been published. I arrived just before their Professor, Sir Ellis Minns, was giving a tea party to Prof. Bosch Gimpera, then a refugee from the Spanish Civil War. I was invited to this party, but as it was the first occasion of that sort that I had attended I was exceedingly nervous, and it was Prof. Bosch Gimpera who managed to put me at my ease. Glyn Daniel praised me from the chair after my lecture; but the following day (Sunday) I was in his rooms at St John's College and happened to pick up his copy of my book, to find it scrawled all over with ruderies showing what he really thought about it. My next lecture at Cambridge was on 25 October 1950, my subject being 'Recent research into Wessex barrows', when the society's secretary was John Hurst, whose interests were then moving from prehistory towards medieval studies.

In the early part of the 1939/45 War I lectured to the Oxford University Archaeological Society probably at New College, also of course about Barrows and related subjects: and shortly after the War I lectured in the Ashmolean to the O.U.A.S. on Wessex prehistory including of course Avebury, Stonehenge, and the surrounding barrows.

I lectured twice, probably between 1974 and 1976, to the Southampton University Archaeological Society, the first on Barrows and the second on the folklore of prehistoric monuments in Britain, about which I had just completed a book. I also lectured to the University of Bristol Spelaeological Society about 1951 on Barrows. There was a departure from precedent in that the Chair was taken not by a student

President but by Dr Dina Dobson-Hinton. Her concluding comment, that the different types of round barrow, 'bowl, bell, disc, saucer, etc.' 'could have been caused by weathering' left me unimpressed. As a lecturer who had never studied at any University I found it a great experience meeting and being dined by students many of whom were destined to become the archaeologists of the future.

Lectures at Public Schools
It has been a pleasure to lecture at four public schools: Aldenham, Bristol Grammar School, Kingswood School (near Bath), and Marlborough College. My lecture at Aldenham School about 1948 was through the good offices of R.A. Skelton, then assistant superintendent of the Map Room in the British Museum. He was an old boy of Aldenham, and his headmaster asked him to get I.E.S. Edwards, of the Department of Egyptian antiquities in the British Museum, to lecture on *The Pyramids of Egypt*, the title of a book that he had just published. Skelton wanted to avoid him for reasons connected not with his scholarship but with his style as a lecturer (constantly saying 'er'), so he asked me instead, knowing that I also had just published a book entitled *Egyptian Pyramids*. My lecture at Bristol Grammar School was to their Archaeological Society in summer 1968. I forget the subject. My first lecture at Kingswood School was on 13 November 1949, the subject being 'Prehistoric Wessex' when I was then working on the first volume of *V.C.H. Wiltshire*. A boy named David Wilson was then at the school and present at my lecture, and he is now Sir David Wilson, Director of the British Museum, and an expert on Anglo-Saxon archaeology. My second lecture at Kingswood School was early in 1952, the subject being 'The Pyramids: how they were built'. My third was on 2 March 1958, on 'The Prehistory of Wessex'. For these lectures the initiative came from Mr John W. Gardner, their master who arranged such lectures and encouraged field archaeology, and to whom I am indebted for these details.

While working on the *V.C.H. Wiltshire* 1949–52 and also I believe on a later occasion I lectured at Marlborough College. On the first occasion I found it a little disconcerting in the Memorial Building where the platform had two lecterns and I could not make up my mind which was the 'real' one, which caused many of the boys to giggle when I walked from one lectern to the other. However, once I got going all was well and I enjoyed talking about the wonderful prehistoric sites almost on their doorstep – at a school which had numbered Grahame Clark and O.G.S. Crawford among its former pupils, and I was well looked after during the weekend by E.G.H. Kempson (a former master) and his wife.

Other lectures
Although I have not prepared and published proper revisions to my surveys of the barrows of Sussex (1934–41) and Berkshire (1935–40), I lectured on Berkshire barrows updated to the Berkshire Archaeological Society at Reading on 21 January 1984, and on 'Sussex barrows in their wider context 1929–1979' to the Sussex Archaeological Society at Lewes in a symposium on archaeology and death on 13 October 1979. It is curious that my regional surveys of barrows have otherwise scarcely ever been the subject of lectures, with one or two exceptions including my paper on bell-barrows, the substance of which was given as a lecture to the Prehistoric Society

of East Anglia in London on 25 October 1933, and my paper on disc-barrows the gist of which was given as a lecture to the Dorset Natural History and Archaeological Society *c.*1974. Many of my lectures have been on more general aspects of prehistory.

Of the various societies and groups to which I have lectured, one of the most agreeable was the Newbury District Field Club when Harold J.E. Peake was their president until his death in 1946. I was in fact the speaker at their first meeting following his death when we stood for a moment in silence in his memory. He had the gift of giving kindly encouragement to the speaker, and unobtrusively prompting him if he forgot some detail. Their meetings were usually followed by a pleasant gathering for tea at a local café.

My lecture to the Cotteswold Naturalists' Field Club on 10 March 1961 was followed by a somewhat painful tea at a local café with Mrs Elsie Clifford and Mrs Helen O'Neil (at daggers drawn with each other) at my table, when neither spoke to the other but both spoke to me, and I had to count my words to each in order to present a façade of impartiality.

In spring 1965 I gave the J.H. Pull Memorial Lecture to the Worthing Archaeological Society, my subject being 'The Amateur in British Field Archaeology': an appropriate subject as J.H. Pull was a distinguished amateur, author of *The Flint Miners of Blackpatch* and numerous papers on the prehistory of the Worthing region.

Throughout my lecturing since the late 1950s, any necessary 35mm slides (apart from those taken by myself) have been made by Jim Hancock of Bristol, who has often also worked the projector for many of my lectures in and around Bristol. He has also done all the enlargements from my negatives, as required for my various publications.

Chapter 8

General Studies on Wessex, Exmoor and the Cotswolds

'Wessex is the core and propelling heart of the whole of prehistoric Britain away from the highland country'.
– Jacquetta Hawkes, A *Guide to the Prehistoric and Roman Monuments in England and Wales*, 1973, 89.

Wessex

I was commissioned by Methuens about 1950 to write a book on the archaeology of Wessex, but by reason of other commitments I did not complete it until 1957 and it was published in summer 1958. The emphasis was on the field monuments nearly all of which I had visited at least once between 1930 and 1957. The work was a natural sequel to my surveys of barrows in Wessex during that time, when my eyes were by no means closed to hillforts, linear earthworks, stone circles, 'henges', and other sites; and for Wiltshire I had already listed all known sites and finds from the palaeolithic down to the end of the pagan Saxon period. *The Archaeology of Wessex* covered just that period for which I had already assembled the Wiltshire material. I took the opportunity to visit outstanding sites in Dorset in the course of my work at weekends completing 'Dorset Barrows' for publication in 1959. Being based on Bristol from 1 February 1952 onwards, my 'Wessex' extended well west of the Wessex chalk country as far as and including most of Mendip.

Inevitably the work reflects the archaeological moods of the 1950s. It was still the 'in' thing to consider the chambered long barrows as resulting from invasions or at least influences from the Iberian peninsula and/or Brittany. Having recently turned professional I had little choice but to follow the current trends in accepting the 'invasion hypothesis' for not only the neolithic but also the Beaker phases and the Early Bronze Age including the Wessex culture. For the latter I emphasized the supposed influences from Ireland, Brittany and Armorica, central Europe and even the Eastern Mediterranean.

The first shock to the invasion hypothesis, to the best of my knowledge, came with Grahame Clark's paper 'The invasion hypothesis in British archaeology' (*Antiquity* XL, 1966, 172–89). It was followed the following year by Colin Renfrew's paper, 'Colonialism and megalithismus' in *Antiquity* XLI, 1968, 276–88 and later writings by the same and other authors.

Yet the radiocarbon revolution, accompanied by several systems of radiocarbon dating and their calibrations into calendar years, has led Colin Burgess to believe that limited contact between the Eastern Mediterranean, especially Mycenae, and Wessex is still possible (*The Age of Stonehenge*, 1980, 108–9); and some of the writings of Prof. Keith Branigan suggest that he also is of an open mind on this problem. Archaeology in this respect is largely affected by the 'swing of the pendulum' and perhaps by each generation of university students tending to react against what they were taught.

As secretary of the Implement Petrology Committee for south-western England I was in a good position to write the section on the stone axe trade in related implements including axe-hammers and battle-axes, brief though this section is (pp. 19–21).

As it is now thirty years since *The Archaeology of Wessex* was published it has to be considered in perspective and inevitably it is now in many respects outdated but not yet replaced. Two books on the archaeology of Wessex before 1000 or 1066 have for some years been in preparation, one by Barry Cunliffe for Longmans, the other by T.C. and Sara T. Champion for another publisher. Meanwhile the slighter book by Peter Fowler, *Wessex* (1967) in Heinemann's Regional Archaeology series, reflects much the same ideas as my own of 1958, because the 'invasion hypothesis' was not seriously questioned in print until mid or late 1966, by which time Peter Fowler's book had probably already gone to press. My own *Archaeology of Wessex* belongs to the period when I was still under the influence of Heywood Sumner, as shown by the style of my North points (Fig. 6)

Exmoor and the Quantocks
I had originally wanted to write only a small book of 60–80 pages on this project, but my publishers David and Charles insisted that I extend it to the length of 200 pages or more. I managed to do this by various methods: extending it to include Norman and medieval periods; including a section on the folklore of archaeological sites in the area; and including appendices on archaeological touring (a) by car and (b) on foot. I also included a set of period distribution maps with accompanying lists of sites shown on them. On Map VIII, Norman and Medieval, I had a symbol for 'Manor houses serving teas in season', which provoked caustic comment from a reviewer. I think the book has served as a useful basis for further work in the region.

The Cotswolds
In the course of my fieldwork on Gloucestershire barrows it came to my notice that the important collection of prehistoric flint implements and other material from the eastern Cotswolds, formed by Rev. David Royce of Lower Swell during the second half of the 19th century, and housed at St Edward's Hall, Stow-on-the-Wold, was in a state of neglect. I decided to remedy this situation and rearranged the collection with showcases lent by Bristol City Museum, and did the fieldwork necessary for writing a paper on the collection, during the early 1960s (Grinsell 1964). One weekend I was doing this fieldwork with a friend when we noticed that Glebe Farm, Condicote, were serving teas. We accordingly entered their tea-room, where we were pleasantly surprised to find it strewn with copies of the periodical *Antiquity*. On my enquiring of the lady serving us how it was that such an unexpected periodical was available there, she replied, 'Oh yes; well you see I have got a funny husband who collects flints and things. Would you like me to bring him in to you?' On my replying 'yes', she brought him in, loaded with several trays of leaf-shaped and barbed-and-tanged flint arrow-heads such as are very common in that part of the Cotswolds. By the time we had finished admiring his collection our tea was cold, but it was a memorable experience the like of which I have never had before or since. This piece of fieldwork comprised my only detailed study of a small area.

Chapter 9

Regional Barrow Surveys Completed and Updated

Barrows
Bowl, bell, disc and saucer –
familiar domestic names;
barrow, hump, tump, tumulus –
those grassy graves
gracefully adorning downland
on smooth-turfed English limestone hills.
          – W.J. Keith, in *The Countryman*, Autumn 1984, p. 173.

In this chapter I resume the story of my barrow surveys where they left off in 1941 (covered in chapter 2). When I returned from Egypt at the end of 1945 and resumed my banking early in 1946 it was only a year before I became Hon. Treasurer of the Prehistoric Society: a task which involved a great deal of routine work and left me with little or no time for archaeological fieldwork until I joined the V.C.H. Wiltshire staff in May 1949. Between then and 1952 I managed to visit the great majority of barrows in Wiltshire as part of the V.C.H. Gazetteer.

Between 1949 and 1952 I devoted my holidays to non-intensive fieldwork on Exmoor, the Quantock Hills, the Lake District and Northumberland for the second edition of *The Ancient Burial-Mounds of England* (1953). From then onwards I devoted many weekends and holidays to the fieldwork on which was based my *Archaeology of Wessex* (1958). The one day per week allowed by the Bristol City Museum for 'the curator's research' was devoted to the tedious but necessary task of converting 1850 latitudes and longitudes to national grid references to enable *Dorset Barrows* (1959) to be published in the most up-to-date form. In this I had valuable assistance from Michael Taylor, a Bristol University geography graduate. Since then the work of the R.C.H.M. and the Archaeology division of the Ordnance Survey led me to prepare *Dorset Barrows Supplement* (1982).

My appointment in Bristol City Museum implied, as far as I was concerned, that I should devote some of my spare time to doing surveys of barrows in Gloucestershire and Somerset. Archaeologically they were both 'sensitive' areas in that it was not very long before I became aware that I was looked upon as something of an intruder. As the opposition seemed less in Gloucestershire than in North Somerset I decided to do Gloucestershire first. The editor of the *Trans. Bristol Gloucestershire Archaeol. Soc.*, Capt H.S. Gracie, was very sympathetic, but the initial problem was to persuade the council of the Society to change the format of their *Transactions* from 8vo to 4to in order to accommodate the lists of barrows in tabulated form printed vertically rather than sideways. This was duly accomplished. It should be added that during the previous 20–30 years there had been a marked tendency for the county archaeological societies to change their format from 8vo to 4to which was more convenient for the increasing number of excavation reports being submitted. Shortly after I told him that my paper was nearing completion, he came to see me and explained that Mrs Helen O'Neil had expressed her intention to offer a paper on the same subject. This predicament was solved by my suggesting a joint paper with Mrs O'Neil's name being put first to give priority to her sex. She had in fact visited and measured many of the round barrows with her late husband, Bryan O'Neil, sometime Chief Inspector of Ancient Monuments, before 1940, and she lent me her cards the information from which added strength to the resulting paper, for the drafting of which I was solely responsible.

Now approaching thirty years afterwards, Dr Tim Darvill and I have produced 'Gloucestershire Barrows: First Supplement', forthcoming. Our ideas concerning chambered long barrows have since 1960 changed in many respects. Many round barrows have been either destroyed or much reduced by ploughing and other activities, and some 'new' ones have been found. Some long and round barrows have been excavated, and all these and many more matters are discussed in this Supplement.

From my first visits to Exmoor and the Quantocks (c.1950), I acquired a special regard for them. Archaeologically they were largely virgin territory apart from four slight papers by H. St George Gray, and there was nobody else covering the Somerset portion. The Devon part of Exmoor was being explored by a charming retired civil servant, Charles Whybrow, who helped me a great deal notably with transport. It was therefore natural that my book *The Archaeology of Exmoor* (1970) should be accompanied by surveys of the barrows in North Devon (1969) and West and South Somerset (1969). The latter was offered to the editor of *Proc. Somerset Archaeol. & N.H. Society*, who stipulated that if his Society published that paper they would eventually expect to be offered the paper on the barrows of North and East Somerset. I had in fact tentatively suggested the idea of a joint paper on the latter with Dr E.K. Tratman, but this presented at least two problems: his use of the word *tumulus* in a broader sense than used by the Ordnance Survey, and more particularly he would stipulate that it be published in *Proc. Univ. Bristol Spelaeological Society*, whose format was 8vo and unsuitable for the tabulated lists which form perhaps the most important part of my barrow surveys. In fact *Proc. U.B.S.S.* is still in 8vo. So was *Proc. Somerset A & N.H. Society* until they changed to 4to in 1968, largely at my suggestion. The result was that Parts I and II of Somerset Barrows appeared in the *Proceedings* of the latter society.

One of my most exciting field days on Mendip was on 9 May 1956. During a visit to the southern Priddy Circle, where a trial trench had been dug by a Clifton College boy named Christopher Taylor, I suggested that we go and have a look at the Pool Farm stone cist about 1.5 km to the north, which had been left exposed after the round barrow which contained it ◦was removed in 1930. Prof. R.J.C. Atkinson had discovered various carvings on the sarsen stones of Stonehenge in May 1953 and I thought it just possible that the slabs of this cist might bear carvings. Running my hands over the southern wall slab I found them sinking into corresponding hollows in the slab, and provisionally identified them as carvings of hands. I got Richard

Atkinson to have a look at them during the Prehistoric Society conference in Bristol later in 1956 and he put me right by identifying them as foot carvings similar to those at the Calderstones near Liverpool and various others in Scandinavia. I identified six foot carvings on the Pool Farm slab, and in 1977 Mike Pitts found a 7th foot carving shallower than the others. The slab is in the City of Bristol Museum but a cast is on the site.

I had always wanted to follow my early paper on 'Bell-barrows' (*PPSEA* vii, 1933) and the more mature 'Bronze Age round barrows of Wessex' (*PPS* vii, 1941) with a paper on disc-barrows: unquestionably the most beautiful of all the 'Wessex' barrow types. With my county barrow surveys now completed for Berkshire, Dorset, Gloucestershire, Hampshire and the Isle of Wight, Somerset, Surrey, Sussex and Wiltshire, I was in a strong position to perform this task. The resulting paper, 'Disc-barrows' appeared in *PPS* 40, 1974. My chief recollection connected with preparing this paper is that when drawing the plans of types of disc-barrow (Fig. 1 of that paper), I became so absorbed in drawing the circles and doing the hachuring in the style of Heywood Sumner, that I quite forgot that I had left my kitchen tap running; and within a few minutes the tenant of the flat beneath mine called on me and drew my attention to the fact that his flat was being flooded with water from mine, which was also being flooded. It was my great regret that the Editor did not allow the distribution map (Fig. 2) to be printed in two colours. As it is, the symbols for the towns tend to get confused with those for the disc-barrows except that the former are larger.

As the greatest concentration of barrows of 'Wessex' types occurs around Stonehenge, there appeared to be a need for a popular guide to these groups, in the hope also of reducing visitor pressure on Stonehenge and encouraging the visitor to see the monument in its context. It is probably an under-statement that not one visitor in a hundred visits the surrounding barrow groups, although since 1985 the National Trust in association with other organisations has developed a series of signposted walks incorporating the Cursus group, the Winterbourne Stoke Crossroads group and parts of the Normanton group. It was to meet this need that I wrote a 48-page monograph entitled *The Stonehenge Barrow Groups* (1978), published by the Salisbury and South Wiltshire Museum. In 8vo format, it is more compact than the RCHM publication *Stonehenge and its Environs* (4to, 1979), which with its pocket of folded maps is more suitable for the study. While preparing it I learned a good deal about the policy of Hoare and Cunnington in deciding which barrows to open. They tended to avoid those bearing evidence of having already been opened, those planted with trees, and those under standing corn.

It was not practicable to write a 3rd edition of *The Ancient Burial-Mounds of England*. The Greenwood Press (Westport, Conn.) reprinted the 1953 edition with a fresh introduction, and the slighter book *Barrows in England and Wales* was published by Shire Archaeologies (1979; 2nd edn 1984). The third edition of the latter, largely rewritten, is now in the press.

After retiring in April 1972 at the age of 65, I decided to prepare a survey of Dartmoor barrows: no light undertaking as the number of known examples is around 650 and there are doubtless many smaller examples awaiting discovery. I was fortunate to have done about half the fieldwork during the dry summers of 1975 and 1976. My policy was to spend two or three days mid week on this work, when the country bus services are better than on Sundays and it is easier to get accommodation than at weekends. I managed to visit all the sites personally except a couple of dozen very remote sites which were visited on my behalf by Joe R. Turner who has an uncanny sense of location on Dartmoor, and who took me to several sites difficult to find. Dartmoor is the ideal area for cairns enclosing a central stone cist and bordered by a retaining circle of stones, there being as many as 125 stone cists and 132 retaining circles listed in my paper, which includes 56 cairns having a stone row extending almost always downhill. It was a pleasure to do fieldwork on Dartmoor without feeling that one was 'treading on the toes' of others; for not even R. Hansford Worth (died 1950) was mad enough to walk all over Dartmoor to visit every barrow.

The Royal Commission on Historical Monuments completed their survey of Dorset with the publication of volume V in 1975. The fieldwork of their investigators, together with that of those from the Archaeology division of the Ordnance Survey and of various private field archaeologists, resulted in the addition of about 360 'new' sites to my *Dorset Barrows* (1959). I put these together in my *Dorset Barrows Supplement* (1982). During my fieldwork on 15 May 1980 I caught a young man red-handed digging into a round barrow west of Culliford Tree, following his use of a metal-detector.

There remained the task of completing Devon by doing the fieldwork and research for 'The barrows of south and east Devon' (*Proc. Devon A.S.* no 41, 1983). This involved some duplication with the surveys by Lady Aileen Fox on the Broad Down (Farway) barrow cemetery and the Upton Pyne group, but these both required updating in the light of the later work of the Archaeology Division of the Ordnance Survey and for other reasons. There were also various barrows in other parts of south and east Devon, notably the Woodbury area, Great and Little Haldon, and the South Hams, to be visited. They form an interesting and varied series of rather more than 300 sites. The re-use of a barrow for sepulchral purposes as recently as 1921 is illustrated by CHUDLEIGH 3, one of a linear barrow group, in which the body of Sir Edward Chaning Wills of Harcombe in Chudleigh was interred at his request as an intrusive burial in a coffin covered by an appropriately inscribed grave-slab. He endowed the Chaning Wills Chair of Geology in Bristol University and was a benefactor to Exeter Museum. A search through the drawings by P.O. Hutchinson in the Devon Record Office at Exeter introduced me to the lighter side of barrow study (Fig. 8).

A group of three or more anomalous mounds east of Dornafield (IPPLEPEN 1–3 and perhaps, 4, 5, the former (1–3) in an improbable valley situation, somehow did not look right. I consulted Prof. Allan Straw, Professor of Geology, Exeter University, who after visiting them expressed the opinion that they are natural and 'an expression of contrasts in resistance of different types of rock that outcrop in the area'. This shows the importance of liaison between archaeologists and geologists in cases of doubt.

With the completion of the barrows of Devon my county surveys have probably come to an end except for revisions and updatings. Those for Somerset and Gloucestershire have already been described. One of my earliest county surveys, 'An analysis and list of Surrey barrows' (1934) was totally revised and re-written because of the new material which had since come to hand and the extensive administrative reorganisation of the county in 1974, and because the Surrey Archaeological Society were willing to publish a totally rewritten paper: 'Surrey Barrows 1934–1986: a reappraisal' (*Surrey Archaeol. Collect.* 78, 1–41).

My regional barrow surveys would now seem to have come to an end. R.F. Jessup and I visited a few sites and got together a few notes on the barrows of Kent before 1940, but these notes were destroyed by enemy action during the 1939–45 war. Cornwall is too large a county and too far west for me to tackle, but the information is probably in the Sites and Monuments Record at Truro; that is however not the same thing as having it published. I do intend, if spared for another year or two, to prepare a paper on the use made by the Anglo-Saxons of barrows as boundary-points in their land charters. Since I last made a comprehensive statement on this subject (*Dorset Barrows*, 1959, 60–64), much more information has become available and a fresh study is well worth doing, although a valuable contribution has since been made by Della Hooke ('Burial features in West Midland charters', *English Place-Name Society Journal*, 13, 1981).

It remains to add a note on my methods of measuring barrows. I normally carry a reel-tape (30 metres = 100 feet) and have as a general principle always used it for measuring long barrows and the rarer types of round barrow (bell, disc, saucer and pond). When alone I have tied one end of the reel tape to my rucksack and held the other end. I have usually measured ordinary bowl-barrows by pacing only. I have checked my pacing at frequent intervals. Until I was around 70 my 'stretched' pace was near enough to three feet. Since then it has been getting a little shorter. In 1988 it was 0.83 metres, based on a measurement of 30 metres (36 of my paces).

The advantages of pacing are manifold. Time is saved in unwinding and winding the reel-tape; the risk is eliminated of getting the reel-tape muddy on ploughed fields in winter, or fouled on cow pasture. In areas such as Dartmoor where most of the round barrows have a retaining circle of stones, measurements by tape are more meaningful except that these barrows are seldom exactly circular. On the chalk downs of Wessex and elsewhere the precise diameter of round barrows is not ascertainable unless a surrounding ditch is visible, and then my measurement has always been of the mound excluding the ditch. The 'Grinsellpace' was described by John Coles in *Field Archaeology in Britain* (1972), p. 62.

Until about 1935 I used to carry a folding five-foot rule to estimate heights. Since then I have been content to estimate them by comparison with the height of my eyes above ground (5ft 6 inches).

Chapter 10

International Prehistoric Congresses

'At a Conference of representative prehistorians, held at Berne on 28th May 1931 it was decided to form a new *Congrès International des Sciences préhistoriques et protohistoriques*.'

– Preface to *Proceedings of First International Congress, 1932* (1934)

I attended the First International Congress of Prehistoric and Protohistoric Sciences, held at King's College, *London*, 1–6 August 1932, but was merely a passenger and did not offer a paper. The subscription was £1 which included the volume of *Proceedings*, 322 pages long, published in 1934, and a reception at Lancaster House. I spent the whole of my time in Section III, the Neolithic, Bronze and Iron Ages in the Ancient World, under the able chairmanship of Prof. H.J. Fleure.

The conference opened on the Monday evening 1st with the Presidential address, by Sir Charles Peers, on the origins of prehistoric studies in Britain. On Tuesday evening Cyril Fox delivered his masterly address on *The Personality of Britain*, published that year as a book which passed through several editions. I well remember the impact made by his statement (p. 33 of 1938 edition) that 'it is the tragedy of British prehistory and history, and the key thereto, that the most habitable and most easily conquerable areas are adjacent to the shores whence invaders are most likely to come'. His lecture was largely a commentary on a series of distribution maps, many of them by Lily Chitty, and my own emphasis on distribution maps dates from this lecture. I did not attend the evening lectures on Wednesday (Thurlow Leeds on Celtic art) and Thursday (T.D. Kendrick on the crafts in ancient Britain), being in those days (and also today) mainly a 'Neolithic and Bronze Age person'.

During each day there were short papers, I believe often limited to 20 minutes or so, grouped into sessions. I have been told that one speaker, on Life in the pre-Roman Iron Age in Britain, devoted almost all his 20 minutes to profusely apologizing for having the impertinence to lecture on such a subject to so many learned people, so that by the time he had started on his subject the chairman told him his time was up.

On Tuesday there was a rather disappointing lecture by Miss V. Collum on the Tressé *allée couverte* in Brittany, which she attributed to the Iron Age. It was not well received, and it is now accepted that the Iron Age interments which she found in it were intrusive. There was a fascinating lecture by Miss Florence Ayscough on her photography of carvings on megalithic monuments in Guernsey, either by moonlight or by electric light at night (compare P.R. Giot's nocturnal visit to the statue-menhirs in Guernsey, described in the next chapter).

On Wednesday H. St George Gray lectured on his excavations at Avebury done mostly before the first world war, and financially rather on a shoestring. Alexander Keiller joined in the discussion and pointed this out by way of contrast to his own excavations there with his own almost unlimited resources. Mrs Cunnington lectured on her work on timber circles, of course with special reference to Woodhenge. A deep impression was made by Prof. A.E. Van Giffen of Groningen, with his lecture on the round barrows enclosed by timber circles in the Netherlands. I was to meet him again in the British Museum later in the 1930s and also at Avebury in 1949 during my work for V.C.H. *Wiltshire*, and finally at the Rome congress in 1962. Another speaker in this particularly interesting session was W.J. Varley on the Bleasdale timber circle in Lancashire.

I believe it was on this day that W.J. Hemp lectured on the Bryn Celli Ddu chambered tomb in Anglesey, and Lindsay Scott grossly overran his time speaking on the megalithic tombs in the west coast of Britain, but fortunately he was the last speaker before lunch.

On Thursday Dr E.C. Curwen spoke on his excavations in the neolithic causewayed enclosures of Whitehawk and the Trundle in Sussex, and Alexander Keiller on his excavations on Windmill Hill in Wiltshire. For me the most memorable lecture was by Father Christian Burdo on his excavation at *Le Pinacle* in Jersey, delivered in French but with great clarity and with the key words translated into English so that he could be readily understood by all. We shall meet him again in the next chapter. Stuart Piggott spoke on the relative chronology of the British long barrows.

This week being part of my annual holiday from my bank, I broke off from the Congress to do archaeological fieldwork in Wiltshire for the rest of the week.

The great advantage of my attending this congress was that I got to know many of the leading archaeologists of the day, including Mrs Cunnington, Lily Chitty, H. St George Gray, and O.G.S. Crawford.

I did not attend the 1936 congress in *Oslo*. It was held shortly after the publication of my *Ancient Burial-Mounds of England* in April that year. Mrs Clifford told me that she was reading my book on the ship on the way to Oslo when Prof. Gordon Childe edged up to her and asked to have a look at the book she was reading. He went straight to the index, but on finding that his name was not mentioned in it he had no further interest in the book and handed it back to her.

The next congress that I attended was in *Rome* (29 August–3 September 1962). It was preceded by a week's archaeological tour of Sicily which will be described in the next chapter. I did not offer a paper on this occasion but I derived some benefit from getting to know more archaeologists, including Sabine Gerloff of Berlin.

I attended the *Prague* congress (21–27 August 1966) and gave a paper on archaeological distribution maps, an abstract of which was published in the *Actes du VII Congrés International des Sciences Préhistoriques et Protohistoriques*, Prague 1966 (1970), I, 64. There was an excellent concert of Czech music, given probably by the Czech Philharmonic Orchestra, which I attended; but I felt a little embarrassed when an attendant showed me into a seat in the front row next to the President (Jan Filip) and his wife.

I was to have been present at the *Nice* congress of 1976, but after submitting an abstract of my paper on 'The folklore of prehistoric sites in Britain', I withdrew as the cost became prohibitive. However, the abstract of my paper was published in the Congress *Proceedings* (vol. I, p. 12, 1976).

I attended the World Archaeological Congress in *Southampton* 1–7 September 1986. The admission fee was £200 without *Proceedings* publications except for whichever of its 24 volumes covered the participant's main interest; and I seem to remember that enrolment before a certain date carried a reduced fee of £180. I believe I was the only person from the U.K. who attended this congress who was also present at the London congress of 1932. This was largely because several British prehistorians who might have attended stayed away because of the exclusion of the South Africans from the congress on the apartheid issue. Largely through the influence of the organiser Prof. Peter Ucko, there was a considerable emphasis on the archaeology and anthropology of the Third World, which I found difficult to relate to the prehistory and Roman and later history of Western Europe including the British Isles.

I believe that until the 1986 congress the authors of papers held their own copyright. For the Southampton congress the copyright on all papers was assigned to the publishers Allen and Unwin. It was because of this that the paper which I submitted, on *The Impact of Christianity on Prehistoric and other pagan sites*, which was at first provisionally accepted, was rejected by the chairman of the section to which it was allocated, because my abstract included a statement that an extended version would be published in *Landscape History*, the annual volume of the Society for Landscape Studies. The chairman in question was a lecturer in French and in my opinion hardly the most suitable chairman for such an occasion. I think that the situation could have been covered by some statement such as 'For an extended coverage prepared for a different readership, see *Landscape History*, vol. 8 for 1986 (1987), pp. 27–37'.

Of the 26 papers which I attended, 11 of their lecturers were absent, some probably because of the high cost, others on account of the apartheid issue. On Monday there was an excellent lecture by Sean McGrail on the Bronze Age boats of North-West Europe. The sessions that I most enjoyed however were on matters concerning Stonehenge. These opened with the Tuesday evening lecture on 'Stonehenge observed: the Middle Ages to 1986', by Christopher Chippindale (appropriately wearing a pullover embroidered with a picture of Stonehenge). In the Nuffield Theatre the whole of Thursday morning was devoted to Stonehenge and the problem of its management. The speakers ranged from Francis Golding (Head of Properties in Care) at one end to the lunatic fringe at the other. The Wednesday tour to Danebury included the Andover Museum but we were disappointed that the Museum of the Iron Age was not yet ready. I was pleased to note Egyptology well represented by Prof. John Baines who lectured on literacy in ancient Egypt on Thursday and on ancient Egyptian concepts of the past on Friday.

Many of the papers read were understood in inverse proportion to the quantity of technical jargon used by the speakers. At the end of one of the sessions on 'Value, ranking and consumption in the Bronze Age', one of the audience commented that some of the speakers had tried to show their own ranking and supremacy over their audience by using jargon, the meaning of which was known only to the few.

I would sum up the advantage derived from attending this congress by emphasizing the value of renewing contact with old colleagues, strengthening personal relationships with them over lunch and dinner and on other occasions; meeting younger archaeologists who help to keep one abreast of the times; and the discussions between the lectures are often more useful than the lectures themselves. There was a splendid display of archaeological literature recently published, put on by Alan Sutton, Academic Press, Allen and Unwin, British Museum publications, Cambridge University Press, Thames and Hudson and others, which enabled us to keep up to date with the most recent literature on our subjects.

It was a pity that the Council for British Archaeology, having withdrawn their support for the congress on the apartheid issue, felt unable to participate even to the extent of exhibiting their publications for sale.

Chapter 11

Out with the Prehistorians

'Is Mr Everard Bone there?' 'My son is at a meeting of the Prehistoric Society.'
'Oh, I see. I am so sorry to have bothered you.'
— Barbara Pym, *Excellent Women* (1952), 29–30.

On 26 October 1908 a group of primarily flint-hunting enthusiasts held the inaugural meeting of what they called the East Anglian Society of Prehistorians; the following year they changed their title to the Prehistoric Society of East Anglia. I joined this society in October 1929 under the dispensation by which a new member paying his subscription of fifteen shillings in advance to cover the following year was entitled to attend the meetings held between October and December the previous year. That is why according to the Membership lists (not published since 1971) my membership dates from 1930.

In those days I was in a state of transition from flint-hunting to barrow-hunting. My paper on 'Bell-barrows' was published in *PPSEA* vii for 1933, after it had been rejected by the *Wiltshire Archaeological Magazine* as it contained 40 per cent of non-Wiltshire material (but I suspect that another reason was that I was considered something of an intruder). Either late in 1934 or early in 1935 I received a letter from Grahame Clark, then editor of *PPSEA*, saying that he hoped that I would vote in favour of changing the name of the Society from the Prehistoric Society of East Anglia to the Prehistoric Society. I was indignant at being advised how to use my vote, but none the less did vote in favour of the change, and the Society became the Prehistoric Society from 1935. It published my paper 'The Bronze Age round barrows of Wessex' in *PPS* vii, 1941.

I believe the original PSEA had occasional outdoor meetings, but by reason of my banking commitments in London I could not have attended them. After the 1939/45 War, when Sir Lindsay Scott became President, the present series of field meetings began, and after becoming the Society's Hon. Treasurer in 1947, a position which I held until 1970, I attended most of the Society's Summer Meetings, as well as some of the *Study Tours* sponsored by the Society since the late 1970s.

First of all it needs to be stated that my own appraisals of these conferences are inevitably slanted to my own interests which are largely in megalithic monuments, barrows and cairns, and I have therefore tended to understate or even omit the Iron Age hillforts and other settlement sites visited. Except for the Danish conference of 1963 when for the most part we had student guides, almost all our speakers at sites have been the acknowledged authorities on each monument.

The first summer conference was held at *York* in 1947 and comprised lectures only apart from a tour of medieval York led by Dr Kathleen Kenyon. I had to miss the

Carlisle meeting (3–6 Sept 1948). The *Exeter* meeting (23–26 Sept 1949) included a memorable lecture by R. Hansford Worth on the prehistory of Dartmoor. The most entertaining item however was the unplanned intrusion of a 'fringe' archaeologist in the person of G.E.L. Carter whose (for that time) bizarre observations led Lady Aileen Fox to walk out of the lecture hall and slam the door behind her, followed a minute or so later by O.G.S. Crawford and in dribs and drabs by various others, so that within five minutes or so the hall was half empty. Unfortunately, his main point: that prehistorians tend to be imprecise in their terminology, often describing megalithic rings as stone circles when they are often ellipses, has since been upheld by the late Prof. Alexander Thom and his followers; and Carter is presumably having a laugh on us from his grave (he died aged 88 in 1974). On 23 September the members, guided by Lady Fox, visited Hembury Fort and some of the round barrows on Farway Down (one of which is the first barrow that I ever saw – in the mid 1920s). This conference, held jointly with the Devonshire Association and the Devon Archaeological Exploration Society, was described by Gerald Dunning in the *Archaeological Newsletter*, vol. 2, 110–16.

In 1950 the summer conference was held at *Brighton* (22–25 September), jointly with the Sussex Archaeological Society. We were welcomed by the Mayor, who in his address remarked, 'I don't know what good you people think you are doing, but I am pleased to see you.' The introductory lecture was given by Dr E. Cecil Curwen on the prehistory of Sussex. There were other lectures and visits to Whitehawk neolithic enclosure, Church Hill (Findon) flint mines, the Devil's Dyke, Combe Hill neolithic enclosure, and visits to the museums at Lewes and Worthing. The local organisers were G.P. Burstow and G.A. Holleyman.

The 1951 summer conference was held in *Dublin and Limerick* (10–15 September) and was among the most memorable of all. At the start a gentleman named Aland Ussher joined the meeting: a kinsman of the Archbishop Ussher who in the mid seventeenth century invented 4004 B.C. as the date of the creation of the world. Two young local lads – George Eogan and Etienne Rynne – joined as Associate members: both destined to become eminent prehistorians. The sites visited included the passage graves in the Boyne Valley, the Four Knocks megalithic tomb, and Tara, guided by Paddy Hartnett, Sean O'Riordain and others. In Limerick, Ruardhri De Valera composed and sang a song entitled *The Prehistoric Foundations of Ireland,* (a skit on *The Prehistoric Foundations of Europe*, by our then President Prof. Christopher Hawkes), set to the tune of *Cockles and Mussels* (Trad.) It began:

> In the pale Palaeolithic
> The ice was a bit thick
> On Ireland's fair country for people to dwell;
> So we've no Acheulean,
> No Aurignacian.
> No Magdalenean and Thank God no Creswell!

Chorus: Thank God No Cresweh-ell, Thank God No Cresweh-ell,
> No Magdalenean and Thank God No Creswell'.
> [In the Mesolithic we ate Cockles and Mussels]

> . . . You see how this mess'l
> Produced the Food Vessel . . .
>
> . . . Here's an end to my ditty,
> *Three cheers for Miss Chitty.*

Except for the line in square brackets this is the version remembered by Christopher Hawkes.

While emerging from the hotel in Limerick where we had lunch, Miss Chitty had the misfortune to be stung twice by a wasp which got caught in the folds of her blouse, and she had to be taken back into the Hotel for bluebag treatment. A day or so later Prof. Childe sent a postcard to our former president Sir Lindsay Scott, who had been unable to attend the meeting; the only piece of information that it contained was that Miss Chitty had been stung by a wasp: nothing whatever about the prehistory. I was one of the signatories on this card. The meeting was fully described in the *Archaeological News Letter*, 4, 71–6.

The next summer conference was held at *Sheffield* (18–21 Sept 1952). In those days prehistory was not taught in the University but was an extra-mural subject for which A. Leslie Armstrong was the lecturer. In the course of his lecture to the Society he mentioned the skull of a palaeolithic woman whose brain case showed that she had a lot more brains than the average women of today. Mrs Dobson-Hinton (author of *The Archaeology of Somerset*, 1931) enquired what the capacity was and Armstrong replied, 'About 1400 ccs'. Mrs Dobson Hinton commented, 'That would be about the same as mine'. The lectures included one by Mrs Margaret Fowler on Thomas Bateman and his barrow-diggings in Derbyshire and Staffordshire, and our visit to the Derbyshire Dales included a pilgrimage to his grave behind the nonconformist chapel at Middleton-by-Youlgreave: his tomb appropriately crowned by a stone-carved model of a Bronze Age collared urn. We also had a lecture by J.P. Heathcote on his excavations of the round barrows on Stanton Moor. A full account of the meeting, by F.L. Preston, is in the *Archaeological News Letter*, 4, 167–74.

The summer conference in 1953 was at *Salisbury* (10–13 September). The lectures included one by H. de S. Shortt on the Celtic coinage of Wessex. The field trips included one to Stonehenge and Salisbury Plain where we saw the Tilshead 'Old Ditch' long barrow – in my opinion the largest and finest long barrow in Southern England. The trip to Cranborne Chase included the Pitt Rivers Museum, Wor Barrow, the long barrows on Thickthorn Down (Stuart Piggott), and the Woodyates group of round barrows.

The conference in 1954 (13–18 Sept) was based partly in *Edinburgh* and partly on *Kilmory Castle* (Argyll). It was our first summer conference to have a *Field Guide*: 42 pages long in A4 format, edited by Richard Atkinson who was also secretary for the meeting, which was extremely well run. There was a reception at Holyrood Palace. The sites visited included the Cairnpapple 'henge', the hillfort of Dunadd, and the extensive cairn cemetery and associated sites near Kilmartin. I did not accompany the optional trip to Orkney which followed the conclusion of the meeting.

At the *Cambridge* conference (15–18 Sept 1955) the prehistoric field monuments were inevitably minimal but included the 'henge' monument at Arminghall outside

Norwich. We also saw the Bartlow Hills Roman barrows and the Devil's Ditch nearby. The meeting was organised by Grahame Clark.

In 1956 the conference was in *Bristol* (13–16 September) and based on the City Museum. We saw the stone circles and associated monuments at Stanton Drew; the Priddy Circles and other sites on Mendip; and a visit to the Cotswolds included the Uleybury hillfort (John Brailsford), Hetty Pegler's Tump and Nympsfield long barrows, and the Bulwarks earthworks on Minchinhampton Common, finishing up with an excellent tea at the Moor Court Hotel.

The society paid its first visit to the *Channel Islands* from 16 to 21 September 1957. In Guernsey (16–18) our tours included the Dehus chambered tomb and the statue menhirs. We transferred to St Helier on 18th and had a lecture on La Cotte de St Brelade by Father Christian Burdo, whose irrepressibly cheerful personality infected all of us throughout the meeting. On 19th we saw the chambered tombs of *Mont Ubé*, *Faldouet*, and *La Hougue Bie* where we had a reception. On 20th we had lectures by P.R. Giot on the statue menhirs, and by Dr Colbert de Beaulieu on the pre-Roman coinage of the Coriosolites, followed by a tour which included the prehistoric tombs at *Ville es Nouaux* and *Le Couperon*. On 21st Father Burdo addressed us at the multi-period site of *Le Pinacle*, and we saw the chambered tombs of *Mont Grantez* and *La Sergenté*. The Société Jersiaise marked the occasion by publishing *A General Description of some Jersey Antiquities*, and the Jersey part of the meeting is fully described in the *Bulletin de la Société Jersiaise*, 17(ii), 109–112.

The *Penzance* conference (10–13 April 1958) included a reception at the Museum of the Royal Institution of Cornwall in Truro. I was asked by the Curator, Mr. H.L. Douch, how much he ought to offer for a Late Bronze Age sword found locally which had just been submitted for identification. I referred the enquiry to H. St' George Gray, whose reply was characteristic of the man: 'The General would have offered £20 for it in 1900'. We visited the Stripple Stones circle which Gray had excavated in 1905. At only a few minutes' notice he gave a brilliant lecture on the spot although then aged 86.

The conference was at *Bangor* in 1959 (29 August–1 September). One day was devoted to the megalithic sites in Anglesey including *Bryn Celli Ddu*, *Bryn yr Hen Bobl* and *Barclodiad y Gawres*; another to sites in Caernarvonshire including the stone axe factory of *Mynydd Rhiw*. During the reception in Bangor Museum I was delighted to meet Canon Ellis Davies, author of the splendid books on the prehistoric and Roman remains of Denbighshire and Flintshire.

In 1960 the Society held its first conference in the *Netherlands*, under the excellent guidance of Dr P.J.R. Modderman, supported by Prof. W. Glasbergen and Prof. H.T. Waterbolk and others. It was our first meeting on the continent, and lasted from 3 to 10 September. There was a splendid *Conference Handbook*. For me the highlights of this conference were the hunebeds (the Dutch equivalent of our chambered long barrows), of which we saw those at Eext, Rolde, and *Papeloze Kerk* (the church without a priest), the latter under the guidance of their leading authority Prof. A.E. Van Giffen. Of equal interest were the round barrows of *Nordse Veld*, *Bergeyk* and *Toterfout Halve Mijl*, many of them with their post-rings reconstructed, and some with their crouched burials showing as stains in the soil. Dr Waterbolk demonstrated the technique of spraying the vertical sections of the barrows with a liquid plastic enabling them to be peeled off and exhibited in museums, notably in the Museum of Groningen University. A report of this conference, by J.J. Butler, appeared in the *Archaeological News Letter*, 7, 16–19.

The 1961 conference (30 August–6 September) was based on *Dublin* and *Sligo*. It went well and field trips included the classic sites in the Boyne valley and various prehistoric sites in Sligo; but the beds in Sligo Grammar School were a bit short and the taller members had their feet protruding from the bottom of the beds. The society met in *Dorchester* 6–9 September 1962 but I missed the meeting, having only just returned from the International Prehistoric Congress in Rome.

I find *Denmark* (5–12 Sept 1963) the most difficult of all our field meetings to discuss. The weather was consistently fine. The prehistoric sites were excellent, and included chambered tombs (*Knebel; Troldkerchen; Tustrup; Grønhøge*; and the round barrows of *Maglehøge* in Zealand. For good measure we also visited important Viking sites including *Fyrkat* and *Trelleborg*, the royal barrows at *Jellinge*, and the *Ladby* ship barrow, and (most exciting of all) the great Viking cemetery at *Lindholm Høje*. On the debit side many administrative problems arose before, during and after the meeting. It had not been properly planned, and we had to collect money on the coaches each day to pay for packed lunches; money to pay hired student guides whereas it has always been our custom to be guided by more mature local scholars (in fact the local experts); and the cashier of the hotel where we stayed refused to accept the Society's cheque in payment on the last day, and I had to borrow a lot of cash from various members. We sustained a heavy loss on this meeting. The outcome was that a *Meetings Secretary* was appointed for the first time w.e.f. 1964. I did not attend the 1964 conference which was at *Wooler* in Northumberland, 30 August–6 September.

In 1965 (30 August–4 Sept) the conference was held at *Swansea* under the able secretaryship of Prof. Richard Atkinson. There was an excellent coverage of megalithic tombs including Tinkinswood and St Lythans west of Cardiff; Arthur's Stone, *Parc Cwm* and Penmaen Burrows at Gower; and *Carreg Coetan Arthur, Cerrig y Gof* and *Pentre Ifan* in the Presely area. Our only regret was that we were not permitted to approach nearer to *Carn Meini*, the supposed source of the Stonehenge Bluestones, than the *Gors Fawr* stone circle, our guide fearing that some of us might pick up bits of bluestone and scatter them over the countryside, thereby falsifying future distribution maps: and this in spite of the Presely Ridge being a public right-of-way.

In 1966 the society met at *Reading* (Friday to Sunday 25–27 March to avoid clashing with the International Prehistoric Congress in Prague the following August). On Friday evening 25th I gave the introductory lecture, on the history of archaeology in the area from Francis Wise 1738 onwards. The Saturday tour included Blewburton hillfort and Grimsditch and was followed by a reception in Reading Museum, whose gallery of prehistory had just been rearranged. Sunday was devoted to a tour of the Berkshire Downs including Wayland's Smithy, Uffington Castle and the Blowing Stone. An account of the meeting was published in the *Berkshire Archaeological Journal*, 63, pp. 90 – 91.

In 1967 (26 Aug–2 Sept) the society held their summer conference in *Ulster* in association with the Ulster Archaeological Society, based on Belfast, the year before the troubles began. We had the rare experience of being shown the Radiocarbon dating laboratory in the University and also the excellent display of prehistory in the

Belfast Museum. The sites visited included the neolithic hilltop enclosure on Lyles Hill, the Tievebulliagh stone axe factory site, various megalithic tombs, and the stone circles, stone rows and cairns at Beaghmore. There were receptions at Government House Stormont, and Belfast University and Museum. The *Field Guide* was edited by P.V. Addyman.

The 1968 conference (1–7 Sept) was in *Bristol* and coincided with the completion of Bristol City Museum's new Gallery of South-Western Prehistory, and publication of the *Guide Catalogue to the South-Western British Prehistoric Collections*, both of which were completed only just in time. The field trips began with a rather wet afternoon at the Stanton Drew stone circles and associated sites. A whole day was spent on the Cotswolds. We had morning coffee at the Bisley home of our President J.D. Cowen, and the sites visited included the hillforts of Sodbury and Painswick. Other days were devoted to the Iron Age and Roman sites at Butcombe, the Abbot's Way in the Somerset Levels, and Avebury, Overton Hill and Fyfield Down. Another day was devoted to sites in Gwent including the long cairn at Heston Brake (Portskewett) specially cleared of vegetation for the occasion, the chambered tombs of *Y Garn Lwyd* and *Ty Isaf*, and the Grey Hill stone circle. On a pre-conference visit to *Y Garn Lwyd*, I was told by the lady of the house nearby where I had requested permission for our visit, 'It is a pity those people of yours can't find summat better to do!'. The programme included a memorable lecture by Dr E.K. Tratman on 'Fifty Years of work on Mendip prehistory'. Peter Fowler and I were joint secretaries for the meeting.

I did not attend the 1969 conference (26 Aug–4 Sept) which was based on *South Germany*. I also missed the conference for 1970 which was in *Sheffield* (23–29 August), having attended the 1952 conference there.

The conference for 1971 (23–27 April) was based on *Douglas* (Isle of Man). The highlights included the Meayll stone circle, the megalithic tombs of *Cashtal yn Ard*, King Orrey's Grave and Ballakelly, South Barrule hillfort, the Braaid circle and related sites, and the Tynwald. Our guides were Peter Gelling, Audrey Henshall, Basil Megaw, and A.M. Cubbon who edited the excellent Guide. There was no meeting in 1972. It was to have been held in *Cork* (30 August–5 Sept) but was cancelled because of the sensitive political situation.

The conference for 1973 (23–27 April) was at *Glasgow*, in association with the Glasgow Archaeological Society. We explored the impressive cemetery of cairns and standing stones at Kilmartin, first visited by the society in 1954, and were delighted by the manner in which it is presented. I included a plan of the area in *Barrow Pyramid and Tomb* (1975), 224–6, together with a description. We also saw the Dunadd hillfort and the Cairnpapple 'henge' (Stuart Piggott) and went over to Arran for a day where we saw the various stone circles and the Tormore I Clyde cairn. I did not attend the meetings of 1974 (*Southampton* 1–7 Sept) and 1975 (*Silsoe, Chilterns* 1–6 Sept).

In 1976 the conference (29 Aug–4 Sept) was based on *Cardiff*, and among the sites studied were the chambered tombs of Tinkinswood and St Lythans, Gelligaer Common with its several cairns including *Carn Bugail*, *Parc Cwm* and Arthur's Stone in Gower, Castle Ditches near Llantwit Major, and the Welsh Folk Museum at St Fagans. *The Field Guide* was edited by J.G. Evans.

Our conference for 1977 was at *Penrith* (27 Aug–3 Sept?) and was rather wet. We included King Arthur's Round Table and Mayburgh, and the Keswick Carles and

Castlerigg stone circles under the guidance of Miss Clare Fell and others. Some amusement was caused by a young archaeologist, speaking at one of the sites recently excavated, stating that the excavation report had been published in the *Cumbersome and Wearisome Transactions*. I missed the 1978 conference which was in *Edinburgh* (26 Aug–2 Sept).

For 1979 (7–12 September) we met at *Cheltenham* with Alan Saville as Local Secretary. The *Cotswold Conference Handbook* was exceptionally good but describes rather more than we actually saw. We had the unusual experience of visiting the Sites and Monuments Record in the Oxfordshire County Museum at Woodstock. The sites explored included the chambered long barrows of Hetty Pegler's Tump, Nympsfield and Belas Knap, the Hull Plantations round barrow group, and the hillforts of Uleybury and Sodbury. We also visited the Rollright Stones.

I did not attend the conference in *Dublin* (31 Aug–7 Sept 1980) having been to those of 1951 and 1961.

Our conference for 1981 (31 Aug–5 Sept) was held at *Exeter*, Miss Bryony Orme being local secretary. The tours to Dartmoor included the excavations then in progress on Shaugh Moor, where we had the unusual experience of seeing the footprints of Bronze Age horse, cow and sheep. The tour from Exeter to Exmoor was via the Exmoor National Park headquarters at Dulverton, where the Secretary, J.S. Haynes, gave a splendid lecture on the National Park organisation with special reference to its archaeological aspect, and we were shown many air photographs, some in stereo, of the principal antiquities. For the Exmoor sites I was in charge and on my way to the stone setting on Almsworthy Common found an unrecorded small round barrow. On another day we visited Kent's Cavern under the guidance of Prof. Allan Straw.

I skipped the *Orkney* conference (1982, 24–31 July) having already been there.

The *Channel Islands* conference (26–31 March 1983) included the barrows on *Le Petit Monceau*, Herm, as well as Guernsey and Jersey. It was a pleasure to visit the new Candie Gardens Museum (successor of the Guilles Allés and Lukis Museums in Guernsey) and the Museum beside *La Hougue Bie*. In addition to the usual monuments we saw the recently excavated megalithic tomb of *Les Fouillages* under the guidance of its excavator Ian Kinnes, whose monograph *Les Fouillages and the Megalithic Monuments of Guernsey* had just been published and was distributed at the meeting. There was an excellent *Field Guide*.

I missed the *Truro* conference (1984, 26 May–2 June) when I was in Minorca.

For 1985, the 50th anniversary year of the Prehistoric Society in its present form, a 50th anniversary indoor meeting at Norwich 29–31 March was followed by a *Study Tour of Wessex* (20–27 April) which replaced the usual annual summer conference. Andrew Lawson was Local Secretary and it was based on Rushmore School, formerly the home of Lt. Gen A.H.L.F. Pitt-Rivers, except for those members who put comfort foremost and stayed at the Grosvenor Hotel, Shaftesbury. It was in every way a special occasion. Sunday 21 April was devoted to a Seminar on Wessex Prehistory concluding with a lecture by Mark Bowden on General Pitt-Rivers. The afternoon comprised a tour of the General's archaeological sites in Rushmore Park ending with a Reception at Rushmore by the Trust for Wessex Archaeology.

On Monday 22 April the chief archaeological sites on Cranborne Chase were visited under the leadership of Richard Bradley and others; these included Bokerly

Dyke, the Oakley Down barrow group, the Dorset Cursus, Wor Barrow, the Ackling Dyke Roman road, and Martin Green's excavations at Down Farm north of Gussage Hill. Hod Hill and Hambledon Hill were then visited under Roger Mercer. On Tuesday 23rd we were up with the lark in order to reach Stonehenge when the enclosure is open to visitors (then early Tuesday mornings only). Richard Atkinson was our guide there. We afterwards visited neighbouring sites including Woodhenge, Durrington Walls (Geoff Wainwright) and Robin Hood's Ball, and finished with a tour of Danebury led by Barry Cunliffe. There was a reception at Salisbury and South Wiltshire Museum.

On Wednesday 24th we moved eastwards to the Chichester area and saw the Roman palace at Fishbourne and the Butser ancient farm project, and those interested in the Lower Palaeolithic visited the recently discovered site at Boxgrove. Thursday 25th was devoted to the Dorchester area including Maiden Castle, Poundbury and Maumbury Rings, but included the Martin's Down and Poor Lot barrow groups, and concluded with a reception at Dorset County Museum. On Friday 26th we saw the Marden earthwork with Geoff Wainwright, and Avebury, the Kennet Avenue, Silbury Hill and the West Kennet long barrow under the guidance of Richard Atkinson and Stuart Piggott.

In short, we visited most of the classic sites under the guidance of the leading authorities, all of whom made themselves available for our archaeological education. We heard the latest interpretations of each site (no matter if few or none are likely to last until the year 2000), and had excellent weather except for a few spots of rain at Stonehenge.

In 1986 (5–12 July) we had a highly successful conference at *Buxton*, with Ken Smith as local secretary. Sites visited included Creswell Crags, the mesolithic site in Lismore Fields (Buxton), the Nine Ladies stone circle and other remains on Stanton Moor with Clive Hart as our guide, and Bee Low, the Five Wells barrow, Green Low and Minning Low, in addition to Arbor Low. We were given a reception at Chatsworth by the Duke of Devonshire. I did not attend the conference for 1987 which comprised a tour of the cave paintings in *Northern Spain*.

The Summer Conference for 1988 was based on *Aberdeen* and covered much of North-East Scotland (27 August–3 September). The Sunday began with lectures including one by Ian Shepherd on the prehistoric sites in general and one by Aubrey Burl on the recumbent stone circles (RSC's). During the afternoon we saw the Broomend of Crichie henge and the RSC's of Loanhead of Daviot with its circular cremation cemetery almost adjoining, and Balgorkar/Castle Fraser.

On Monday 29th we visited the Cullerlie cremation circle and three RSC's: Sunhoney, Midmar Kirk and Old Keig, each with its own characteristics. The Midmar Kirk RSC is in a churchyard which seems to date only from the eighteenth century. The hillfort of Dunnideer was also visited. In the evening we received civic hospitality in Aberdeen City Art Gallery and Museums.

For me the highlight of the whole week was the Tuesday visit to the Balnuaran of Clava cairns. In the morning we saw the Burghead promontory fort and the Pictish Sueno's Stone and we had lunch in the Inverness Museum and Art Gallery and inspected its local prehistoric collections. The afternoon was devoted to the Balnuaran of Clava cairns. As the speaker (Graham Ritchie) gathered the main party around the NE cairn where he addressed them, the two or three keenest photographers (including myself) were free to photograph the central and south-western cairns, and to cover the north-eastern cairn when the party moved away from it. We were impressed by the excellent condition of these cairns and their surroundings, and with the unique phenomenon of the three walls projecting from the central cairn. In the evening we visited the Anthropological Museum of the University of Aberdeen, with its collection of beakers and bronze implements.

On Wednesday we saw the Glassel stone setting, described by Aubrey Burl as an 'Economy' RSC but without the recumbent stone, and later we saw the Tomnaverie RSC, the Woods of Finzean long cairn, and the Nine Stanes RSC. The excursion concluded with an inspection of the magnificent Pictish carving known as the Rhynie Man, beautifully displayed in Woodhill House, Aberdeen, and acquired in 1988 by the Aberdeen Regional Council. Thursday 1 September was very wet and I remained in the coach except for the lunch interval in Dundee Museum. I skipped the Friday excursion to spend the day in the University and City Libraries. With fine weather on five of the six days it was a satisfactory week. The extremely thorough Excursion Guide, by Ian Shepherd and Graham Ritchie, distinguished between sites visited (in normal type) and sites seen only from the coach (in italic type).

Since 1978 the Society has also run *Study Tours* through the Travel Organisation Ltd. These have included *Brittany* (June 1978 and September 1981), the *Dordogne* (1980), *Denmark* (1981), the *Balearic Islands* (1982), and *South-Eastern Spain* (1984). I attended both those covering Brittany, but these are described in chapter 15. I missed the tours to the Dordogne and Denmark. The Study Tour of the *Balearic Islands* (8–15 May 1982), directed by William Waldren, covered both Majorca and Minorca but not Ibiza. It provided a useful introduction to the prehistory of the two islands, although rather slanted towards the director's own largely pre-Talayotic interests. For me it was marred by an obvious omission to go over the ground beforehand and at least find the proper way into each site. At Trepuco for example, a mile or so south of Mahon, we were expected to follow our leader by climbing over a farmer's wall into the site instead of approaching it by the signposted path. There was no site guide.

The study tour to *South-Eastern Spain* (19–26 October 1984) included the *Cueva de Menga* and *Cueva de Viera*, close to one another north-east of Antequera, and the *Cueva de Romeral* two km further east towards Granada: each of them rivalling Gavr'inis and Maes Howe in impressiveness and among the masterpieces of megalithic sepulchral architecture. The tour also included some of the dolmens at *Montefrio* and the extensive settlement and cemetery at *Los Millares*, all under the guidance of Robert W. Chapman assisted by a local prehistorian.

As the Prehistoric Society's lectures are scarcely ever preceded or followed by refreshments (except the Spring Conferences), these summer conferences and study tours are the main occasions when members can socialize. This account of the sites visited may therefore conclude with a note on some of those who have taken part in them. Only a minute proportion – less than 5% – of the total membership normally take part in these meetings, the total membership being anything up to 2,000. One tends to remember the 'characters': the more unusual people. Gordon Childe was a fairly regular attender, occasionally in home-made shorts but with short socks supported by suspenders. Lt/Col R.H. Cunnington, author of *Stonehenge and its Date*

(1935) and a descendant of the William Cunnington who was Colt Hoare's 'coadjutor' on the excavation of Wiltshire barrows betwen 1800 and 1810, attended almost every meeting and was recognizable by his white hair and black moustache, until shortly before his death in 1959. Another 'regular' was W.F. Bushell, son of W. Done Bushell who wrote papers on the stone circles of Pembrokeshire and especially Presely (1908–11). Lily Chitty (replete with shooting stick and numerous handbags) came frequently, often with her sister-in-law Mrs Derwas Chitty. Among the most regular of all was John A. Inglis, an ex-schoolmaster who had assisted on archaeological excavations in every English county and many of those in Scotland and Wales. His annual subscription was always accompanied by a closely-written letter of several pages, narrating his archaeological autobiography for the past year. Florence Nankivell (always on the lookout for new members of the Cornwall Archaeological Society of which she was Secretary) came to the meetings in the Netherlands, Ireland, Denmark and several others. Mollie Bull, our Assistant Secretary 1952–75, attended almost every meeting and acted as unofficial courier to smooth out such difficulties as arose. These meetings were seldom if ever without their 'Lunatic fringe' members who shall remain nameless. For me they have usually added interest to the meetings and I would not wish the society to be without them.

Chapter 12

Out with the Cambrians

'Although as hardy Cambrians we were of course indifferent to weather, it is always pleasant to start out on the first excursion of the week under a smiling sky'.
– Evelyn Lewes, *Out with the Cambrians*, 1934, 143.

I joined the Cambrian Archaeological Association in 1961, but did not attend any of their Annual Meetings (as they call their Summer Meetings) until 1974. As an Englishman I half expected to be given an icy reception, but was from the start welcomed as one of themselves. I believe the reason is partly that whereas the Prehistoric Society is composed largely of specialists, the Cambrian Archaeological Association comprises mostly Welsh people interested in all cultural aspects of the principality, who are keen on getting to know every part of it and the areas with which it has affinities.

Their meetings tend to be extremely well organised. This is partly because they have a system of *stewards*, usually sons or daughters of senior members of the Association and often university students, who make sure that everything runs smoothly and to time. Among other details they check that everybody is in each coach before it leaves each site, and at each lunch break hand out the packed lunches from the boot of the coaches, and they act as 'sheep dogs' to ensure that people get back into the coaches on time after visiting each site. The activities of these stewards (supervised by a *Chief Steward*) add greatly to the success of each meeting. As with the Prehistoric Society meetings, the speakers at each location visited by the Cambrians are almost invariably the leading authorities of the day on each site.

The meetings normally begin with a Saturday evening lecture on reminiscences of the previous year's meeting, and the Sunday evening is devoted to an introductory lecture on the region now being visited. The excursions are usually A (ecclesiastical and domestic architecture and medieval sites generally); B (field archaeology often involving some walking); and sometimes C (industrial archaeology). Until recently I have tended to concentrate on B (field archaeology).

The first meeting that I attended was *South Brecknock* (1974), based on Hereford (17–24 August). For me the highlights were the Brecknock Museum, Frank Noble's public lecture on Offa's Dyke, and the visits to the Pipton long barrow and *Pen-y-Wyrlod* cairn II, both described by H.N. Savory. On Thursday we went to Llanthony Priory and on Friday we visited Hay Castle and R.G. Booth's various bookshops.

Every few years the Association holds an annual meeting outside Wales, which should prevent them from becoming over-parochial. The second meeting I attended was *Winchester* (9–15 August 1975). It included evening lectures on aspects of the relations between Wales and Wessex in antiquity, by Prof. C.F.C. Hawkes, W.F. Grimes, and H.N. Savory. There were visits to Winchester Cathedral, Wolvesley Palace, the hospital and chapel of St Cross, and the great hall of Winchester Castle. Outside Winchester we saw the Butser Hill ancient farm project, H.M.S. Victory and Portchester Castle, and Silchester (guided by George Boon) and the Reading Museum for the Silchester collection. We also visited Barry Cunliffe's excavations at Danebury hillfort; the Dorset Cursus, Knowlton Circles and Badbury Rings, Tidpit Common and Grim's Ditch (all with H. Collin Bowen as our guide). On the Friday we visited Stonehenge, where in my opinion our guide (Major Vatcher) spoke so long that we did not have enough time to see the monument properly. We also visited Salisbury Cathedral and Romsey Abbey.

I believe I missed *South Pembrokeshire* (1976) and *Aberystwyth* (1977).

The Annual Meeting for 1978 was in *Gwent and the Forest of Dean* (12–19 August), based on Caerleon. On Sunday we visited Caerleon with George Boon as our guide. On Monday we went to the Grey Hill stone circle which was described by H. Stephen Green. On Tuesday I selected the visit to Grosmont and Skenfrith castles. On Wednesday we visited Harold's Stones (Trellech) and Trellech church, and on Thursday the Heston Brake (Portskewett) long barrow, followed by the rare delicacy of morning coffee at Speech House in the Forest of Dean, after which we visited Lydney with George Boon. On another day we had afternoon tea at the St Pierre golf club house.

I missed the 1979 meeting (*Lleyn and Snowdonia*) as it coincided with the British Association's meeting in Bath which I attended.

In 1980 the Annual Meeting was in *Swansea, Gower and West Glamorgan* (16–23 August), based on Swansea. On Monday we visited Swansea Museum and Castle and surroundings. On Tuesday we gained access to the Margam Museum of Early Christian stones, including the BODVOC stone which I had for long wanted to see. On Wednesday we saw the megalithic tombs of *Parc Cwm* and *Penmaen* and also the Iron Age hillfort of Thurba. On Thursday Douglas Hague was our entertaining guide at Burry Holms, and W.F. Grimes showed us Samson's Jack standing stone and Cilifor Top hillfort. On Friday we explored Oystermouth Castle and village and in the churchyard some of us saw the grave of Rev. Thomas Bowdler who 'Bowdlerised' Shakespeare.

In 1981 the Association was in *Chester and North-East Wales* (15–22 August). We experienced the glories of medieval Chester by devoting Monday to it including a visit to the Grosvenor Museum. On Wednesday we went to Northwick including the Weaver's Hall Museum, and Nantwich. On Friday there was little to interest me in the programme and Dennis Petch drove me to the Bridestones megalithic tomb at Congleton.

1982 saw the Association in *Cumbria and the Lake District*, based on Lancaster University Halls of Residence (14–21 August). The sites visited included on Monday various prehistoric sites near Crosby Ravensworth (Frances Lynch), and on Tuesday Hardknott hillfort (Tom Clare). On Wednesday we visited Long Meg and her Daughters, Little Meg Circle, King Arthur's Round Table and Mayburgh, both the latter with Clare Fell, and the early hogback tombs in Penrith churchyard (Tom Clare). On Thursday we had a day in the Wordsworth country at Grasmere, and on

Friday a day in Coniston with a choice of visiting John Ruskin's house Brantwood or the Ruskin Museum in Coniston. As a museum curator I found the latter a little disappointing and unworthy of its subject.

In 1983 the Association was in *South Glamorgan*, but I was attending the British Association meeting in Brighton.

In 1984 the Association covered *Anglesey*, based on the Normal College in Bangor (18–25 August). On the Sunday we had the memorable experience of exploring Conway Castle and town walls and Carnarvon Castle with Arnold Taylor, and in the evening we had an introductory lecture by Donald Moore. On Monday we saw the hillfort of *Bwrdd Arthur* (Arthur's Table). On Tuesday a visit to the two remaining of the original five barrows at Llanddyfnan was followed by the more exciting chambered tomb of *Lligwy* with its enormous cover-slab (Frances Lynch). On Wednesday we first visited *Llyn Cerrig Bach*, the lake from which the celebrated hoard of Celtic metalwork was dredged in 1943. Among other sites visited were the prehistoric hut-circles at *Ty Mawr* and the chambered tomb at Trefignath. On Thursday we saw three more chambered tombs: *Barclodiad y Gawres* (the Giantess's Apronful); *Ty Newydd* and *Presaddfed*.

For me Friday was the best day. It included three famous chambered tombs, all explained by Frances Lynch. *Bryn Celli Ddu* (the hill of the dark grove) has been reinterpreted at least once since my earlier visit with the Prehistoric Society (1959); *Bryn yr Hen Bobl* (the hill of the old people), with its extraordinary projecting 'tail' compared by its excavator W.J. Hemp to a phallus; and *Plas Newydd*, an impressive and often illustrated chambered tomb which I had not previously seen.

The 1985 meeting covered *Old Carmarthenshire* and was based on Carmarthen (17–24 August). In contrast with Anglesey 1984 there were few megalithic sites: just the Gours standing stone (*Maen Llwyd*, the Hoar Stone) and the chambered tomb of *Twlc y Filiast* (Kennel of the Greyhound Bitch), excavated in 1953 by H.N. Savory who spoke at the site. It was a memorable experience to attend the reception by the local archaeological societies and related bodies at the Carmarthen Museum, notable for its early association with George Eyre Evans, a thumbnail sketch of whom is given in Sir Mortimer Wheeler's *Still Digging* (1955 edn., 80–82). What everyone remembers who attended this meeting was that it poured with rain on several occasions, usually at the most inconvenient moments when we were on tops of hills exploring medieval castles.

In 1986 the meeting covered *Avon* and was based on the Salisbury Hotel, Weston-super-Mare (16–23 August). On Sunday we visited the Banwell Bone Caves (which I had not seen before), led by J.H. Tucker, and Worlebury Iron Age hillfort led by Miss Jane Evans (curator of the Woodspring Museum). In the evening there was the introductory lecture by Prof. Desmond Donovan. On Monday we explored Wookey Hole under the guidance of Christopher J. Hawkes. There seemed rather more to see than when I was last there several years previously. In the afternoon we visited Wells Cathedral, the Bishop's Palace and the Museum. The evening was occupied by George Boon's Presidential Address followed by the President's Reception.

Tuesday was devoted to Glastonbury and the Somerset Levels. Dr Ralegh Radford addressed us at Glastonbury Abbey and Prof. Philip Rahtz on his excavations on Glastonbury Tor, and some of us also visited the Glastonbury Museum.

On Wednesday we visited the stone circles and related monuments at Stanton Drew under my guidance, but unfortunately an unexpected traffic diversion conspired with other circumstances to delay our arrival at Stanton Drew by 30–40 minutes and this time was deducted from our stay there, causing us to omit the Cove and the south-western circle. We then proceeded to Camerton Church where W.J. Wedlake addressed us on the Rev. John Skinner of Camerton (1772–1839) and the hundred volumes of his Journals in the British Library describing his numerous antiquarian researches. Mr Wedlake slightly overran, and we arrived rather late for lunch at the George Inn, Norton St Philip, where Commander E.H.D. Williams addressed us on the architecture of the George Inn. In the afternoon we visited the Stoney Littleton long barrow under my guidance, and Maes Knoll hillfort and Wansdyke led by Prof. Philip Rahtz, who also gave the public lecture in the evening on 'Dark Age Somerset illuminated'.

On Thursday we explored Mendip. The guide whose name was on the programme did not turn up, but Christopher Richards led a highly competent tour of Dolebury hillfort, our President led us over the Charterhouse-on-Mendip Roman settlement, and Mr Ed Dennison showed us the remains of nineteenth century lead-mining. I described the Priddy Circles and barrow groups but the weather had by then deteriorated and the visit to them was curtailed.

On Friday Party B went to Steep Holm, and I went on Party A to architectural sites including Nunney Castle (D. Cathcart King) and Downside Abbey.

The meeting in 1987 was based on *Hereford* (17–21 August), where we stayed at the College of Further Education as in 1974. On Monday we explored the Cathedral under the guidance of the architect, master mason and librarian, and we also visited the City Museum and Art Gallery, where the Woolhope Naturalists' Field Club entertained us. In the evening there was the introductory lecture by S.C. Stanford on 'Colonisation and Conquest in the Central Marshes'. Among the sites visited on Tuesday were Arthur's Stone passage grave (Dorstone) with Stephen Green as our guide, Kilpeck Norman church and castle, and Abbey Dore. In the evening there was the Presidential Address by Emeritus Prof. J. Gwyn Williams, on 'The Castles of Wales during the Civil War 1642–47'.

Wednesday included a visit to Croft Ambry hillfort led by S.C. Stanford, followed by visits to Croft Castle and church. In the evening I gave a short lecture on 'The Rise and Fall of the Old Straight Track', which will soon be published in *Transactions of the Woolhope Naturalists' Field Club*. During one of our visits to Hereford I showed a few of our members the bronze plaque outside the home of Alfred Watkins near the Cathedral. Thursday included a walk around Pembridge with its numerous timber-framed houses. On Friday we visited Treago Castle where we were received by Sir Humphrey and Sir Roger Mynors and their wives. We stopped briefly at the Hangman's Stone near St Weonards, where I spoke on standing stones so-called and their associated traditions. We also visited Goodrich Castle.

A characteristic of this meeting was the contribution of J.W. Tonkin who spoke at a dozen of the churches and other buildings visited, and contributed in other ways to the success of it, as also did Mrs Tonkin. On the Friday evening, at the College of Further Education, I showed two video tapes about Alfred Watkins, one entitled ''Mornin' Mr Watkins', the other 'The strange affair of the Old Straight Track', which dealt more particularly with his antiquarian interests. Both were kindly lent by the Hereford Public Library.

The meeting in 1988 was in *Leinster* (13–20 August), based on a school in a suburb of Dublin. The Sunday visits included the National Museum (mostly in course of modernisation and rearrangement) where there were excellent displays illustrating the treasures of Irish archaeology from the Bronze Age to the Early Christian period and the recent excavations in the extensive Viking settlement on the borders of the River Liffey: as far as known the origin of Dublin. There were welcome receptions by the Royal Society of Antiquaries of Ireland (President: Etienne Rynne) and the Kilkenny Archaeological Society. Prof. Michael Herity gave the introductory lecture on the archaeology of Ireland, and on the following evenings Miss Frances Lynch gave her Presidential Address on 'Wales and Ireland in Prehistory' and Dr Patrick Wallace lectured on 'Excavations in Viking and Medieval Dublin'.

On Monday 15th the tour was to the Boyne Valley and surroundings, and included the passage graves of New Grange and Knowth (the latter described by its excavator Prof. George Eogan), the Four Knocks passage grave (where we were reminded that it is one of four sepulchral cairns in that locality), and the Early Christian monuments at Monasterboice. On Tuesday we covered the Wicklow area including the Athgreany stone circle and its outlier and the Early Christian monastic site at Glendalough. On Wednesday we were in the Kilkenny/Kildare areas, including Castledermot where I was delighted to see the Christianized holed standing stone which I had known of for many years from early illustrations. Thursday was devoted to the Meath area including Kells with its Early Christian monastic sites. A group of good walkers including myself climbed the *Slieve na Calliagh* (the Hag's Mountain) and inspected Cairn T with its decorated cruciform interior almost rivalling that of New Grange, and its two nearest neighbours. Friday was devoted to a tour of Dublin which included a sight of the Book of Kells in Trinity College Library and the old-established Marsh's Library. The week was very well organised by Rory O'Farrell, Miss Debby Wheeler and others.

An incident at one of the summer meetings is worth recording. Mr David Cathcart King used to bring along two of his young students to these meetings, on the first day of which a distinguished geographer would give a rather lengthy geographical introduction to the region. I once saw Cathcart King advise his students: 'If I were you I would sit right at the back; you will find the lecture awfully boring and if you find it too much you will then be able to slip away without being noticed'. I do not remember whether the students stayed the course. At the conclusion of the lecture Mr Cathcart King, who was in the chair, said, 'Well ladies and gentlemen, I am sure you will all agree that we have been held spellbound and enthralled by a most fascinating account of the region we are about to explore' – or words to that effect.

Chapter 13

County and Local Archaeological Societies

'A feature of . . . the Society's Annual General Meeting for many years was the Temporary Museum. Some of the exhibits were curious rather than important – a brick from Babylon and King Charles I's toothpick, for example . . . [The Secretary] reserved to himself the right of dunning certain distinguished defaulters, such as the Archbishop of Canterbury'.
                    – F.W. Jessup, in *Archaeologia Cantiana*, 70 (1956), 11, 19.

On 19 July 1950 I attended the AGM of the Wiltshire Archaeological and Natural history Society held at the Town Hall, Devizes. During the meeting and without warning me beforehand, their Secretary, C.W. Pugh, asked me to propose the re-election of the Committee *en bloc* (*W.A.M.* 53, 443). In the course of my year or so working on *V.C.H. Wiltshire* in the library of the Society I had already formed the opinion that the Society was badly in need of new blood on its Committee, and it was therefore with some diffidence that I complied with the Secretary's request.

To a varying extent it can probably be said that most of the county archaeological societies, normally formed in the mid-nineteenth century to cater for the interests of a membership largely comprising clergy, lawyers, medical doctors and school teachers, with antiquarian rather than archaeological interests, were in a state of transition following the end of the 1939/45 war, which brought in its train an immense amount of damage to ancient earthworks by the introduction of more drastic agricultural machinery and the needs of the developer often accompanied by the bulldozer. At the Society's AGM on 25 July 1951 I drew their attention to the serious damage caused by those riding tanks over the round barrows on Snail Down in the parish of Collingbourne Kingston (*W.A.M.* 54, 221–2).

Soon after assuming my duties in Bristol City Museum on 1 February 1952, having already become a member of the Bristol & Gloucestershire Archaeological Society, I attended one of their Bristol branch lectures, which was of course on an aspect of archaeology (I forget the exact subject). I was surprised when the Chairman stated that he knew nothing whatever about archaeology when introducing the speaker. The chairman was in fact a historian, and I wondered whether Historical Societies were accustomed to put in as Chairmen those who know nothing whatever about history. Discretion caused me to refrain from asking this question during the discussion time.

During my first few years in Bristol City Museum I did a good deal to make my presence known to the B & G.A.S., partly by regularly attending their Bristol lectures and partly by writing up archaeological papers and notes for publication in their *Transactions*, e.g. in vols. 72, 75, 76, 77 and 79 between 1953 and 1960; and subsequently in vols. 83, 85, 86, 91 and 97 between 1964 and 1980.

I had rather expected that the curator in archaeology at Bristol City Museum would eventually have been considered a suitable person to be one of the 9 representatives from the Bristol area on the council. However, I was once told by one of the Society's senior officials that the Bristol City Museum had to be represented by its Director [whether he was an archaeologist or not]. I believe it was about the beginning of 1962 when I ventured to write to the Chairman of the Council pointing out that of the 9 council members from Bristol, not one had ever had a paper published which had been included in the annual bibliographies published by the Council for British Archaeology; also that neither the department of Classics and Archaeology in Bristol University, nor the department of archaeology in the City Museum, was represented on the Society's Council.

This resulted in Prof. J.M. Cook of the Classics Department of the University being put on the Society's Council, and either then or very soon afterwards I was invited to join their Excavations and Buildings Committee, and accepted. However, shortly afterwards I had occasion to report to that Committee the formation of the Bristol Archaeological Research Group; and I was forthwith dropped from the said Committee (but without my being informed).

The circumstances which led to the formation of B.A.R.G. must now be given. Concern at what seemed a failure of the B & G.A.S. to respond adequately to the changing needs of such societies was not confined to its younger members. Indeed Dr F.S. Wallis opened his Presidential Address (March 1960) with the words:

May I put in a plea for a fuller awareness of the young people in our midst? . . . There is a tremendous urge to know more about prehistoric and historic times. But with young people this urge is accompanied by a desire to *do* something as distinct from passive reading and listening . . . Already another Society in Bristol is discussing possible schemes and it is for this body to probe the situation and provide a solution. (*TBGAS* 79 ii, 155).

Dr Wallis told me afterwards that his remarks in this context were met with black looks from certain quarters.

The other society that he had in mind was the Bristol Naturalists' Society. About this time I was invited by Mr R.G. Payne, secretary of their Geological section, to be secretary of an archaeological section which they proposed to form, of which Mrs Margaret Fowler, a trained archaeologist and wife of Dr G.N. Fowler of the Physics department in the University, had agreed to be Chairperson. I declined partly because of other commitments but largely because such an arrangement would have left her with the kudos and me with most of the work. The Annual Report of their Geological Section states that consideration had been given to the formation of an archaeological section but the idea had been rejected for the time being (*Proc. Bristol Naturalists' Society for 1959–63*, 96).

I was also conscious that a group of rather militant young local amateur archaeologists had it in mind to form an archaeological group more active in field archaeology, led by someone who I regarded as something of a menace.

At this juncture I received a letter, around the turn of 1961/62, from Charles Browne, suggesting the formation of an archaeological society or group in the Bristol area. I immediately discussed that proposal with my recently appointed Museum

Director Alan Warhurst and one or two others and we decided to proceed without further delay with the formation of such a group. We got together a steering committee comprising interested people from the University, the City Museum, and the private sector. At a meeting of this committee I lectured on the archaeological situation in the region, and showed a distribution map indicating the traditional county societies with black spots and the smaller and recently formed groups, mostly of 'splinter' type, with spots of another colour. I was unconscious of the double meaning until Mr Warhurst drew my attention to it afterwards. After due consideration we came out in favour of calling it an archaeological research group in preference to an archaeological society because the latter might reflect the image of the county archaeological societies mostly formed in the mid-nineteenth century. Since then the creation of the county of Avon out of areas formerly north Somerset and south Gloucestershire has led initially to our changing our title to Bristol and Avon Archaeological Research Group and finally to the change to the Bristol and Avon Archaeological Society and we have come into line with the other county archaeological societies. My work as editor of the publications of the Bristol Archaeological Research Group and its later manifestations is discussed in chapters 17 and 18.

I now have to discuss my more recent relations with the Bristol and Gloucestershire Archaeological Society. A few years after the formation of B.A.R.G., the members and others in the Gloucester area were so impressed by our progress that they formed the Gloucester and District Archaeological Research Group which continues to flourish to this day. I was made a vice-president of the Bristol and Gloucestershire Archaeological Society in 1971; but I found it necessary to resign from that position on 26 September 1977 because I was unable to accept the decision of their Council, on the motion of their Hon. Treasurer, to default with all or part of their institutional subscription to the Council for British Archaeology – because to have done so would have jeopardised their right to submit papers to that body for publication grants. They made this decision on 28 June that year but revoked it after receiving my resignation (and that of Peter Fowler) on that issue.

That the Society were still tending, in my opinion, to put the emphasis on history rather than archaeology as late as 1976 is shown by the title, as well as most of the contents, of their centenary volume: *Essays in Bristol and Gloucestershire History*, edited by two historians.

It must however in fairness be stated that the Society's Editors, Dr Joan Evans (1949–58), Captain H.S. Gracie (1959–72) and their successors have readily accepted papers on archaeology if of the right standard, for the Society's *Transactions*.

The Local Government reorganisation of 1974 was followed by the creation of county archaeologists within the planning departments of the counties, but in Gloucestershire not until 1982, when a county Sites and Monuments record was established, and this was followed by the appointment of Jan Wills as Gloucestershire's first County Archaeologist in 1985. In recent years the absorption of younger and distinguished archaeologists including Alan Saville as joint Editor, and Dr Tim Darvill, has resulted in a far more satisfactory balance between archaeological and other interests in the BGAS, and this was shown, for example, by the publication of *Archaeology in Gloucestershire*, dedicated to the memory of Mrs Elsie Clifford and Mrs Helen O'Neil (divided in life but thus united in death), in 1984. The Society's dedication of vol. 104 of their *Transactions*, issued in March 1987, to me to mark by 80th birthday, gave me much pleasure.

My relations with the Somerset Archaeological and Natural History Society have been entirely satisfactory. I was put on their Council from 1960 and was their President in 1970–71, and devoted my Presidential Address to 'The past and future of archaeology in Somerset' (*Som. A & NH* 115, 29 –38). The Society welcomed the formation of B.A.R.G. as they have always encouraged the establishment of such groups because it tends to increase the number of effectively interested people. My most recent act for that Society was to lead a group of their members on a field trip to the Quantocks on 11 July 1987, when we visited Fyne Court, Dowsborough hillfort, and finished with tea at the Combe House Hotel at Holford.

On 3 December 1928 the Devon Archaeological Exploration Society was initiated to give more positive direction to archaeological research than was being provided by the Archaeology section of the Devonshire Association for the Advancement of Science. Roland MacAlpine Woods, an old friend of my father, was on the Executive Committee of the D.A.E.S. and his wife Gertrude was joint secretary from 1929 to 1932. They persuaded me to join and I was a member in 1930–31 when I resigned for financial reasons. I rejoined it in 1952 when I joined all the county archaeological societies in south-western England following my appointment to Bristol City Museum. Distance from base has precluded my attendance at more than an occasional meeting, but I attended their 50th jubilee meeting in 1979. I also attended their 60th anniversary meeting on 3 December 1988 and was one of the three earliest members present. The introduction by the President, Henrietta Quinnell, was followed by a delightfully reminiscent lecture by Dr Ralegh Radford (a founder member) on the origins of the Society and its early work, and a lecture by John Allan of Exeter City Museum on archaeology in Exeter since the 1939/45 War. A reception at the Guildhall by invitation of the Mayor who was present included an excellent lunch as well as appropriate speeches. In the afternnon there were lectures by Lady Aileen Fox who dealt mainly with the Society's excavation at Hembury hillfort under Dorothy Liddell in the 1930s, and by Prof. Thurstan Shaw who also took part in the Hembury excavations. The tea break was followed by lectures by Henrietta Quinnell on the Society's activities since 1970 and by Simon Tymms on the Society's current activities. It was a particular pleasure to meet so many old friends during the refreshment breaks. My survey of Devon barrows was published in three parts by that Society, now re-named the Devon Archaeological Society.

I joined the Cornwall Archaeological Society in 1961, but distance from Bristol has precluded my attendance at any of their meetings. My only contribution to *Cornish Archaeology* is a short note on the Rillaton barrow (vol. 8, 126–7).

Chapter 14

Folklore and the Folklore Society

We have but to scratch the rustic
to find the barbarian underneath.
– Edward Clodd, in introduction to Lady E.C. Gurdon, *County Folklore: Suffolk*
(1893), xii.

My interest in folklore originated in the study of the folk traditions associated with barrows, notably in Sussex where my fieldwork began, where I was told by a shepherd about 1928 of the tradition that a golden calf was buried somewhere in the Sussex downs, whether or not in a barrow. My first article on folklore, 'Barrows and their Folklore', was published in the *Sussex County Herald* on 23 January 1931.

I was formally elected a member of the Folklore Society on 21 November 1934. At one of their first meetings that I attended, probably in 1935, Lady Alice Gomme was present: the widow of Sir Laurence Gomme, one of the founders of the Society (the other being W.J. Thoms) in 1879. I joined the Society's Council on 17 February 1937, after my suitability had been checked by the Secretary, Harold Coote Lake, with my young friend R. Rainbird Clarke of Norwich, with whom in the summer of 1937 I spent a fortnight's holiday on a 'barrow-crawl' in Norfolk. I had already included a chapter on barrow folklore in my book *The Ancient Burial-Mounds of England*, published in 1936. By 1937 I had reviewed the three-volume *Corpus du Folklore Préhistorique en France et dans les Colonies Françaises* (1934–6) for *Antiquity* (March 1937) and *Folk-lore* (March 1937). On 17 March 1937 I lectured to the Folklore Society on 'Some aspects of the folklore of prehistoric remains', – a paper to which I devoted a great deal of thought during the previous two or three months. The audience included Dr J.H. Hutton, A.D. Lacaille, Glyn Daniel (then a rising star), Stuart Piggott and Alexander Keiller. The paper was printed in *Folk-lore* 48 (Sept 1937), 245–59.

On the eve of the outbreak of the 1939–45 war, I prepared 'A Scheme for recording the folklore of prehistoric remains', which was printed in *Folk-lore* 50 (Dec 1939), 323–32. Needless to say, the project was shelved until some years after the war had ended, except that Dr Edith Guest assembled notes covering the material for the Northern English counties, now in the archives of the Folklore Society.

After spending four years with the R.A.F. in the Middle East, based at Heliopolis outside Cairo, my first contribution to folklore after my return was to read a paper on 'the folklore of ancient Egyptian monuments' to the Folklore Society on 12 February 1947, which was afterwards printed in *Folk-lore* 58 (1947), 345–60. To my delight it was attended by a group from the Department of Egyptology in University College, led by Prof. Černy, whom I had met in Cairo during the war.

Early in Sept 1947 I lectured on the folklore of prehistoric sites at the Dundee meeting of the British Association for the Advancement of Science (Section H, Anthropology and Archaeology), where it was well received. The following week I gave a similar lecture at the first Summer Meeting of the Prehistoric Society, held at York. I was equally conscious that my lecture there was a flop and it was in fact cut short by the President who was in the Chair.

On 23 April 1949 I resigned from my employment in Barclays Bank and from 1 May I joined the staff of the *Victoria County Histories* as assistant to Prof. C.F.C. Hawkes and Prof. Stuart Piggott for preparing the Archaeological Gazetteer which eventually constituted vol. I (Part i) of the *V.C.H. Wiltshire*, the publication of which was delayed until 1957 although my Gazetteer was completed by 1952. This caused me to move to Devizes until 1952 when, on taking up my appointment as Curator in Archaeology and Ethnography at Bristol City Museum, I moved to Bristol. Inevitably my move to the provinces led to a curtailment of my activities in the Folklore Society.

This is a suitable occasion to refer to the more social aspects of the Folklore Society's activities. Their meetings were then preceded by modestly-priced dinners at University College, where it was possible to meet one's folklore colleagues and discuss matters with them more satisfactorily than at the meetings. These occasions brought me into contact with many interesting people including Lord Raglan, Dr Moses Gaster and his son Theodor Gaster, and Prof. Edwin Oliver James, who was Editor of *Folk-lore* for many years. Among the more unusual members was Dr G.B. Gardner, who created a witchcraft museum in the Isle of Man, was author of a book called *Witchcraft To-Day* (1954), and used to take part, dressed as a modern Druid, at their midsummer meetings at Stonehenge. These occasions were very convenient for those members residing in the London area and the home counties, but not for those living further afield.

On 18 April 1951 I lectured to the Folklore Society on 'Prehistory, tradition and superstition', printed under the title of 'Early funerary superstitions in Britain' in *Folk-lore* 64, 271–81, 1953. In the audience were my then chief Prof. C.F.C. Hawkes and Kenneth Oakley who was perhaps at that time the only other archaeologist known to me with a keen interest in folklore. It was not among my most satisfactory papers, but it was a stage in my transition from Egyptology to British archaeology and folklore.

Looking back on the various papers given by others to the Folklore Society, my impression is that the most interesting of them all was that by Prof. David Brunt, F.R.S., on 'Meteorology and weather lore', given on 20 February 1946, in which he showed the extent to which 'red sky at night, shepherd's delight' and so on have a factual basis, with parallels in other languages.

My appointment as curator of archaeology and ethnography in Bristol City Museum w.e.f. 1 February 1952 quickly led to an increased interest in numismatics, as most of the enquiries dealt with the identification of coins, often dug up in the gardens of suburban residences. This led to my next paper, 'The ferryman and his fee', printed in *Folk-lore* 68, 257–69 (1957), dealing with Charon's obol and related matters among the Romans; and to my review of Radomersky's book *The Dead Obolus of the Slavs in Bohemia and Moravia* (*Folk-lore* 69, 209–10, 1958). The former dealt with the ferryman of the dead in ancient Egypt, Greece, Rome and in medieval and later contexts. Another paper with a numismatic slant was 'Barrow treasure in fact, tradition and legislation (*Folklore* 78, 1–38 (1967)), which dealt with the practice of depositing hoards of coins in barrows during times of political disturbance.

Between these related papers came 'The breaking of objects as a funerary rite' (*Folklore* 72, 475–91, 1961; supplementary notes in *Folklore* 84, 111–14, 1973). This subject has been regarded with suspicion by some orthodox archaeologists, perhaps because their wilder colleagues have been unable to resist the temptation of attributing to funerary ritual objects most likely broken accidentally (perhaps even by the later barrow-diggers), probably in order to make their own papers more interesting. However, unknown to me a distinguished Italian prehistorian, Dr Editta Castaldi, had a much more exhaustive paper on the same subject 'La frammentazione rituale in etnologia e in preistoria') published in *Rivista di Scienze Preistoriche*, XX (i), 1965, 247–77.

During the ten years following my retirement on 13 April 1972, I enjoyed writing five of the West Country Folklore monographs published by J. Stevens Cox for the Toucan Press in Guernsey:

No. 5. *The Folklore of Stanton Drew* (1973);
No. 9. *The Legendary History and Folklore of Stonehenge* (1976); also printed in *Folklore*, 87, 5–20, following delivery as a lecture to the Society in December 1975;
No. 10. *The Rollright Stones and their Folklore* (1978);
No. 11. *The Druids and Stonehenge: the Story of a Myth* (1978);
No. 15. *Mitchell's Fold Stone Circle and its Folklore* (1982).

The Legendary History and Folklore of Stonehenge was put on sale at Stonehenge from 1976 until about 1980 and brought me a handsome return from a 10 % royalty on a sale price of 30 pence as about 900 copies a year were sold there. A change of management policy at Stonehenge about 1979 stopped this, and the Stonehenge authorities would not put on sale *The Druids and Stonehenge* which had then just been published, because they considered that to have done so would have caused problems with the modern Druid Orders who would have wanted their own publications to be put on sale there (Chippindale in *Antiquity* 57 (1983), 177). I enjoyed writing these monographs which dealt with the folklore of four of our most important megalithic monuments.

Ever since about 1930 I had been maintaining a card catalogue of folklore attached to prehistoric sites in Britain – mostly England, to which I added in the course of my reading. It had always been my hope, since publication of my 'scheme for recording the folklore of prehistoric remains' in December 1939, to produce an inventory of this material, preceded by an analytical introduction. This was eventually achieved, at least for England, Scotland, Wales and the Isle of Man, by the publication of my *Folklore of Prehistoric Sites in Britain* (1976, David & Charles), which was followed by addenda in *Folklore* (Sept 1979). A task outstanding is to compile a similar inventory of the folklore of Roman and later sites. The material certainly exists but its collection would involve searching all the literature as I did for the prehistoric material. I made a minute contribution to this end with my paper on 'Hangman's Stones and their Traditions' (*Folklore* 96, 217–22, 1985).

My other studies in folklore include 'A century of the study of the folklore of archaeological sites' (in V. Newall, ed., 1980, 213–17), originally delivered as a lecture at the Centenary Conference of the Folklore Society at the Royal Holloway College, 17–21 July 1978. My contributions dealing more particularly with foreign folklore include 'folklore of archaeological sites in Corsica' (with Dorothy Carrington), in *Folklore* 93: i, 61–8 (1982); 'The popular names and folklore of prehistoric sites in Menorca' in *Folklore* 95, 90–9 (1984); and 'The Christianization of prehistoric sites', covering Mediterranean, Iberian and French as well as British material, in *Landscape History*, 8, 27–37 (1986).

My publications with a marginal folklore interest include 'Wayland's Smithy, Beahhild's Byrigels and Hwittuc's hlaew', an attempt to show that the legend of Wayland the invisible smith had imprinted itself not only at the Wayland's Smithy long barrow but also at several other sites used as boundary points in the Saxon charters. It was published in *Trans. Newbury District Field Club*, 8, 136–9 (1940).

Of my activities on the Council of the Folklore Society from 1937 onwards little need be said. They followed their normal course from 1937 to 1941 when I was posted to Egypt with the R.A.F., but I resumed my service on the Society's Council on my return. All went well until the early 1950s. Mrs H.A. Lake Barnett, to whom the Society is indebted for generous benefactions and an immense amount of hard work, became both Secretary and Treasurer from late 1949; but her singleness of purpose in the interests of the Folklore Society was such that she was not the easiest of colleagues. As far as I was concerned matters came to a head about January 1953 when I decided to resign from the Counil. In 1969, when Mrs Venetia Newall had succeeded her as Hon. Secretary, the constitution of the Society was re-modelled, the old Council became the Committee, and a new Council was formed as an advisory body, which I joined in December 1969 and have remained on it ever since.

My folklore activities have not been restricted to the Folklore Society. In 1957 the British Association for Advancement of Science held their annual meeting in Dublin and I was Recorder of Section H (Archaeology and Anthropology). It was decided to devote an afternoon session to the folklore of 'these islands' (the phrase was J.H. Delargy's who was director of the Irish Folklore Commission). It comprised Seamus O'Sullivan who covered Ireland and the Isle of Man; Stewart F. Sanderson who covered Scotland; Peter Opie who covered England; and Iowerth O. Peate who covered the Welsh material. The session was chaired by Prof. Delargy. A slight difficulty arose while the programme for the Folklore session was being developed. Dr Margaret Murray, then aged 94, offered to give a paper on Irish Fairies; but when I discussed her offer at the preliminary meeting with Prof. Delargy in Dublin, he warned me that he would refuse to take the Chair at the Folklore session if we were going to have Dr Murray among the speakers. I then referred the matter to our President of Section H, Prof. Christopher Hawkes, and suggested that perhaps we might fit her into one of our archaeology sessions; he replied 'Fairies are folklore; and if the folklorists won't have her, that is no reason why the archaeologists should!' She was therefore omitted from the Folklore programme. However, the folklore session finished with 20 minutes or so to spare, and Delargy moved that the time be devoted to discussion, and invited someone to open it. Dr Murray then got up and virtually read her paper on Irish Fairies, and Delargy had no choice but to sit it out.

1931 'Barrows and their folklore'. *Sussex County Herald* 23 January.
1936 *The Ancient Burial-Mounds of England*, chapter 3.
1937 Review, *Corpus du folklore préhistorique en France et dans les Colonies françaises.*
       Antiquity, March; *Folk-lore*, March. 'Some aspects of the folklore of prehistoric
       monuments'. *Folk-lore* 48, Sept., 245–59.
1939 'Scheme for recording the folklore of prehistoric remains'. *Folk-lore* 50, Dec.
       323–32.
1940 'Wayland's Smithy, *Beahhild's Byrigels* and *Hwittuc's Hlaew*: a suggestion'.
       Trans. Newbury Dist. Field Club 8, 136–9.
1946 Review, 'Ship of the dead in textile art'. *Folk-lore* 57, 199–200.
1947 'The folklore of ancient Egyptian monuments'. *Folk-lore* 58, 345–60. Lecture,
       'The folklore of prehistoric monuments'. British Assoc. Dundee meeting.
1953 'Early funerary superstitions in Britain'. *Folk-lore* 64, 271–81.
1957 'The ferryman and his fee'. *Folk-lore* 68, 257–69.
1958 Review. *The Dead Obolus of the Slavs in Bohemia and Moravia*, by P.
       Radomersky. *Folklore* 69, 209–10.
1961 'The breaking of objects as a funerary rite'. *Folklore* 72, 475–91.
1966 Review, *Somerset Folklore*, by Ruth Tongue. *Proc. Somerset Archaeol. & Nat.
       Hist. Soc.* 110, 116.
1967 'Barrow treasure, in fact, fiction and legislation'. *Folklore* 78, 1–38.
1973 *The Folklore of Stanton Drew*. Toucan Press.
1973 'Witchcraft at prehistoric sites'. *The Witch Figure*, ed. V. Newall, 72–9.
1976 *Legendary History and Folklore of Stonehenge*. Toucan Press. 'Legendary history
       and folklore of Stonehenge'. *Folklore* 87, 5–20. *Folklore of Prehistoric Sites in Britain.*
       David & Charles. 'Folklore of prehistoric sites in Britain'. U.I.S.P.P. Congress,
       Nice. I, 12.
1978 'The county of Avon and the Druids'. *Avon Archaeological Newsletter.*
       The Rollright Stones and their Folklore. Toucan Press.
       The Druids and Stonehenge: the story of a myth. Toucan Press.
1979 'The folklore of Exmoor antiquities'. *Exmoor Review* for 1979. 'Notes on the
       folklore of prehistoric sites in Britain'. *Folklore*, 90, 66–70.
1980 Reviews, Marie de Garis, *Folklore of Guernsey*; J. Stevens Cox, *Prehistoric
       Monuments of Guernsey and Associated Folklore*. *Folklore* 91, 247. 'A century of the
       study of the folklore of archaeological sites'. *Folklore Studies in the Twentieth Century*,
       ed. V. Newall, 213–17.
1982 'The stone at Snivelling Corner, Ashbury'. *Trans. Newbury Dist. Field Club.* 12
       (vi), 54–5.
       Mitchell's Fold Stone Circle and its Folklore. Toucan Press. 'Folklore of archaeological
       sites in Corsica' (with Dorothy Carrington). *Folklore* 93, 61–9. 'The later history of
       Ty Illtud long barrow'. *Archaeol. Cambrensis* 130 for 1981, 131–9.
1983 'Stanton Drew: from folk tradition to the New Archaeology'. *Avon Past*. 8, 4–8.
1984 'The popular names and folklore of prehistoric sites in Menorca'. *Folklore* 95
       (i), 90–99.
1985 'Hangman's Stones and their traditions'. *Folklore* 96 (ii), 217–22.
1987 'The Christianization of prehistoric sites'. *Landscape History* 8, 27–37.
   Review of J & C. Bord, *Sacred Waters. Landscape History*, 8 (for 1986), 100–101.

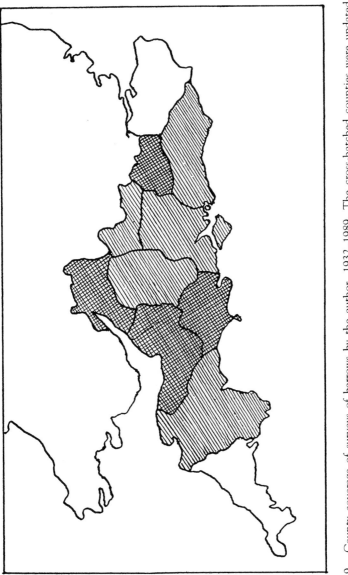

9. County coverage of surveys of barrows by the author, 1932–1989. The cross-hatched counties were updated 1982–9.

10.   The author at porthole-entrance dolmen, Montplé,
Minorca, spring 1980. Photo: José Mascaro Pasarius.

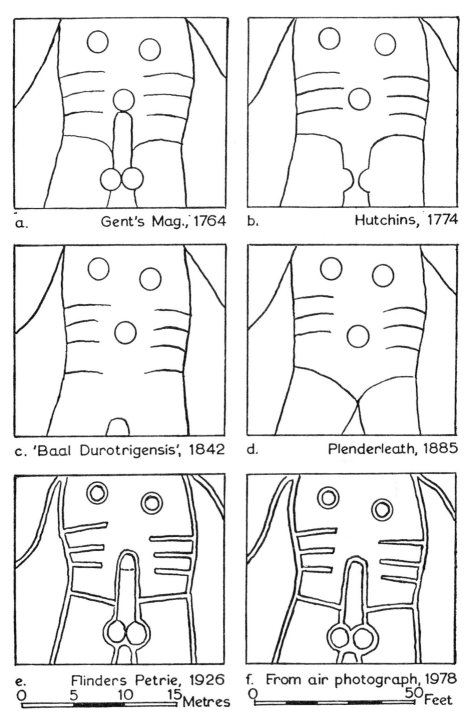

a.   Gent's Mag., 1764   b.   Hutchins, 1774

c. 'Baal Durotrigensis', 1842   d.   Plenderleath, 1885

e.   Flinders Petrie, 1926   f.   From air photograph, 1978

0   5   10   15 Metres   0   50 Feet

11.   Plans of the giant of Cerne Abbas from 1764 onwards.

Triumph of CHRISTIANITY *over* DRUIDISM.

12. A Christianized megalithic tomb at Carnac, Brittany. Ex R.C. Hoare, *History of Modern Wiltshire*, II, 1826, facing p. 49.

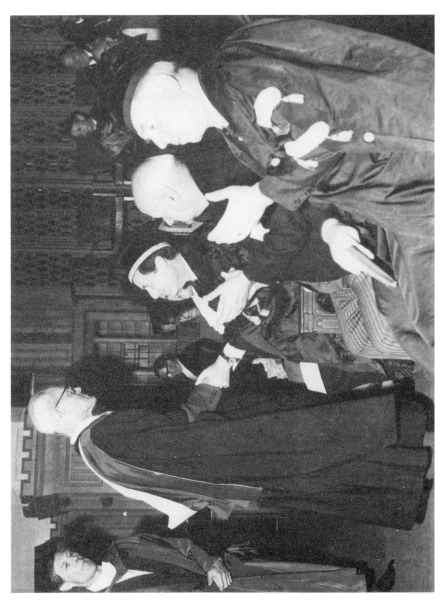

13. The author receiving an Honorary M.A. degree from Bristol University, 1971. Photo: Bristol Evening Post.

14. The author receiving a cake crowned with 50 chocolate 'barrows', to mark 50th anniversary of publication of *Ancient Burial-Mounds of England*, at Spring Conference of the Prehistoric Society, April 1986. Photo: Clive Gamble.

15. The author receiving 80th birthday presentation of specially bound copy of *The Bristol Mint*, February 1987. In background: Foot-carved cist-slab from Pool Farm, Mendip, found by the author, 9 May 1956. L to R: Mike Ponsford, Jennifer Stewart, L.V. Grinsell, Nicholas Thomas. Photo: Bristol United Press Ltd.

16. The author in front of Wayland's Smithy long barrow, Oxon.

Chapter 15

Mediterranean Holidays (1)

'The conquest of the Mediterranean Sea must . . . be included as a civilising factor. The Phoenician, Greek, Minoan . . . and Roman fleets carried between them knowledge of their cultures to all parts of the Mediterranean and beyond. Their mariners brought back new ideas, new products, and new information about foreign customs and ways of life.'
— J.J. Branigan & H.R. Jarrett, *The Mediterranean Lands*, 1969, 99.

My first holidays in the Mediterranean were undertaken chiefly to enable me to widen the scope of my extramural courses to include Mediterranean archaeology. The first tours that I joined were run by Wings, originally a branch of the Ramblers' Association. These early tours comprised about 40–45 passengers with aircrew and an excellent Wings courier. My first tour (1958) was to Rome, Naples, Pompeii and Athens, from which we explored the Acropolis, Mycenae and Delphi. The passengers were by no means exclusively archaeological, and the trip from Naples to Pompeii was via a cameo factory where more time was spent than at Pompeii. My second Wings holiday was to Greece, Crete and Rhodes in March 1959. This was so enjoyable that I repeated it in 1960 when we included Tiryns as well as Mycenae and Knossos. Although these tours enabled me to widen the scope of my extramural classes, they did not permit the freedom required for any more detailed archaeological fieldwork.

Lebanon

In 1961 I went on an organised tour comprising a week in Egypt and a week in Jordan and Lebanon, when I paid my first visit to Byblos. In 1964 I spent a fortnight's Christmas holiday in Beirut, and a member of my Mediterranean archaeology class, a Bristol University student, asked me if I would visit Byblos in more detail and give a lecture on it on my return. I should have done this anyway, but I spent two or three whole days at Byblos and duly gave a lecture on it to my class. The student who asked for it was not present as she was away taking part in some antics connected with the University Rag Week which was about to take place. These visits to Byblos were of great interest to me because from about 3000 B.C. until the Roman period it had very close contacts with Egypt, being the capital of a sort of client kingdom, largely because the cedars of Lebanon were exported from Byblos to Egypt where they were in great demand for shipbuilding and other purposes. I was particularly interested in visiting the royal cemetery including the tombs of the client kings, notably Abi-Chemou and Ip Chemou Abi, the rich grave-goods from which are in the Beirut Museum, whose Director, Maurice Chehab, gave me every facility to photograph them. I might have included a chapter on them in *Barrow Pyramid and Tomb* but these tombs are unspectacular and difficult of access.

On my way from Beirut to Byblos, in both 1961 and 1964, I stopped at *Nahr el-Kelb* (The Dog River), so-called from the presence at its mouth of a rock shaped like a dog, which according to folk tradition barks loudly on the approach of enemies from overseas. The cliffs on either side of the river are covered with inscriptions commemorating victories, or supposed victories, of Ramesses II (1290–1224 B.C.) which I have not seen as they are up a side valley, Ashurnasirpal (*c.* 842 B.C.), Nebuchadrezzar II (*c.* 600 B.C.), Caracalla (A.D. 211–17), the Egyptian mameluke Barquq (1382–99), and French and British inscriptions of October 1918. I know of nothing like this inscribed valley anywhere else.

In 1964 I also visited Tyre and Sidon. At Tyre the ruins of the old harbour protrude from the sea, and at the time of my visit numerous columns of Roman temples were still standing. At Sidon, I saw remains of the Land Castle, the Sea Castle, and the Phoenician temple of Eshmun; but was particularly interested in Murex Hill, composed almost entirely of shells of Murex used by the Phoenicians for their purple dyes.

Cyprus

My first visit to Cyprus was for the fortnight including Christmas 1963 and the New Year. We arrived at Nicosia airport and our car from there to the Catsellis Dome Hotel, Kyrenia, had a police escort. I sat next to the driver who explained to me that trouble had broken out during the day between the Turkish and the Greek Cypriots. The rest of the fortnight was extremely tense, more so than I had ever experienced since the Alamein crisis of mid 1942. On coming down to breakfast two or three mornings later we found the hotel surrounded by men armed with rifles, and were told by the chief receptionist that they were provided for our protection.

In spite of the tense situation I was fortunate to meet an excellent and charming young Greek Cypriot, Andreas Kourtellides, with his own chauffeur-driven car, who soon became my friend as well as my chauffeur and took me on several days during that fortnight to visit some of the chief antiquities in the island. We missed only those few days when we were advised by the British consul to stay put. Among the sites that I was taken to by Andreas were Vouni Palace, Myrtou Pighades, excavated in 1950–51 by Joan du Plat Taylor, and the Bronze Age cemetery of rock-tombs at Karmi/Palaeolona with its relief of 'Marianna' at the entrance to one of the tombs.

By a happy coincidence Prof. Einar Gjerstad, director of the Swedish Cyprus Expedition, was staying with his wife at the same hotel and I had several conversations with him. I also met Sir Harry Luke, a former British consul in Cyprus and author of *Cyprus: a Portrait and an Appreciation*. I also read *Bitter Lemons*, the well-known book on Cyprus by Laurence Durrell, and saw his house at Bellapais nearby.

I was again at the Catsellis Dome Hotel in Kyrenia for Christmas 1966 and the New Year. On 23–4 December I had a two-day tour of archaeological sites of the island put on by the Cyprus Tourist Board: in a chauffeur-driven car with an interpreter and all for a modest price. The sites visited included the neolithic town or large village of Khirokitia, the Temple of Apollo and other remains at Curium, and the Tombs of the Kings at Paphos. On 28 December I visited the Bronze Age cemetery at Vasilia with the local archaeologist Andreas Stylianou.

For Christmas 1968 and the New Year I stayed at Famagusta, and made a study of the 'Royal' necropolis at Salamis, and the tomb at Enkomi attributed to Nicocreon, in sufficient detail to form chapter 16 of *Barrow, Pyramid and Tomb* (1975). Although my Publisher's Agreement to write this book is dated 4 November 1970, I believe that I already had it in mind well before this date. My more recent visits to Cyprus are described in chapter 16.

Greece

For Christmas 1969 and the New Year I stayed for the first week in Athens and the second at Nauplion. The week at Nauplion enabled me to go by the local buses via Argos to Mycenae and visit the nine tholos tombs there and study them in the detail required for chapter 15 of *Barrow, Pyramid and Tomb*. (I once visited Mycenae on a set tour from Athens which includes only the Treasury of Atreus among the tombs; when I asked our Guide why we were not taken to see any of the other tholos tombs, she replied that the Treasury of Atreus was the only one really worth seeing!). I found this such an enjoyable excursion from Nauplion that I did it twice, each time having lunch at the Belle Helene where Schliemann, Sir Arthur Evans, Alan Wace, and many others had stayed and signed the visitors' book; and then spending the whole afternoon touring the nine tholos tombs. On my second visit I was accompanied by a delightful young Chinese student, I think from Formosa, who was studying for a degree in Mycenean archaeology: and how I envied him! On another day I walked the couple of miles from Nauplion to Tiryns and visited not only the citadel but also the tholos tomb which has since been published in detail.

Sicily 1962

Before the Prehistoric and Protohistoric Congress in Rome in 1962 there was a week's excursion to Sicily, led mostly by Prof. Bernabo Brea, which I joined. We spent the first night at Milazzo at the Hotel Moderne (where there was scarcely any water) and the next morning we crossed over to Lipari, where Prof. Bernabo Brea welcomed us with his assistant Mme Cavalier, and conducted us around his splendid centre of prehistoric studies. We then returned to the mainland and visited Messina and Taormina where of course we saw the Greco-Roman Theatre. We then went south to Syracuse where we visited the archaeological museum and a selection of the archaeological sites. Prof. Brea got us up fairly early the next morning to enable us to visit a selection of the five great necropoli of rock-tombs at Pantalica before the heat came on, which we almost succeeded in doing. There are more than five thousand tombs in all, ranging in date from thirteenth century B.C. to late eighth or seventh century B.C. From there we proceeded to Gela where we visited the National Museum. As it was founded as recently as 1958 we were invited to inspect the storerooms where everything was in perfect order as no state of chaos had been inherited. We next visited the impressive Roman mosaics at Piazza Armerina, and continued westwards to Agrigento where we saw the Temple of Concord and several other temples, as well as the gigantic recumbent statue of Atlas. We next followed the coastal road to the Temples of Selinunte and Segesta and took in Monreale Cathedral *en route* to Palermo where we visited the National Museum. As one keen on Egyptology I was horrified to find the Palermo Stone, with its extremely important

Egyptian king-list, so unsatisfactorily displayed. From Palermo we went by ship to Naples and by train to Rome for the Congress. I doubt whether I have ever known so many archaeological sites of such outstanding importance to be crowded into one week as in this week in Sicily.

I spent Christmas 1962 and the New Year at the Hotel Paradiso in Taormina, from which I explored some of the archaeological sites including the Catacombs in Syracuse.

Etruscan Italy 1962–1972
During the Rome Congress of September 1962 I paid my first visit to the Banditaccia necropolis of sculptured tombs at Cerveteri on an organised tour. I revisited it in April 1964 and again in October 1972 and the material from these visits forms part of chapter 17 of *Barrow, Pyramid and Tomb*. During the Rome Congress visit the delegates were permitted to explore beyond the Monumental Enclosure to which the public are confined, and which forms only part of this great necropolis. My visit of October 1972 included the Museo Nazionale di Cerveteri, which was opened in 1967 and provides an excellent overview of the necropolis as a whole. I also entered the Regolini-Galassi tomb, which when explored in 1836 yielded the richest known grave-group from any Etruscan tomb – so large that it fills one room of the Gregorian Etruscan Museum in the Vatican. In April 1964 I also visited the fine Pietrera tomb near Vetulonia and the necropolis of tumuli behind Populonia, a coastal town of Etruscan origin.

In October 1972 I stayed at the Sunbay Park Hotel at Civitavecchia, which made an excellent base from which to visit Tarquinia on several occasions to study the numerous painted tombs on the Monterozzi, a short account of which forms the rest of chapter 17 of *Barrow, Pyramid and Tomb*. This necropolis comprises many thousands of tombs, mostly chambered. Since 1955 the Lerici Foundation, applying geophysical methods to locate the tombs and periscope photography to record their contents and their wall paintings, have located at least 6,000 more.

Of course the painted chambered tombs of Tarquinia were never intended by their makers to be visited by hordes of tourists. The paintings were done to satisfy the supposed needs of the dead; to provide them with representations of their requirements and pleasures of this life in the vain hope of securing them in the next; although latterly their faith in a future life declined and is reflected by wall paintings less optimistic in character.

The effect of having many of these tombs open for visitors for more than a century (although at the time of my last visit in 1972 during mornings only) is to create atmospheric conditions inconsistent with the preservation of the tomb paintings, some of which have been removed to the *Museo Communale* in Tarquinia for better preservation. It is a question whether flash photography should be discouraged or forbidden as it can do no good to the paintings, and good colour slides of the better known tomb paintings are on sale locally. The expansion of archaeological tourism is probably partly counterbalanced by improvements in conservation techniques. Of course I combined morning visits to the tombs with afternoon visits to the *Museo Communale* where among many other treasures I saw the celebrated terracotta models of horses from the frontal elevation of a local temple.

My advice to visitors to the tombs on the Monterozzi is to include the Tomb of Hunting and Fishing, whatever else they miss.

Sardinia

In May 1971 I had a fortnight in Sardinia, based on Alghero, at a hotel only a couple of minutes' walk from both bus station and railway station. Unfortunately both buses and trains seemed to leave very early in the morning for the places that I desired to visit, especially between Macomer and Bonorva with the Giants' Tombs in their vicinity. I had no objection to catching buses or trains at 4 a.m. or 5 a.m., but I was given queer looks by the hotel receptionist as I left so early each morning, in shorts and carrying my rucsac: so unlike the sort of tourists to whom they were accustomed.

A high priority among the sites that I wished to visit was the necropolis of rock tombs at Anghelu Ruju. On one of my visits there I met a couple of young Sardinian students who had with them a descriptive booklet in Italian about the necropolis. I asked them where I could get a copy, but they insisted on giving me theirs, saying that they could easily get another. I have always wished that I had taken their names and addresses so that I could have written to thank them and perhaps sent them a photocopy of the relevant portion of *B.P & T.*.

I went on the usual organised excursion from Alghero to the nuraghe of St Antine followed by a visit to the Elephant Rock, a rock shaped like an elephant's trunk. Our Guide was quite unaware that it is riddled with Bronze Age rock tombs including one with stylised reliefs of bulls' heads on each inside wall (*B.P. & T.* fig. 113).

Among the easiest Giants' Tombs to visit is that of Molafá, 200 yards from the railway station of that name next to Sassari. Although my photograph of it shows clearly three holes above the doorway (*B.P. & T.* fig. 116), I did not notice them until Editta Castaldi subsequently drew my attention to them as a normal feature of Giants' Tombs. I also visited the Giants' Tombs at Imbertighe (*B.P. & T.* fig. 115) and Santa Gavino, both near Borore. The purpose of these three holes is unknown.

Corsica

In June 1973 I spent a fortnight in Corsica based on Propriano, a good centre for the concentration of megalithic sites in the south-west of the island. Corsica however is not noted for its prehistoric tombs in the same way that Sardinia is famous for its Giants' Tombs, and I should not have devoted a section to Corsica in *B.P. & T.* if it were not that it is sister island to Sardinia (although the former is French and the latter Italian). I had bought Roger Grosjean's *La Corse avant l'Histoire* when it appeared in 1966, and Dorothy Carrington's *Granite Island: a Portrait of Corsica* (1971), and had corresponded with Lady Frederica Rose (whose pen-name is Dorothy Carrington).

From Propriano there was a weekly excursion to Filitosa and it was also possible to get there by bus. On my first visit to Filitosa the son of the proprietor Jean Cesare was on duty at the entrance. I showed him a letter from Lady Rose and was automatically admitted free of charge and extremely well looked after. The son of the proprietor of the hotel where I was staying introduced me to one of the leading Corsican prehistorians, Prof. George Peretti, headmaster of a school at Sartène, who drove me to the various sites which I needed to visit, among the chief being the dolmen at

Fontanaccia. He also took me to the dolmen at Settiva, enclosed within a roughly circular stone setting and essentially a chambered round barrow with a menhir associated. We also visited the stone alignments at Palaggiu, Renaggiu and Stantari, numerous stone cists (coffres), and several other archaeological sites including Cucuruzzu not strictly relevant to the book that I had in mind. I also visited Lady Rose in Ajaccio, where we decided on preparing a paper on the folklore of prehistoric sites in Corsica (Carrington and Grinsell 1982).

Greece including Messenia 1971–2

For Christmas 1971 and the New Year I spent a week or so in Athens followed by a few days in Messenia for the express purpose of gathering material for chapter 15 of *B.P. & T.* In Athens I visited the Kerameikos Cemetery which includes several circular tumuli. I linked up with the British School at Athens whose Assistant Director was then Peter Warren who took me to see the tholos tomb at Menidi north of Athens, and the following day to the Tumulus of the Plataeans and other tombs on the plain of Marathon. At the British School I met Roger Howell, then Secretary of the Minnesota University Expedition to Messenia, who accompanied me to see a selection of tholos tombs in Messenia. We flew from Athens to Kalamata and hired a car from there to visit various tholos tombs between Kalamata and Pylos. These included one at MIROU/Peristeria with linear A signs on its left door jamb (*B.P. & T.* fig. 92, where however the signs are all but lost in the reproduction), one of those at CHORA/ Volymidia, and the restored tholos tomb of fifteenth-century B.C. near the Palace of Nestor at Pylos. We also visited Pylos Museum where we saw some of the finds from these and other local tholos tombs.

The Balearic Islands 1965–74

Ibiza

The archaeological character of Ibiza is totally different from that of Majorca and Minorca, Ibiza being Punic/Carthaginian whereas the larger islands are Talayotic. My only visit to Ibiza was at Christmas 1967 when I stayed at San Antonio. I found little of interest to me beyond the great Carthaginian cemetery of many thousands of tombs on the *Puig des Molins* (Windmill Hill) south-west of Ibiza town. Here I noted tombs exposed in the cuttings made to form one of the roads beside the hill. I found both Museums well worth visiting: that opposite the Cathedral, and the then new Archaeological Museum beside the Carthaginian necropolis, arranged on modern lines.

Majorca

In December 1965 I paid my first visit to Majorca and stayed at a hotel west of Palma. One day I hired a chauffeur-driven car for most of the day for £6 to do an archaeological tour of the island. This included the Manacor Museum, the talayotic village of Ses Paisses, Arta Museum, Alcudia Roman theatre and Archaeological Museum, and several other sites. During that fortnight I also saw the talayot of Sa Canova, the Son Real naviform structures on the east coast, the talayotic site of Son Oms near Palma Airport, and talayotic village of Capocorb Vey on the south coast.

At Christmas 1970, a few weeks after I had signed my agreement with Thames and Hudson for *Barrow, Pyramid and Tomb*, I spent a fortnight at the Molins Hotel at Cala San Vicente, only *c.* 25 minutes' walk from the group of a dozen or so rock tombs first published in English by W.J. Hemp (*B.P. & T.* fig. 119). On New Year's Eve, two friends from the hotel accompanied me to these tombs with a bottle of wine, and we drank the New Year in within the best of these rock tombs (no. 7), *B.P. & T.* fig. 120. A short story entitled 'Pam and Mark explore caves', by Margaret Orford, based on my visits to these tombs on this occasion, appeared in *The Christian Science Monitor*, 19 August 1972.

At Christmas 1972 and the New Year I spent a fortnight at the Illa d'Or Hotel in Pto Pollensa. I was helped enormously by Sr José Mascaro Pasarius, of Palma, a noted Balearic archaeologist, who took me to see various sites which he was particularly keen that I should visit for my book. These included the cave tomb of Son Caulelles, the group of cave tombs at Son Sunyer and Son Toni Amer, and cave-tombs of special interest because of their slots for closing slabs, including Son Boscana and Sa Figuera: just the sort of information needed to add strength to chapter 19 of *B.P. & T.*

I was again at the Illa d'Or Hotel in Pto Pollensa for Christmas 1973 when I saw the probable rock-tombs on the edge of the medieval town of Alcudia. One day José Mascaro Pasarius took me to see the Taula-like pillar (originally one of a pair) at Almaluttx on the north coast opposite Minorca: the nearest approach to a Minorcan Taula so far known in Majorca, and surely showing influence from that island.

I have paid several more recent visits to Majorca: Christmas 1974, 1976, 1982, 1983 and 1987, always staying at the Illa d'Or Hotel at Pto Pollensa. On these occasions I have visited Son Boquer (the ancient town of Bocchoris) just north of Pto Pollensa, and in December 1976 José Mascaro Pasarius took me to see the *Punta de sa Dent* on the south coast: thought to be either an ancient quern quarry or a quarry for the lids of sitjots (grain storage pits), and similar to quarries in Minorca notably on the coast at Binibeca. On my last visit (December 1987), I was able to get into the Pollensa Museum where I was particularly impressed by their wooden carving of a bull, attributed to fourth or third century B.C., found not far from the so-called 'Roman Bridge'.

Minorca (1966 onwards)

For my first visit to Minorca (April 1966) I stayed in Villa Carlos just east of Mahon. I soon visited the *Museo de Bellas Artes* which included the archaeological museum and the library, under the directorship of Sta Maria Louise Serra who was also Director of the Antiquities Service. It was in the Plaza de la Conquista just off the Abundancia, the flight of steps going down to the sea front. Sta Serra was very kind to me and on two occasions took me out on field trips. On one occasion she took me to the necropolis of rock tombs at Cales Coves and showed me the Roman inscriptions on one of the rock faces there, and we went on to the palaeochristian basilica at Son Bou. On another day she took me on a tour of the navetas (boat-shaped prehistoric tombs) between Alayor and Mahon – Argentina, Biniac, and Rafal Rubi NW and SE. She accompanied me into three of these – I believe the first three, but remained in her car while I visited the fourth. After entering the tomb I soon discovered that it was flea-ridden and after returning to my hotel that evening it was some time before I got back to normal. I last met her at the International Prehistoric Congress in Rome in 1966. A year or two later she died while still only middle aged. Shortly after her death the Museum had to be closed as the building was declared structurally unsafe. Now renovated, it was opened in 1988 as a fine *Biblioteca Publica*. The library and collection of the distinguished Minorcan archaeologist and historian Juan Hernandez Mora, who died in 1986 aged 84, constitute a Museum off Miranda Square in Mahon, open on weekdays 11 a.m. until 2 p.m. at the time of writing. The Archaeological Museum is being developed at Mahon next to the church of San Francisco in the west part of the town.

Minorca is my favourite island in the western Mediterranean. It is not yet too overrun by tourists and is full of prehistoric sites, many of them reasonably accessible from the road between Ciudadela and Mahon. It is architecturally delightful though small scale, and to some extent a blend of Minorcan and good quality British elements introduced during the British occupation from 1713 to 1802, the buildings originating from the British occupation being painted brick red. A characteristic is the tendency for the doorways and window frames of most of the houses to be painted olive green.

Although Minorca does not officially have a winter season, I spent a week or so at Mahon in January 1973 when I visited among other sites Sa Torreta on the east coast, with its talayot and naveta excavated by Dr Margaret Murray in 1931.

Since 1980 I have spent a fortnight in Minorca in late spring or early summer every year except 1983 and 1986. It must suffice to mention the highlights of these visits from the archaeological angle. In April 1980 José Mascaro Pasarius took me on a tour of the dolmenic cists including those at Alcaidus, Montplé and Ses Roques Llises: off the beaten track but of interest to specialists in prehistoric tombs. About the same time I studied the *Naveta dels Tudons* near Ciudadela in sufficient detail for an article published in *Antiquity* (Nov 1981), and its folklore associating it with a local well for a paper in *Folklore* (1984). On 24 May 1984 Mr & Mrs Ken and Doris Roe of Ciudadela drove me to see the naveta of *La Cova*, an impressive monument near the south-west coast but difficult to reach and little known. It was excavated by Cristobal Veny in 1973 and has the unusual feature of an entrance through a perforated slab.

From 1980 onwards I made several day trips to Cales Coves, the necropolis of around a hundred caves popularly known as 'troglodyte dwellings' but considered by reliable archaeologists to have been mostly originally tombs. These visits culminated in one with a local archaeologist, Juan Morales, in May 1984, when we were invited into that known as La Solita and used as a weekend retreat by its owner. My visits to these caves enabled me to write an article, 'Cales Coves: dwellings, tombs or both?' for the Minorcan English Magazine *Roqueta* (October 1984), and to review the book about them by C. Veny Melia (*Antiquity*, July 1984).

Malta and Gozo 1961

At Christmas 1961 I spent a week at the Phoenicia Hotel in Valletta. It was fortunate that David Trump was then Curator of the National Archaeological Museum at Valletta, Charles Zammit (son of Sir Themistocles Zammit) being Director of the Antiquities Service. There was then an extremely good bus service covering most parts of the island, and I used this except for a few sites difficult to approach, which David Trump drove me to on a couple of afternoons. These included his own site of

Skorba and some of the more remote cart tracks. I was particularly impressed by the cart track which runs into the sea by Borg en Nadur. I was well looked after by the Trumps who entertained me on Christmas Day. Charles Zammit took me over to Gozo for one day when we visited the north and south temples of Gigantija and the recently established Museum.

On the first morning of my stay at the Hotel, a copy of *The Maltese Times*, Thursday 21 December 1961, was pushed under my bedroom door. Under 'Social and Personal' was the statement,

'Mr L. Grinsell, coming from Britain, arrived yesterday for a week's stay at the Hotel Phoenicia'.

Unfortunately the parallel notice, that after my week at the Hotel Phoenicia I had now returned to Britain, was not published until after my departure and I did not get a copy of it. To the best of my knowledge this is the only occasion when I have ever appeared in a Social and Personal column of any newspaper.

Although the temples of Tarxien and many others are very impressive I did not see enough sepulchral archaeology to justify a chapter in *B.P. & T.*

Chapter 16

Mediterranean and Other Holidays (2)

'Evans had come to the site [Knossos] in the hope of finding a seal impression and
a clay tablet, and Time and Chance had led him to discover a civilisation'.
　　　　　　　　　　　　　　– Joan Evans, *Time and Chance* (1943), p. 338.

Crete 1975/6 and 1978/9

I had visited Crete on Wings' Tours in 1959 and 1960, but of course these did not
permit any individual research. I did not include Crete in *Barrow Pyramid and Tomb*,
because rightly or wrongly I was under the impression that not enough prehistoric
tombs of spectacular type were sufficiently accessible to be included in that sort of
book.

In December 1975/January 1976 I spent three weeks at the Astoria Hotel,
Heraklion, two minutes' walk from the Archaeological Museum which was open most
days over the Christmas period. At Knossos I went beyond the normal tourist area and
among other things visited the Temple Tomb. From Knossos I went by bus on two
occasions (24 and 30 December) to Arkhanes from which I visited the Arkhanes/
Phourni site with its Minoan buildings including the two tholos tombs and the ossuary
which had contained 196 human skulls probably transferred from a cemetery. One of
these tholos tombs contained, when excavated in the mid 1960s, the only unplun-
dered Minoan royal burial found until that date. This is considered the most important
Minoan cemetery so far known. It was an experience to see this site free of other
tourists and to see the finds from it in the Archaeological Museum at Heraklion.

I also went to Phaestos and stayed the night at its Rest House, from which I was
taken by the chief antiquties custodian to see the three tholos tombs at Kamilari, and
my visit to Hagia Triadha included the two tholos tombs as well as the villa.

For Christmas 1978 and the New Year I spent a fortnight at a hotel a few km east of
Rethymnon: the most disappointing experience that I have ever had in the
Mediterranean. The hotel reception staff told me that there was no winter bus service
and that I should need a taxi to get around. Within half an hour or so I found out that
I had been misinformed; there was a bus stop just outside the hotel and there was a
good and reliable bus service along the coast road between Khania, Rethymnon and
Heraklion, winter and summer. By this bus I visited all three towns and their
museums.

Rhodes (1977–8)

I first visited Kamiros, Lindos and Yalysos on a Wings' tour in March 1959. I revisited
Rhodes during Christmas 1977 and the New Year, based on a hotel in Rhodes city.
During my stay I admired the architectural achievements of the Knights of St John in

the old city, and visited the Archaeological Museum in the Hospital of the Knights of St John near the Commercial Harbour. During the 1939–45 War one of my duties was to prepare the bomb damage assessment reports covering the Eastern Mediterranean. On one occasion a small calibre bomb aimed at the shipping in Rhodes harbour happened to hit the ceramics gallery in the Archaeological Museum. The walls of this building are so thick that the damage was probably confined to the one room and the pots had most likely been moved elsewhere during the War. During my examination of the air photographs I sometimes yielded to the temptation to apply the stereoscope to the Palace of the Grand Master with its splendid patterned quadrangle, never expecting that one day I should actually walk over it. The Roman and Byzantine mosaics on the floors of the various rooms in this Palace are somewhat misleading in that most of them were moved by the Italians from the island of Kos during their occupation 1912–45. My walks in and around Rhodes city included a visit to Monte Smith with its Temple of Apollo, Theatre and Stadium.

I revisited Kamiros, which although said to be the smallest of the three city states (the others being Lindos and Yalysos) enables one to get the best idea of the layout of a Hellenistic town because so much of the foundations is exposed. It was a pleasure to return to Lindos and walk up the path to it past the famous relief of the prow of a Hellenistic trireme, emphasizing the seafaring aspect of both these towns. In addition to the spectacular Hellenistic remains on the hilltop, the village beneath has much to offer in the way of domestic architecture especially of the seventeenth century, and streets of cobbled mosaic patterns.

Southern Cyprus (1984 to date)
After Northern Cyprus fell to the Turks in 1974 I did not resume my holidays in that island until 1984. Since then I have spent each Christmas and New Year there except 1987/8. I have stayed at a hotel in Paphos except for Christmas 1986 when I stayed at one outside Larnaca.

Paphos is an excellent centre for archaeological exploration, there being such a variety of important sites within walking distance. The city was founded *c.* 320 B.C. when it succeeded Salamis as the island's capital. It held this position until the fourth century A.D. when, following severe earthquake damage, the capital reverted to Salamis. The city and its environs are rich in remains of all periods from Hellenistic onwards.

The Hellenistic is represented by the pebble mosaic, probably fourth century B.C., on which the House of Dionysos is partly superimposed, and by the fine series of tombs comprising the so-called Tombs of the Kings, which date from the third century B.C. onwards. Some continued to be used into the early Christian period, either for burial or in one instance (no. 5) perhaps for Christian worship, as a cross is carved on one of the pillars and there are traces of frescoes elsewhere. The neighbouring tomb (no. 6) is known locally as *Palaeoeclisha* (the old church), but I was told by the Inspector of Antiquities for Paphos that it got this name because until a few decades ago it was the most conspicuous ruin in the cemetery. There are remains of a Hellenistic theatre a short distance east of the catacomb of Ayia Solomoni.

West of the Harbour and just north of the coast road are the remains of an amphitheatre which might be Roman in view of its proximity to the three important groups of Roman mosaics: the House of Dionysos, the Palace of Theseus, and the House of Aion, in course of excavation. Near the Lighthouse is the Roman theatre (Odeon) now restored and in use during the summer, and to the east of it are remains of the Agora (marketplace). Remains of the mole of the Roman harbour can be seen limiting the seaward side of the present harbour.

North of the road from St Paul's Avenue to the House of Dionysos is the Byzantine fortress, composed largely of columns from Roman buildings and therefore getting its nickname *Saranda Colones* (Forty columns).

Of the later monuments, I have a soft spot for the three sacred caves, Ayios Agapetikos, Ayios Lambrianus and Ayia Solomoni. The first, south-east of the Rock of Dighenes, comprises a prominent outcrop containing a chamber in which are various pictures of saints and usually a candle burning whenever I have been there. Ayios Lambrianus, on the west side of the road opposite the Apollo Hotel, comprises a cave almost resembling a Hellenistic tomb. Ayia Solomoni, on the opposite side of the road, comprises caves over a sacred spring, above which is a sacred tree, on the branches of which those wishing to be cured, or to have a wish fulfilled, tie a bit of their clothing or an old rag. Part of this cave is converted into a Nativity scene by the good Christians of Paphos every Christmas and is much visited.

There are similar sacred bushes with rags tied all over them at Belvedere on Troodos near the Tomb of Archbishop Makarios. They were mentioned by writers on Cyprus several decades before the death of the Archbishop, and I saw a sacred rag tree somewhere near the north coast between Kyrenia and Famagusta in the mid 1960s.

The highlights of my visit to Larnaka for Christmas 1987 were a good look at Kition and at the contents of the District Museum and above all at the Pierides Collection of Cypriot Antiquities, handpicked items acquired by several generations of Swedish consuls and housed in the Swedish consulate next to Barclays Bank. My recent stays at Paphos have of course included the well organised District Museum and the private Museum of George Eliades outside of which is a rock tomb.

Finally, those staying at the Paphos Beach or Annabelle Hotels have excellent Hellenistic tombs in front of their hotels, including the tomb of a doctor or surgeon as identified by the grave-goods; this tomb has a carved pediment and is beside the Grecian Restaurant Tavern. It is indeed difficult for a builder to dig the foundations of any new building in this part of Paphos without uncovering yet another Hellenistic or Roman tomb. The Alexander the Great Hotel, opened Spring 1988, has Hellenistic tombs in its grounds.

Tunisia (1979)

From the archaeological angle my holiday in Tunisia was extremely cursory for various reasons. Tunisia's strong suits – Punic and Roman remains – are not mine; the distance of most of the sites from my base at Hammamat was considerable; and I was largely limited to going on the official tours. The one tour to Carthage devoted about half-an-hour to Carthage and a considerable time longer to a village full of souvenir shops. The tour of Roman sites was on a day of thunderstorms but we did see Thuburbo Majus with its fine mosaics and the Lybic-Punic mausoleum at Dougga. As an afficionado of Muslim architecture I was also pleased to visit Kairouan. In Tunis I enjoyed the Bardo Museum with its very fine series of mosaics.

Portugal (1981)

For Christmas 1981 and the New Year I stayed at Estoril in Portugal. The Archaeological Museum in Lisbon was closed, but there was an excellent display of Treasures of Portuguese Archaeology at a Museum in Belem nearby, with a large quantity of Bronze Age and later goldwork. Belem also has a world-famous Coach Museum. From Estoril it is a walk of half an hour to Cascais, a lovely little town with its own Museum – the Guimaraes Museum, in a small palace in a park. In the basement is the Archaeology Gallery with local finds including those from the tombs of Alapraia. I visited the rock tombs at Alapraia and was interested in noting that the local square is named Largo do Alfonso do Paco, from a famous Portuguese archaeologist who excavated these tombs.

However, the highlight of my visit to Portugal was the set tour to the monastic sites of Batalha and Alcobaca, following in the footsteps of William Beckford. As there were only five of us in a chauffeur-driven car, I managed to persuade the driver and the other passengers that we could substitute Alcobertas for Alcobaca, the difference being that Alcobertas is a church dating from fourteenth century (but possibly on an earlier site), which was built to incorporate a magnificent dolmen. This dolmen is used as a side chapel and Sunday schools and other events are held in it. As an example of the Christianization of a pagan site it ranks on a small scale with Syracuse Cathedral, and I found it equally impressive.

Finistère and Brittany

I have had three tours of Finistère and Brittany of one week each: in September 1974 with the Wiltshire Archaeological Society, June 1978 with the Prehistoric Society, and June 1981 with Oxford University Department of External Studies.

Rather than give a bare catalogue of sites visited it seems preferable to mention the details which interested me personally on these tours. The Wiltshire Archaeological Society tour was exceptionally well organised and was the only one of the three to include Gavrinis. My impression of that remarkable structure, with its interior so richly decorated, is that it may have been a place for ritual rather than burial. The tour also included the multiple tomb of Barnenez, the Dol menhir, the Carnac alignments and a good selection of chambered tombs. The Penmarch Museum was also visited, with its various megalithic tombs and grooved stone cists reconstituted in the garden.

The Prehistoric Society tour of 1978 was led by Ian Kinnes of the British Museum and concentrated on the megalithic tombs, and included a fair selection of those in Finistère and the Morbihan. At Essé we saw the Roche des Fées: not only one of the finest of the passage graves but with the added attraction of its folklore: that young lovers about to get married repair to that site and count the stones, the man on the right and the woman on the left. If they get the same number or within two they can look forward to a happy marriage. If they are more than two out, it is a bad sign. For me, another of the highlights of this tour was that after staying a night or two at Auray, we proceeded to Carnac via the chapel of St Avoye, in which is a probably neolithic saddle-quern traditionally supposed to be the stone boat on which St Cornely fled across the river from the pagan army represented by the Carnac alignments, after turning them into stone. I had wanted to see this ever since reading about it in Zacharie Le Rouzie's book *Carnac: Légendes, Traditions, Coutumes et Contes du Pays* (Vannes, 1934), p. 166.

The tour of June 1981, run by Oxford University Department of External Studies, was slighter and more general in character. I got the impression that the leader had not done his 'homework' very carefully. While he was addressing us at the Kermario alignments, I played truant and photographed three girls in Breton costume reclining in front of the Kermario passage grave. When we visited the Dol menhir he seemed unaware that it had been Christianized by having a cross incised near its base – quite apart from the cross which periodically gets inserted into the socket in the top and as often removed by the younger element.

Scilly

Scilly is included here for several reasons. It is 'overseas' and my visit was for an archaeological holiday as distinct from a systematic survey of the numerous chambered cairns on the islands (which has been done by others). My tour lasted from 6th to 10th April 1984. I went by helicopter from Penzance and stayed at a guest house in Hugh Town, and my visit was confined to St Marys. On 7th I walked from Hugh Town along the coast path northwards to Bants Carn and the prehistoric settlement nearby, and continued eastward to the Upper and Lower Innisidgen cairns. After seeing various other cairns I returned along the main road from Normandy to Hugh Town. On 8th I went to the Archaeological Museum, and called on Gibson's the well-known photographers of everything connected with Scilly, where I had the distinction of being photographed and my portrait added to their Archaeological Rogues' Gallery. On 9th I walked from Hugh Town to the group of chambered cairns on Porth Hellick Down. It was a memorable tour of some spectacular sites in a beautiful setting.

Chapter 17

Related Topics

'Saw *Twelfth Night* acted well, though it be but a silly play, and not related at all to the name of day'.

— Samuel Pepys. *Diary*, 6 January 1662–3.

Excavation

I have never taken to excavation. I have tried to do so on several occasions, the first being in April 1933 when I cut a section across the berm and ditch of one of the bell-barrows on Bow Hill, West Sussex, to ascertain whether there were any post-holes on the berm, similar to those found by Van Giffen around the barrows in the Netherlands, as reported by him at the International Prehistoric Congress in London in 1932. We found there were not. In this work I was helped and guided by the brothers Hamilton who had experience under the Curwens, and the excavation was visited by Dr Cecil Curwen. (Sussex Barrows, Supplement II, *Sx A.C.* 82, 115–23). In November 1941 I took part in excavation of Barrows in the New Forest directed by Mrs Piggott.

After returning from Egypt and resuming my duties in Barclays Bank I spent one or two weekends assisting (?) Richard Atkinson on his excavations at Dorchester-on-Thames. For part or my annual holiday about 1947 I joined Kathleen Kenyon's excavation of the Iron Age hill-fort of Sutton Walls north of Hereford. Frankly I found it very boring remaining in one place all the time – the boredom relieved only by the evenings with Kathleen Kenyon and the other diggers, and by the company of my companion digger Prince Subhadradis Diskul of Siam (Thailand). I missed the varied scenery experienced by non-excavational fieldwork.

After assuming my duties in Bristol City Museum, I devoted part of my annual leave to joining Nicholas Thomas's excavations at Thornborough Rings near Ripon. I was so bored that I pushed off with one of the other diggers, who had a car, and we surveyed the barrows in the vicinity of the Thornborough Rings and the similar rings on Hutton Moor (Grinsell 1955). I also joined his excavations in the round barrows on Snail Down, Wiltshire, in 1953. After these efforts I decided that excavation is not my 'thing' and since then my archaeological activities have been non-excavational.

The Kivik Cairn, Scania

In 1941 I spent much time studying the incised slabs of the Kivik cairn, an enormous sepulchral cairn 75 metres in diameter, broken into for the stones in 1748, which yielded a series of carvings the most likely interpretation of which is in terms of a funerary procession. My study was of course done from illustrations as the originals are in Sweden. As nearly all the literature is in Swedish or German and I could then read neither, I did my best at laborious word-for-word translations. Reflecting the archaeological thought of the time, I sought comparison with the Minoan sarcophagus of Hagia Triada: the only other adequate representation of a Bronze Age funeral ceremony known to me outside Egypt (Grinsell, 'The Kivik Cairn; *Antiquity* XVI, 1942, 160–74). A recent monograph, *The Kivik Tomb*, by A-C-A Moberg, Stockholm 1963, wisely confines itself to a description of the scenes and avoids theorising on oriental or any other influences.

The Cerne Giant and Other Hill-figures
In 1979, while looking at a number of the *Dorset Magazine* devoted to this figure, I happened to notice that the illustrations of it could be divided into two groups: an earlier group showing the navel, and a later group with the penis lengthened by being added to the navel which no longer had a separate existence. Thus arose my only contribution to pornographic archaeology: 'The Cerne Abbas Giant: 1764–1980' (*Antiquity* LIV, 29–33).

Two years earlier, my friend Owen Legg, whom I first met when he was a boy of 14 walking over Salisbury Plain when I was visiting barrows on Silk Hill for *V.C.H. Wiltshire*, produced a folio volume of lino-cuts entitled *Cut in the Chalk*, comprising a couple of dozen reproductions of our chalk-cut hill-figures: white horses, the Cerne Giant, the Whiteleaf and Bledlow crosses and the Laverstock panda. For this work I wrote the descriptions of each hill-figure: a purely factual statement culled from the most reliable sources. He presented me with a copy of it for my 70th birthday.

Archaeology in Literature and Fiction
My first incursion into this subject was in 1940 when my paper 'The archaeological contributions of Richard Jefferies' appeared in *Trans. Newbury District Field Club*, 8, 216–26. On 3 December 1979 I lectured on 'Richard Jefferies and Archaeology' to the Richard Jefferies Society at Swindon. My note on an attempt to identify the barrow of 'The Man in the Tumulus' of *The Story of My Heart* was published in the Wiltshire Archaeological Society *Newsletter* March 1981. I concluded that it may not have been a barrow, but a mound of some other kind, as no known barrow seems to fit the context.

My note on Thomas Hardy's advice on the maintenance of the Giant of Cerne Abbas appeared in *Notes & Queries for Somerset & Dorset* March 1980, 38. My short article on 'Rainbarrows and Thomas Hardy' was published in *The Thomas Hardy Journal* II, 2, May 1986, 59–61, unfortunately spoiled by my not being sent proofs and several lines of my text omitted.

On 10 May 1985 I lectured at the Weston-super-Mare congress of the West Country Writers' Association on 'The Past in West Country Literature', a summary of which was published in their *Newsletter* (pp. 12–15) later that year. The Wiltshire part of it was published in revised and extended form as 'Wiltshire prehistoric sites in recent fiction' in *Wiltshire Archaeological Magazine* 80 for 1986, 234–7. It grouped the material into three sections: i) novels which try to reconstruct the past (David Burnett, *The Priestess of Henge*; Mary John, *Blue Stones* and Harry Harrison and Leon Stover, *Stonehenge, where Atlantis died*); ii) novels which use prehistoric sites as a setting for recent episodes (J.R.L. Anderson, *The Nine Spoked Wheel*; Penelope Lively, *Treasures of Time*); and iii) a novel which invokes the return of a neolithic goddess (Michael Hyndman, *Nine Lost Days*). The novels in the first category demonstrate the ability of the writer to put flesh and blood over the dry bones unearthed by the archaeologist. I found the book by Hyndman, centred on Avebury, the most enjoyable of them all.

It was not until several years after 'Somerset Barrows: North and East' was published (1970), that I learned of the novel by John Jarmain, *Priddy Barrows* (1944), which fell rather flat because of the preoccupation of almost everyone with other matters at that time; and the author sadly lost his life during the Normandy invasion on the morning of 26 June 1944 near Caen where he is buried. My note on 'John Jarmain and *Priddy Barrows*' appeared in *Notes & Queries for Somerset & Dorset*, March 1987. In the course of my work on this article I had the pleasure of meeting Jarmain's widow, now Mrs Beryl Ditchfield, in Swanage where she now resides. The novel deals with the headmaster of a school for backward boys, not far from the Ashen Hill barrows and the Priddy Nine Barrows, which the headmaster spent his spare time digging into. As Jarmain was developing this novel in the mid 1930s soon after these barrows were scheduled under the Ancient Monuments Acts in July 1933, it is a question whether they might have been scheduled to kerb the activities of some such local menace.

The Christianization of Prehistoric and other Pagan Sites
As early as 1937 I had much to say about the Christianization of prehistoric sites, especially in Britain, in my first paper to the Folklore Society (Some aspects of the folklore of prehistoric monuments, *Folk-lore* 48, 245–59). My wartime sojourn in Egypt introduced me to various instances of the conversion of parts of the ancient Egyptian temples, notably Luxor, to Christian usage, and during a visit to the Coptic Museum in south Cairo a friend drew my attention to the Coptic crosses converted from the ancient Egyptian *ankh* (key of life) hieroglyph. Throughout my Mediterranean and other holidays from 1958 to the present I have kept on the lookout for Christianized prehistoric sites. In 1975, with Stephen Cogbill, I studied the crosses and other symbols incised on the walls of the chambered cairn of *Ty Illtud* (the hermitage of St Illtud), and concluded that they represent the Christianization of a pagan site (The later history of Ty Illtud, *Arch. Cambrensis*, 130 for 1981, 131–9).

In 1985–6 the Society for Landscape Studies, jointly with the Council for British Archaeology, were contemplating a conference on Religion in the Landscape, and asked me to contribute a paper on the Hill-figures. As I did not consider this to be sufficiently on their subject, I offered them a lecture on the Christianization of prehistoric sites. They accepted this, but the conference was cancelled through lack of support. Some months later, two groups dealing with speculative archaeology, one of them *Earthlines*, the other *Northern Earth Mysteries*, ran a joint conference on much the same subject, at an adult education centre at Burton-on-Trent on Saturday 25 October 1986, and I gave my lecture on the Christianization of Prehistoric Sites on that occasion. The substance of it was published in *Landscape History*, 8, 27–37. As the material that I collected was mostly from prehistoric tombs and ritual sites the paper covers the subject only partially. There are probably more instances of Christianization of prehistoric monuments in Brittany than anywhere else.

The Preparation of Archaeological Reports

A chain of circumstances led to the production of what I believe to be my most useful contribution to archaeology, albeit I am only its part author. Early in 1962, a new archaeological group was formed in the Bristol area by archaeologists who felt the need for a more positive approach to local problems than was being made by the existing societies, whose structure dated from the late nineteenth century. In this way the Bristol Archaeological Research Group (now the Bristol and Avon Archaeological Society) was born. When the news was broken to one of the county archaeological societies, one of their council members asked the rhetorical question, 'What reason have we got to think that this new-fangled group of young upstarts would ever publish anything they did or dug?' – or words to that effect. Arising from this comment, I arranged through Bristol University Department of Extra-Mural Studies a course of six lectures on 'The preparation of archaeological reports'. These were given two each by Philip Rahtz, Alan Warhurst and myself, in Bristol City Museum. Duplicated editions of the revised text of these lectures were produced in 1963 and 1965, and a revised printed edition was published by John Baker in 1966. A much improved edition was published by Adam & Charles Black Ltd under the imprint of John Baker in 1974, in 4to format, with a slightly different authorship, David Price Williams replacing Alan Warhurst for the chapter on illustrations. There was an additional chapter by myself on distribution maps, a subject which I had covered in more detail elsewhere (*Prehistoric Man in Wales and the West*, Essays in honour of Lily F. Chitty, ed. Frances Lynch and Colin Burgess, 1972, 5–18). As a non-digging archaeologist my own contribution to this book was concerned mainly with preliminaries, the body of a non-excavational report, and the final stages. It is hoped that this book has been of use to those many archaeologists who find the writing of the report so much more difficult than doing the excavation. With the advances in the new technology a revised edition should be undertaken by younger people.

The Lunatic Fringe and its Borders

My first encounter with the lunatic fringe (or at least its borders) was when, about 1938, being progamme arranger for a small archaeological group in London, I invited Major F.C. Tyler, a prominent member of the Straight Track Club, to lecture to us on his pet subject. His lecture was afterwards published by him under the title *The Geometric Arrangement of Ancient Sites* (1939).

In 1953 the subject of the Spring Conference of the Prehistoric Society was 'Prehistoric Religion in Archaeology and Folklore'. As I was then the society's honorary treasurer, a member who was a near neighbour, Mr Guy Underwood of Bradford-on-Avon, whom we have already met in chapter 5, informed me that he would like to give a paper at this conference. He had 'always been interested in the religion of the stone age', and had come to the conclusion that the Inner Circle in Regent's Park, where the society then held its Spring conferences, was originally a prehistoric 'henge' monument, and that John Nash when landscaping it into Regent's Park 1811–1830 adapted a pre-existing 'henge' with its enclosed barrows (i.e. the mounds upcast from the ornamented ponds within the Inner Circle). He had been inspired to reach this conclusion because it was paralleled by his study of Budbury at Bradford-on-Avon, with its two enclosed mounds which he thought were barrows.

The Budbury earthwork has since been shown by Geoff Wainwright to be the remains of an Iron Age promontory fort and the enclosed mounds not to be barrows. We reluctantly (?) informed Mr Underwood that our programme was already full but that we would keep him in mind for another occasion, which fortunately never arose.

My next encounter with the 'fringe' was when I accepted an invitation to take part in a Symposium on *The Alignment of Ancient Sites*, arranged by Tom Williamson and Liz Bellamy, at Emmanuel College, Cambridge, on Saturday 10 September 1983. The programme comprised five orthodox archaeologists (John Barnatt, Aubrey Burl, Christopher Taylor, Tom Williamson and myself), and five 'fringe' people (Michael Behrend (who did not turn up), Paul Devereux, Jeremy Harte, John Michell and Nigel Pennick): an excellent idea in principle. The programme was however put out of joint almost from the start by the first speaker overrunning by some 15–20 minutes and not being stopped by the ineffective chairperson. The timing adjusted itself by the non-arrival of one of the afternoon speakers. My own contribution was on 'The folklore of sites in alignment'. One point that I made was that the credibility of a ley-line is not increased by reports of flying saucers or other UFOs, ghosts, spectral black dogs, phantom funerals, or any other occult phenomena along its course, as some writers on these matters have suggested. I also noted that a very small minority of prehistoric sites really are in alignment, e.g. at Stanton Drew; the linear arrangement of round barrows near Kilmartin; the Priddy Circles and the Thornborough Circles; and the stone rows on Dartmoor including the Erme stone row 3.5 km in length; but this does not justify ley-line enthusiasts claiming that most prehistoric sites are aligned. The percentage in alignment is in fact extremely small. I also mentioned the folly of thinking that all folklore is ancient, in which context I drew attention to Stewart Sanderson's 1969 Presidential Address to the Folklore Society on 'The folklore of the motor car'. I also mentioned the stone circle at Ipsden (Oxfordshire), known to have been built in 1827, which is already known as *The Devil's Ninepins*. I also commented on the supposed 'megalithic' folklore of the *Hoarstone* megalithic tomb (Oxfordshire), whose stones are said to go to drink in the nearest stream 'when they hear the Lidstone church clock strike 12'. Lidstone has never had a church and the most that it can show is a nonconformist chapel (now I believe in use as a garage) which never had a striking clock. My own experience suggests that most 'fringe' archaeologists are such because they lack a critical approach to what they are studying.

I concluded my lecture with an account of the fascinating folklore of the Mitchell's Fold stone circle (Shropshire) and indulged in some adverse criticism of a recent article which put it on a ley-line, not knowing that its author, Jonathan Mullard, was in the audience. He took it so delightfully that we have since been close friends.

My most recent contribution to fringe archaeology was a paper on 'Alfred Watkins and *The Old Straight Track*' given to the Hereford Annual Meeting (1987) of the Cambrian Archaeological Association, and to be published in the *Transactions of the Woolhope Naturalists' Field Club*. In that paper I recalled that soon after *The Old Straight Track* was published, the editor of *Antiquity*, O.G.S. Crawford, refused a paid advertisement for it. In 1957 the editor of the same periodical, still O.G.S. Crawford, announced that his new book, *The Eye Goddess*, would be reviewed in the next issue. In fact he died shortly afterwards, and his successor, Glyn Daniel, decided that *The Eye Goddess* was too far removed from Crawford's usual standard to be reviewed in *Antiquity*.

Chapter 18

Music and Other Things

(An upright piano is) 'a musical growth found adhering to the walls of most semi-detached houses in the provinces'
– Sir Thomas Beecham, quoted in *Beecham Stories*, ed. H. Adkins and A. Newman, 1978, 34.

Music

My mother was musical and played the piano and the mandolin, and we had an upright piano in our home in Crouch End, a London suburb. When in my early years I had a few lessons on the piano, and from then onwards I did my best to teach myself, not very well, and my knowledge of piano-playing has always been elementary in the extreme. During my adolescence my favourite pieces were Liszt's Hungarian Rhapsody no. 2 and certain other items which have an immediate appeal to the young but which one rather tends to avoid in later life.

My father was unsympathetic to my piano-practising, presumably because after returning home from a day at the office he wished to relax. Most of my practising was therefore done when my parents were at the cinema, which fortunately occurred once or twice weekly. Following the death of my mother in October 1932, I inherited her piano and had it moved to my room at the Bloomsbury House Club, London WC1, where my repertoire was extended especially to include more Beethoven and Chopin.

From my late teens until the outbreak of the 1939–45 War I sometimes attended concerts. These included, on a ticket given me by a relative, a recital at the Albert Hall by Chaliapine, but his only song not above my head was The Song of the Volga Boatmen. I derived much more benefit from a violin recital by Fritz Kreisler in the Dome, Brighton, in the late 1920s or early 1930s. About this time I also heard a piano recital by Claudio Arrau at the Wigmore Hall: he was then a rising star. During Arturo Toscanini's stay in London in 1937 I heard him (on the radio) conduct a performance of Beethoven's Eroica Symphony, his rendering of the slow movement of which still haunts me.

It was my custom to attend a few of the Henry Wood Promenade Concerts each season, usually picking those containing piano concertos. A memorable occasion was a performance of Beethoven's Emperor Concerto by Wilhelm Backhaus. About a fortnight before the outbreak of the 1939/45 War I heard a performance of Beethoven's violin concerto by Albert Sammons, so superbly played that for the time my mind was taken off the forthcoming conflict.

I was also accustomed, from 1932 to 1941 and from 1946 to my removal to Devizes in 1949, to attend the Sunday evening concerts of the South Place Ethical Society, held at their premises in Queen Square, WC1. It was here that I first heard Grieg's violin sonata opus 45. It was also here that I heard the pianiste Johan Stockmarr, who many years earlier had played Grieg's piano concerto with Grieg himself conducting. In a lighter vein I always made a point of attending the annual concerts of music by Albert W. Ketelbey conducted by the composer, at the Kingsway Hall in London WC1.

I arrived in Heliopolis, a suburb of Cairo, in January 1942, a few weeks after a Services centre called Music for All was formed in Cairo. Until 30 April it was directed by Gerhard Willner, a highly accomplished pianist, who on two occasions between 1942 and 1945 performed all of Beethoven's 32 piano sonatas at the rate of three or four for each concert. He was supported by his wife Dora Willner, a soprano who sang songs chiefly by Beethoven, Brahms, Schubert and Schumann. From 1 May 1942 the musical director was Clifford Harker, who broadened the repertoire. In addition to the Beethoven recitals by Gerhard Willner I remember the splendid recital given by the pianist Pouishnoff. While in Cairo I also heard for the first time a performance of the Schumann piano concerto by the Palestine Symphony orchestra with Pnina Salzman as soloist, at the Opera House. On other occasions Music for All put on piano recitals by artists including Gina Bachauer, Lance Dossor, Gerald Gover, Ignace Tiegermann, and the blind pianist Georges Themeli. The programmes at Music for All were of course much broader than my own rather narrow tastes for classical piano music. The price of admission to Music for All was five piastres (5 pence of 1988) per day for officers and 3 piastres (three pence of 1988) per day for other ranks, and there was no extra charge for attending the concerts and lectures, and Music for All included a library, reading room, and numerous other facilities including bathrooms.

When I assumed my duties in Bristol early in 1952 it was a pleasant surprise to find that Clifford Harker was organist and Master of the Choristers in Bristol Cathedral and also a leading light in the musical life of Bristol and surroundings, a situation which happily continues to this day except that a few years ago he retired from being the Cathedral organist.

Bristol has a fairly well organised musical life, with concerts at the Colston Hall about once a week between Autumn and Spring, which I attended for the first twenty years or so of my residence in Bristol. Since retiring I have been largely content with the fortnightly evening concerts at the Bristol Music Club in St Paul's Road, only 200 yards from my flat in Clifton. These are of the chamber music type except for an annual orchestral concert in Clifton Cathedral. There are also the lunchtime and other concerts of the St George's Trust on Brandon Hill, and during term there are the Wednesday lunch time concerts in the Wills building of Bristol University. I occasionally attend these but I am not keen on having my normal lunch period disrupted. I did however attend a splendid performance by Craig Sheppard of Liszt's piano sonata at a Bristol University lunchtime concert some years ago.

Between 1952 and my retirement in 1972 weekend concerts were largely out of the question as I gave top priority to archaeological fieldwork at any rate between spring and autumn. I particularly regretted that I did not attend the recitals by Benjamino Gigli at the Colston Hall at Easter between 1952 and 1954, but it was imperative that archaeological fieldwork be done at such times.

In short, music has for me been the chief offset to my archaeological activities: a recreation which has prevented me from getting archaeologically stale and has helped me to lead a more balanced life than could be provided by archaeology alone. I have however been far too keen on working with the radio on and having the Third Programme on as a background instead of listening to it properly.

I often play my baby grand piano for 15 or 20 minutes before retiring: usually two or three easy pieces by Brahms, Beethoven, Chopin or Grieg. I used to play more difficult pieces but as one gets older co-ordination between brain and hands gets slower, unless one devotes much more time to practising.

Appreciation of the Countryside

I have already touched upon fieldwork in Wessex and on Exmoor and the Cotswolds in chapter 8. Here it is desirable to emphasize my appreciation of these contrasting types of landscape, Exmoor including the Quantocks having the advantage, at any rate on their northern parts, of being within sight of the Bristol Channel; the Cotswolds being much more cultivated and developed, and without a prospect of the sea. It was the scenic aspect of Exmoor and the Quantocks that was largely responsible for leading me to write *The Archaeology of Exmoor* (1970) and the pamphlet *Prehistoric Sites in the Quantock Country* (1976). However, as walking country commanding splendid views there is nothing to excel the chalk downs, especially the ridgeways, of Sussex and Wessex, the chalk subsoil being porous so that it absorbs the rain quickly and provides a springy turf, perhaps the easiest on the feet of all types of English soil. The South Dorset Ridgeway, especially between the Hardy Monument on Bronkham Hill and Culliford Tree, is in many ways the best of all and was evidently considered so by the Earlier Bronze Age people who buried their dead along its course beneath one of the most extensive linear barrow cemeteries in southern England.

I am obliged to admit that my appreciation of the countryside is influenced by the availability (or otherwise) of pleasant places for afternoon tea: ideally thatched cottages or cottages of Cotswold stone or their equivalent in other areas. Among those I have patronised have been the Star Inn at Alfriston before the 1939–45 war; the Marigold cottage at Spettisbury (Dorset); The Horse with the Red Umbrella (Dorchester, Dorset); the Manor House, Castle Combe (Wiltshire); the Wishing Well tea rooms (Cheddar); the Mad Hatter at Cirencester; Combe House Hotel, Holford (Quantocks); Primrose Cottage, Lustleigh (Dartmoor); the Polly Restaurant and the Georgian Restaurant (Marlborough); the Lydgate House Hotel, Postbridge (Dartmoor), and the Bay Tree Restaurant in Salisbury.

A café that I have noted down for a visit is the Dagger Restaurant at Pelynt (Cornwall) because it is named from the 'Mycenean' Early Bronze Age dagger said to have been found there.

Running

I developed the habit of the morning run before breakfast while stationed at Heliopolis near Cairo between January 1942 and December 1945, and I continued the healthy habit until my 80th birthday. My distance has usually been not less than two miles and sometimes up to three or four miles. In Heliopolis it was largely running on sand. In

London 1946–9 it was along roads to the Inner Circle in Regent's Park, around the Inner Circle, and back. In Bristol (Clifton), it has been along Pembroke Road to Clifton and Durdham Downs, over those Downs, and back through Victoria Square. A week before my 80th birthday I slipped and fell and sprained a muscle in my hip, which took nearly a month to get right. Since then I have almost given up this healthy pastime.

Treasurerships

i. *The Prehistoric Society* (1947–70).

For most of the period of my treasurership of this Society my job included the routine of billing members in arrear in addition to policy decisions; but from 1954 to 1958 I had J.S. Gilchrist and from 1962 to 1965 Charles Browne, both of Bristol, as Assistant Treasurers responsible for most of the routine; and John Cross assisted me 1966–68.

During 1948 the Society received the sum of £7,250 from the estate of a deceased member, Sir Norman Gray Hill, killed in Sicily in 1943. There were no strings to this bequest, but as Treasurer I considered that it should be invested in stocks approved by Barclays Bank Ltd as Custodian Trustees (whom I had appointed as such), and that at most only the annual income should be available for spending. The President, Sir Lindsay Scott, on the contrary, wanted a substantial portion of the capital to be used to finance the excavation of one or more prehistoric sites in Italy, to be directed by John S.P. Bradford of Oxford University, who had discovered these sites on air photographs during the war. Thus arose the only serious policy disagreement that occurred during my long tenure of the Treasurership. I was backed by a majority of the council, largely through a motion by Grahame Clark that whatever was spent should be in accord with the policies of the recently formed Council for British Archaeology, and therefore exclude major expenditure on foreign excavation. My dealings with the forceful personality of Sir Lindsay Scott were helped by the fact that his son, the late Neil Scott, was one of my best friends at the Middle East (photographic) Interpretation Unit between 1942 and 1945. The account of this episode by C.W. Phillips (*My Life in Archaeology*, 1987, 90) needs correction in that I was an official of Barclays (not the Westminster) Bank, and the Hill bequest of £21,750 was divided into three equal parts of £7,250 between the Prehistoric Society, the Harley Society, and a third organisation the name of which escapes my memory. The Society has in fact always kept the Hill bequest intact and made only the interest from it available for spending.

For about 14 years of my treasurership I had the chores of dealing with the covenanted subscriptions and billing those members in arrear. After a few years I learned how best to cope. The first reminder to those still in arrear on their subscriptions due on 1 January would be sent about May (and in any case well before the start of the summer holidays). The second reminder was sent towards the end of November and worded on the following lines:

Dear Member,

You will be delighted to learn that the volume of *Proceedings* for the current year, one of exceptional interest and containing papers relating to every main period and a variety of subjects, is about to be issued to all paid-up members.

According to my records, however, your subscription for £. . . . is still outstanding. On receipt of this sum by 15 December I shall be happy to add your name to the mailing list.

    Yours sincerely,
      L.V. Grinsell,
        Hon. Treasurer.

In this and similar ways we managed to keep the number of arrearists down to a minimum.

It was my custom to prepare a trial balance early in December and if we were likely to show an appreciable excess of income over expenditure, I would pay something approaching that sum on account to the printers of our *Proceedings*. I would then report at the Annual Meeting that we had only just kept our heads above water, or words to that effect; and there would be enough to cover a substantial part of the *Proceedings* for the following year. In this way I managed to meet the requirements of our Editor.

It was my practice to get the Bank Statements on or about 2 or 3 January, prepare from them our Income and Expenditure account for the previous year, and send it to our Honorary Auditor, H. Senogles of Bangor in North Wales, so that he received it well before the various companies for whom he acted had a chance to send in theirs. The result was that he generally completed our audit well before the end of January and I never failed to present our audited accounts at our A.G.M. which was usually held about the third week each February. There was a splendid partnership between Senogles and myself which lasted for more than twenty years.

ii. *The British School of Archaeology in Egypt*

At the request of Lady Flinders Petrie I became Hon. Treasurer of this declining organisation about 1948. Within two or three weeks I had policy disagreements with Lady Petrie on two issues. She was receiving an honorarium as Honorary Director, which in my view was too much for an honorary position. She also desired to reprint Petrie's book *Ancient Weights and Measures* (1926) as it stood and without bringing it up to date. I got the impression that she was running the organisation for the glorification of Flinders Petrie rather than for the advancement of Egyptology. I therefore resigned and was succeeded as Treasurer by my R.A.F. friend and colleague R. Richmond Brown, who had excavated with Petrie before the 1939–45 War.

iii. *South-western Group/Federation of Museums and Art Galleries*

I followed H. St George Gray as Hon. Treasurer of this co-ordinating body in 1957. Late in 1960 some slight difficulty was occasioned by the fact that our S.W. organisation had always been called a Group, and I was keen to bring it into line with all the others which were known as Federations. I was opposed by Dr F.S. Wallis my former Director but supported by Alan Warhurst my new Director, who agreed that if it were a case of receiving a share of whatever funds were available from a central body, we should stand a better chance if our set-up was in line with the others. Apart from that incident my tenure of the treasurership ran smoothly to the best of my recollection.

Soon after becoming treasurer I attended a meeting chaired by our President A.A. Cumming, Director of Plymouth Art Gallery and Museum, who remarked on the stupidity of some advertisements in the *Museums Journal*, such as 'Retired bank official seeks appointment as curator of a small museum'. I pointed out that I was in fact an ex bank official who had found a museum appointment. At our next A.G.M. when I presented the Federation's Accounts for the past year I reported a substantial excess of income over expenditure which showed the wisdom of ex bank officials re-mustering as museum curators.

At the first meeting after the start of each financial year, it was my custom to hand subscription invoices to the representatives of each museum or art gallery, as those run by local authorities do not pay until invoiced. Sometimes these representatives were chairmen of their museum committees, and they did not always take kindly to being used as errand boys but none the less the system worked, and postages were saved. I held this treasurership until 1962, and was President from 1970 to 1971.

iv. *Council for British Archaeology, Regional Group XIII* (Cornwall, Devon, Somerset, Avon and Gloucestershire).

I assumed the treasurership in 1982 when the affairs of the Group were suffering from several years of a hopelessly incompetent treasurer who failed for several years to bill members in arrear, failed to produce Annual Accounts and Balance Sheets, and failed to attend any meetings. I handed it over to my successor, Ed Dennison of Taunton, on 30 June 1987, to the best of my knowledge in good order.

Editorships

When the Bristol Archaeological Research Group was formed early in 1962 I became their editor, and I remained editor of their *Bulletins* until 1967 when I handed over to Mrs Frances Neale whose interests were to some extent complementary to mine.

During my first four years I also edited the B.A.R.G. *Survey and Policy*, Part I to 1066 (1964) and Part II from 1066 (1965). The Iron Age section was written by Arthur ApSimon, who at first sent me a provisional draft and some months later sent me his final draft. Unfortunately I sent the provisional draft to the printer and ApSimon discovered my error when the work was published. Moral: if ever an editor is sent a revised draft, he must *immediately* file away or destroy the earlier draft. Apart from that error the *Survey and Policy* had an excellent reception and I believe only one or two other regions have produced such a comprehensive work. A second edition of Part I was issued in 1966, incorporating ApSimon's revised text, as well as other improvements. I cannot claim that the effects of the issue of our *Survey and Policy* were very dramatic, but a reader's outlook to our local archaeology is bound to be better informed after reading it than before.

I also edited the B.A.R.G. *Field Guides: Prehistoric Sites* (1966), which I also wrote, second edition 1970; *Roman Sites* by Max Hebditch with L.V.G. (1974); *Medieval Sites* by Philip Rahtz and others (1969); *Earlier Medieval Sites* by Elizabeth Fowler and others

(1980); and *Industrial Monuments* by Neil Cossons (1967). *The Mendip Hills in Prehistoric and Roman Times* (1970), by John Campbell, David Elkington, Peter Fowler and L.V.G., was produced largely with sales at Cheddar in mind. More recently I edited the Bristol and Avon Archaeological Research Group's folder guides: *Prehistoric Sites on Mendip* (1982) by L.V.G., *Roman Sites on Mendip* (1982) by Barri Jones, and *The Stanton Drew Stone Circles* (1985) by L.V.G. *The Preparation of Archaeological Reports* (latest edition 1974) was described in chapter 17. This is surely not a bad output for a small organisation which has seldom or never exceeded more than 300 members and has been in existence for only 27 years. To this have to be added the annual volumes of *Bristol and Avon Archaeology* edited until 1988 by Rob Iles.

Secretaryship

To the best of my recollection I have held only one secretaryship: of the Sub-Committee of the S.W. Group of Museums and Art Galleries on the petrological identification of stone axes. I assumed the secretaryship following the untimely death of Dr J.F.S. Stone in June 1957 and held it until 1965 when I handed over to Dr Isobel F. Smith. My task was to receive implements for sectioning which was done by Mr E.W. Seavill of the Geology Department in Bristol University, to get the sections filled by the Conservation officer in Bristol City Museum and return the implements to their owner, or to those who submitted them. I compiled the list of implements sectioned for the *Fourth Report* (*Proc. Prehist. Soc.* 28, 209–66). I also allocated national grid references to the find-spots of the 710 implements included in the first three reports: a tedious but essential task.

Honours and Tributes received

We are informed by John Aubrey (*Brief Lives*, ed. O. Lawson Dick, 1950, 305) that the seventeenth 'Earle of Oxford, making of his low obeisance to Queen Elizabeth, happened to let a Fart, at which he was so abashed and ashamed that he went to Travell, 7 yeares. On his returne the Queen welcomed him home, and sayd, 'My Lord, I had forgott the Fart'.'

I was awarded the O.B.E. in the Queen's Birthday Honours list in 1972. When I attended on Her Majesty at Buckingham Palace the following 8 November to receive the honour, I naturally took great care not to bow too low. I did not expect that she would say anything to me, but she asked me where I had done my archaeology. I told her, 'mostly in Britain', which was true enough; but it occurred to me afterwards that what she wanted me to say was that I had just retired from the curatorship of archaeology and history at Bristol City Museum.

In 1971 I received an Honorary M.A. degree from Bristol University. I was presented to the Vice Chancellor, [Sir] Alec Merrieson, for this purpose by Prof. Glynne Wickham of the Drama Department, acting as Public Orator. He had to some extent been briefed by Prof. J.M. Cook of the Classics Department and Nicholas Thomas of the City Museum. I know this because they are the only persons to whom I related the episode of my visit to Cley Hill in Wiltshire to inspect and measure the two barrows on that hill (CORSLEY 1 AND 2) for V.C.H. purposes. On reaching one of the barrows I found two lovers nestling in the 'robbers' hollow' on top of the mound. Rather than disturb them I went away and returned a couple of hours later, only to find that they were still *in situ*. On that occasion I gave up and returned to the site another day. In his speech commending me for an Honorary Degree Prof. Wickham mentioned this incident and commended me not only for my erudition but also for my 'extreme consideration for the susceptibilities of others'. In other respects I thought that Prof. Wickham had not done his preparation too well. In the first place he had my name wrong: GRIMSELL instead of GRINSELL throughout and also in the press handout. He referred to me as an 'antiquarian and archaeologist' among other things. I dislike the use of the word antiquarian as a noun, believing it to be properly an adjective as in antiquarian pursuits. Sir Walter Scott got it right with the title of his novel *The Antiquary*. However the modern tendency seems to be to use the term antiquarian for an old-fashioned collector of antiques, and archaeologist for those on the wave-length of modern archaeology. However I was grateful to the University for the honour they bestowed on me.

In 1970 I was elected an Honorary Member of the Prehistoric Society in recognition of my 23 years as their Honorary Treasurer. The same year the Folklore Society elected me as an Honorary Member 'in recognition of distinguished services to the study of folklore', although my main work on the folklore of prehistoric sites in Britain was not published until 1976. I was made an Honorary Member of the South-Western

Federation of Museums and Art Galleries in 1972, and of the Somerset Archaeological and Natural History Society at their AGM on 28 May 1983. In June 1988 I was made an Honorary Life Member of the Bristol Magpies, an association of friends of the City of Bristol Museum and Art Gallery. All these gestures have given me much pleasure.

At the Spring Conference of the Prehistoric Society in London in April 1986, the 50th anniversary of the publication of *The Ancient Burial-Mounds of England* on 16 April 1936, I was presented by the Society with a cake decorated with 50 chocolate barrows, made by Wendy Selkirk (photograph by Clive Gamble, Fig. 14). At the A.G.M. of the same Society on 18 February 1987 I was the recipient of an 80th birthday presentation by that Society. To mark the same event the Bristol and Gloucestershire Archaeological Society dedicated to me vol. 104 (published 1987) of their *Transactions*, and the Bristol and Avon Archaeological Research Group likewise dedicated to me their vol. 5, and their vol. 6 for 1988 contains a bibliography of my writings between 1972 and 1988 compiled by Nicholas Thomas. My 80th birthday was also marked by a luncheon at the City of Bristol Museum and Art Gallery with Nicholas Thomas and my museum colleagues, Prof. Peter Warren, Jim Hancock and others, and by the presentation to me of a copy of my book on *The Bristol Mint* (1986) inscribed and bound in half leather. It was also marked by a dinner party at the home of Jim and Eileen Hancock with various friends. On this occasion I was indeed thoroughly spoiled.

Excursus

Among my books

In the course of some sixty years I have accumulated a good deal of literature largely on the history of the exploration of barrows and other tombs. First of all there is Sir Thomas Browne's *Hydriotaphia, Urne-buriall*, first published in 1658. I have never obtained the first edition, but I have the Noel Douglas replica of it (1927) from the copy in the British Library. I have an edition dated 1669, with the spelling on the title page modernized to *Urn-burial*. I also have the Chiswick Press edition of the text of 1658 together with *Brampton Urns* (1667), with an introduction and notes by Sir John Evans (1893), tailored to the needs of the archaeologist.

In addition to *Ancient Wiltshire* (I, 1812; II, 1819), Sir Richard Colt Hoare compiled *Tumuli Wiltunenses* (printed by J. Rutter at Shaftesbury, 1829), which usefully summarizes the results of the barrow-diggings around Stonehenge carried out by Hoare and his co-adjutor William Cunnington, and includes illustrations of the chief types of barrow and their contents. My copy is in the original half-leather binding.

The Barrow Diggers, a Dialogue in Imitation of the Grave-diggers in Hamlet (London 1839 and Blandford 1839) is by Rev. Charles Woolls, then curate of Sturminster Marshall, although this is not stated in the book. It is a handsome 4to volume and my copy is in the original half-leather binding. The dialogue comprises nearly 40 pages and is followed by 70 pages of notes giving much information on barrows and their contents, especially those in Dorset, with ten appropriate illustrations. It was inspired by the opening of a round barrow (STURMINSTER 1 in my *Dorset Barrows*, 1959) near Shapwick and generally known as the Shapwick Barrow. I acquired a second copy of this, which I presented to the London Library.

A much rarer item is *Barrow-Digging by a Barrow Knight, with Notes by an Esquire* (London, John Olivier, Pall Mall; Bakewell, John Goodwin, 1845). Published anonymously, it is known to be by Rev. Stephen Isaacson, stated in a pencilled note on the title page of my copy to have been 'by no means an ornament to the Church'. The book is in six 'FYTTES' each with notes by an Esquire. A few extracts will indicate the character of this work:

p.10   And all exclaimed, their grog whilst swigging,
        There's naught on earth like barrow digging.
p.34   But who's he armed with shining trowel,
        Who all their labours watches so well?
        If fond of work he does not shew it. –
        Why! That's the barrow digger's POET!

A note to Fytte III quotes from the *Derby Reporter* that 'the hack was inadvertently struck into a necklace of glass beads, only one of which, however, was fortunately broken', and advises adoption by barrow-diggers of the Earl of Onslow's motto *Festina lente*; On slow!

The sixth and final Fytte contains (p. 69) a warning to future barrow-diggers:

And lest some future barrow-knight
A cutting here should make in,
And search in vain from morn till night
For what we've just now taken;

A leaden label we enclose
In pity to such late man,
Where one and all may read, who choose,
Inscribed the name, T. BATEMAN.

This is in fact a delightful poem for every barrow-digger to read while relaxing in the evenings after a day on a barrow excavation.

Another of my treasures is *A Description of the Deverel Barrow, opened A.D. 1825; also a Minute Account of the KIMMERIDGE COAL MONEY, a most mysterious and nondescript article*, published 1826. The barrow is still there, and is distinguished by two of the largest sarsens composing it being inscribed with the initials W.A.M. of the excavator, W.A. Miles. The barrow is MILBORNE 14 in my *Dorset Barrows* (1959). During my twenty years' curatorship of archaeology in Bristol City Museum I had the pleasure of presiding over the eleven urns surviving from this barrow. The 'Kimmeridge coal money' is now known to be a by-product of the manufacture of shale armlets probably of the pre-Roman Iron Age.

Glossary

To assist those readers unfamiliar with the literature of the author's main life study.

Alignment	A row of standing stones, or of barrows in a straight line.
Allée couverte	A chambered tomb comprising an oblong structure with no separate entrance passage or antechamber: common in France.
Barrow	A mound of earth or stones built over one or more human interments: usually prehistoric but occasionally Roman or pagan Saxon.
Bell-barrow	A round barrow with berm or platform between mound and encircling ditch: characteristic of the Wessex culture, q.v.
Beorg, beorh	Anglo-Saxon for a barrow, especially of prehistoric origin.
Bowl-barrow	A round barrow with no berm between mound and quarry-ditch, which may or may not be present.
Cairn	A barrow built mainly or entirely of stones.
Catacomb	A rock-cut underground cemetery, generally for Roman or early Christian burials.
Chambered barrow	A barrow containing one or more stone-built chambers with entrance leading from the outer margin.
Cist	A closed receptacle for one or more human bodies, usually cremated.
Cueva	A Spanish word, in the present context for a chambered tomb.
Currency bar	An iron bar about the length of a sword, used as a medium of exchange in the pre-Roman Iron Age.
Cursus	A linear earthwork of a type normally associated with stone circles or other ceremonial sites.
Deverel-Rimbury	A culture or phase characterized by bucket, barrel and globular urns, which followed the Wessex culture.
Dolmen	A term loosely applied to a megalithic tomb.
Dromos	A passage leading into a built tomb; used especially in the Eastern Mediterranean.
Gallery-grave	See Allée couverte.
Giant's Grave	A term used in Sardinia for megalithic tombs usually comprising a gallery grave with a prominent horned entrance.

Grooved Stone cist	A stone cist with the upright slabs grooved to receive a cover slab: limited to Brittany and the Scilly Isles.
Hangman's Stone	A standing stone bearing a tradition connected with sheep-stealing.
Henge	A prehistoric ceremonial circle of standing stones or earth, usually attributed to late neolithic or early Bronze Age.
Hillfort	A hilltop defensive enclosure limited by one (univallate), two (bivallate), or more ramparts (multivallate), usually Iron Age but occasionally Late Bronze Age in origin.
Hlaew	Anglo-Saxon for a barrow, especially one containing one or more pagan Saxon interments.
Hunebed	A megalithic chambered tomb of a type common in the Netherlands.
Implement petrology	The principle of sectioning a stone implement, grinding down the section to a slide and examining it microscopically to determine the rock source.
Linear A and B scripts	Scripts used in the Bronze Age by the Minoans in Crete and the Myceneans in Greece.
Long barrow/cairn	A long burial mound dating from the Neolithic period.
Megalith	A prehistoric structure of large stone slabs, usually neolithic or early Bronze Age.
Menhir	A standing stone, usually neolithic or Bronze Age.
Naveta	A built tomb in the form of an upturned boat; confined to Minorca.
Nuraghe	A tower-shaped structure common in the Sardinian Bronze Age.
Palstave	A bronze axe, either looped or unlooped, with side-flanges to receive a handle of wood or less probably bone.
Passage grave	A megalithic tomb with burial chamber(s) approached by a passage.
Penannular	In the form of a circle or ring with a break; in the present context applied to ditches or walls encircling round barrows or cairns.
Pond-barrow	A barrow comprising a circular depression surrounded by a raised rim. Barrows of this type are occasionally associated with major barrow groups especially in the vicinity of Stonehenge.
Portal dolmen	A chambered tomb the major element of which is a portal with a slab between the uprights supporting the cover-slab.
Port-hole slab	A vertical slab perforated with a hole, at or near the entrance to some chambered tombs.
Recumbent stone circle	A type of stone circle occurring in North-East Scotland,

	in which there is a recumbent slab in the south-western sector.
Round barrow	A circular barrow; very occasionally neolithic, usually Bronze Age, and occasionally of later periods.
Sarsen	A sandstone from a layer which originally formed a covering over most or all of the chalk downs.
Saucer-barrow	A round barrow comprising a low mound enclosed by a ditch and outer bank.
Section (of stone implement)	See under Implement petrology.
Stater	A pre-Roman gold coin.
Statue-menhir	A standing stone carved to resemble a human figure; especially common in Corsica, France and Guernsey.
Talayot	A prehistoric tower-shaped stone-built structure, usually circular, confined to Majorca and Minorca.
Taula	A T-shaped structure for ritual purposes, usually placed within a U-shaped enclosure; almost confined to Minorca.
Tholos tomb	A beehive-shaped tomb comprising a chamber of stone slabs roofed by corbelling; frequent in the Eastern Mediterranean. Plural: tholoi.
Tumulus	A mound or cairn, usually covering one or more human interments; but in theory the term means a mound of any kind.
Univallate	A hillfort with only one defining rampart.
Wessex Culture	The main Early Bronze Age culture in Wessex and its environs; subdivided into I and II.

Bibliography

i. *Books and papers*

1929 'Lower and middle palaeolithic periods in Sussex'. *Sussex Archaeol. Collect.* **70**, 172–82.

1930 'Long barrows and bell-barrows in Sussex'. *Sussex Notes & Queries* Aug., 69–71.

1931 'Classification of downland tumuli'. *Sussex Notes & Queries*, Feb. 140–43.
'Grave-mound cluster on Mill Hill, Rodmell'. *Sussex Notes & Queries*, Nov., 236–8.
'Sussex in the Bronze Age'. *Sussex Archaeol. Collect.*, **72**, 30–68.

1932 'Some Surrey bell-barrows'. *Surrey Archaeol. Collect.*, **40**, 56–64.
'Sussex in the Bronze Age: addendum and corrigendum'. *Sussex Notes & Queries*, Aug., 85–6.
'Sussex palaeoliths: addenda and corrigenda'. *Sussex Notes & Queries*, Aug., 86.

1934 'Bell-barrows'. *Proc. Prehist. Soc. East Anglia* **7**, 203–30.
'An analysis and list of Surrey Barrows'. *Surrey Archaeol. Collect.* **42**, 26–60.
'Sussex Barrows'. *Sussex Archaeol. Collect.* **75**, 216–75.

1935 'An analysis and list of Berkshire Barrows'. Part I. *Berkshire Archaeol. J.* **39**, 171–91.
'The Lambourn long barrow'. *Proc. Prehist. Soc.* **1**, 149.

1936 'An analysis and list of Berkshire Barrows. Part I addenda and Part II List'. *Berkshire Archaeol. J.* **40**, 20–58.
Ancient Burial-Mounds of England. Methuen.
'The chambered long barrow near Lambourn'. *Trans. Newbury Dist. Fld Club* **7**, 191.
'The Lambourn chambered long barrow'. *Berkshire Archaeol. J.* **40**, 59–62.

1937 'Some aspects of the folklore of prehistoric monuments'. *Folk-lore*, **48**, 245–59.

1938 'Berkshire Barrows: Part III – evidence from the Saxon charters'. *Berkshire Archaeol. J.* **42**, 102–116.
'Hampshire Barrows'. *Proc. Hampshire Fld Club Archaeol. Soc.* **14**, 9–40.

1939 'Berkshire Barrows, Part IV, addenda and corrigenda'. *Berkshire Archaeol. J.* **43**, 9–21.
'Hampshire Barrows'. Part I addenda and corrigenda, and Part II'. *Proc. Hampshire Fld Club Archaeol. Soc.* **14**, 195–229.
'Scheme for recording the folklore of prehistoric remains'. *Folk-lore* **50**, 323–32.
White Horse Hill and Surrounding Country. St Catherine Press Ltd.
The Blowing Stone. St Catherine Press Ltd.
'Some rare types of round barrow on Mendip'. *Proc. Somerset Archaeol. Natur. Hist. Soc.* **85**, 151–66.

1940 'The archaeological contributions of Richard Jefferies'. *Trans. Newbury Dist. Fld Club* **8**, 216–26.

'Hampshire Barrows'. Addenda to Parts I and II, and Part III. *Proc. Hampshire Fld Club Archaeol. Soc.* **14**, 346–65.

'Notes on the White Horse Hill region'. *Berkshire Archaeol. J.* **43**, 135–9.

'References to the Newbury district in Aubrey's *Monumenta Britannica*, *Newbury Dist. Fld Club* **8**, 156–8.

'Sussex Barrows, supplementary paper'. *Sussex Archaeol. Collect.* **81**, 210–14.

'Wayland's Smithy, *Beahhild's Byrigels* and *Hwittuc's Hlaew*: a suggestion'. *T. Newbury Dist. Fld Club* **8**, 136–9.

'Isle of Wight Barrows' (with G.A. Sherwin). *Proc. Isle Wight Natur. Hist. Archaeol. Soc.* **3**, 179–222.

1941   'The Boat of the Dead in the Bronze Age'. *Antiquity* **15**, 360–70.

'The Bronze Age Round Barrows of Wessex'. *Proc. Prehist. Soc.* **7**, 73–113.

1942   'The Kivik cairn, Scania'. *Antiquity* **16**, 160–74.

'Sussex Barrows: Supplement no. II'. *Sussex Archaeol. Collect.* **82**, 115–23.

1943   'The Boat of the Dead'. *Antiquity* **17**, 47–50.

1947   *Egyptian Pyramids*. John Bellows, Gloucester.

'The folklore of Ancient Egyptian monuments'. *Folk-lore* **58**, 345–60.

1948   'Bronze implements in the Avalon Museum, Glastonbury'. *Archaeol. Cantiana*, **61**, 185.

1950   'Prehistoric, Roman & Saxon times', in *Studies in the History of Swindon* (Swindon Borough Council), 9–24.

1951   'A Scandinavian implement from Enfield'. *Trans. London Middlesex Archaeol. Soc. N.S.* **10**, 308 –9.

'Shaving the eyebrows as a funeral custom'. *Man* **50**, no. 231, 144.

1952   'Authorship of *The Barrow Diggers*'. Letter in *Archaeol. Newsletter* **4**, no. 10, 151.

'A palaeolith from Heytesbury'. *Wiltshire Archaeol Natur. Hist. Mag.* **54**, 436–7.

1953   *Ancient Burial-Mounds of England*. 2nd edn. Methuen.

'Early funerary superstitions in Britain'. *Folk-lore* **63**, 271–81.

'A flint dagger from Avebury'. *Wiltshire Archaeol. Natur. Hist. Mag.* **55**, 176; 291.

'A socketed bronze adze from Somerset'. *Antiq. J.* **33**, 203–4.

'The Marshfield Barrows' (with G.L. Gettins and H. Taylor). *Trans. Bristol Gloucestershire Archaeol. Soc.* **72**, 23–44.

1954   'A polished flint axe from Mendip'. *Proc. Univ. Bristol Spelaeol. Soc.* **7**, 42–3.

'A gold stater from Gloucestershire'. *Brit. Numis. J.* **27**, 88–9.

1955   'Death and the after-life' (report of British Association symposium). *Nature* **176**, 809–12.

List of round barrows in area, in N. Thomas, 'The Thornborough Circles, near Ripon, North Riding'. *Yorkshire Archaeol. J.* **38**, table opp. 442.

1956   'Lost and found'. Letter in *Museums J.* **55**, 220.

Stanton Drew Stone Circles, Somerset. (HMSO).

'Three Roman stone coffin burials from Wick, Glos.' (with P.A. Rahtz). *Trans. Bristol Gloucestershire Archaeol. Soc.* **75**, 193–8.

1957   'A decorated cist slab from Mendip'. *Proc. Prehist. Soc.* **23**, 231–2.

'The Ferryman and his fee'. *Folk-lore* **68**, 257–69.

'Archaeological Gazetteer', in *Victoria County History of Wiltshire*, I (i).

'A polished-edge flint knife and a stone axe from Priddy'. *Proc. Univ. Bristol Spelaeol. Soc.* **8**, 44–6.

'A socketed bronze axe from Oldland, Bristol'. *Trans. Bristol Gloucestershire Archaeol. Soc.* **76**, 148–9.

'An inscribed gold stater of the Dobunni from King's Weston', Bristol'. *Brit. Numis. J.* **28**, 175.

'Investigations at Stanton Drew' (with Roger Kendal), *Proc. Univ. Bristol Spelaeol. Soc.* **8** (i), 125–6.

1958 *The Archaeology of Wessex*. Methuen.

'An Early British coin from White Horse Hill' (with P.H. Selwood). *Berkshire Archaeol. J.* **56**, 63–4.

'A perforated stone axe-hammer from Challacombe'. *Trans. Devonshire Ass.* **90**, 215–6.

'Prehistoric objects from Wiltshire in the Lukis Museum, St Peter Port, Guernsey'. *Wiltshire Archaeol. Natur. Hist. Mag.* **57**, 76.

'Marshfield Barrows: supplementary note'. *Trans. Bristol Gloucestershire Archaeol. Soc.* **77**, 151–5.

1959 *Dorset Barrows*. Dorset Natur. Hist. Archaeol. Soc.

'A Saxon bronze strap-end from Blaise Castle Hill'. *Proc. Univ. Bristol Spelaeol. Soc.* **8**, 168–9.

1960 'Children and archaeology'. *Museums J.* **60**, 5–12.

'A palaeolith from Beckford, Worcs'. *Antiq. J.* **40**, 67–8.

'Evidence of Roman ironworking on Exmoor'. *Notes Queries Somerset Dorset* **27**, 192–3.

'Gloucestershire Barrows' (with H.E. O'Neil). *Trans. Bristol Gloucestershire Archaeol. Soc.* **79**, Part i.

'A round barrow on Mendip'. *Notes Queries Somerset Dorset*, **27**, 202–3.

'Work at the Pool Farm cist, Mendip, 1956–8'. *Notes Queries Somerset Dorset* **27**, 243–4.

1961 'The breaking of objects as a funerary rite'. *Folklore* **72**, 475–91.

A Guide to Air Photographic Archaeology in the South-West. C.B.A. Group XIII, Bristol.

1962 *A Brief Numismatic History of Bristol*. Bristol City Museum.

The Preparation of Archaeological Reports (with P.A. Rahtz and Alan Warhurst). Bristol Archaeol. Reseearch Group. Cyclostyled.

'Fourth Report . . . . on the petrological identification of stone axes' (with E.D. Evens, S. Piggott and F.S. Wallis). *Proc. Prehist. Soc.* **28**, 209–66.

(Articles contributed to the periodical *Bulletins* of the Bristol Archaeological Research Group from 1962 onwards are not included. They are mostly of a topical nature. They include numerous reviews of recent publications relevant to the activities of the Group. They may be consulted in the Central Library, College Green, Bristol, and at other well equipped libraries).

1963 'Puttenham: barrow on the Hog's Back'. *Surrey Archaeol. Collections*. **60**, 84.

The Stoney Littleton Lang Barrow, Somerset. HMSO.

1964 'Settlement in prehistoric and Roman times, in *A Survey of Southampton and its*

Region, ed. F.J. Monkhouse for British Association for Advancement of Science, 189–204.

'The Royce collection at Stow-on-the-Wold'. *Trans. Bristol Gloucestershire Archaeol. Soc.* **83**, 1–35.

1964   'A gold stater from Kingswood, Glos.' *Trans. Bristol Gloucestershire Archaeol. Soc.* **83, 143** –4.

A Survey and Policy concerning the Archaeology of the Bristol Region, Part I. Chapters on the Neolithic and Bronze Ages, and on Communications to 1066. Cyclostyled.

1965   'Somerset archaeology 1931–65'. *Proc. Somerset Archaeol. Natur. Hist. Soc.* **109**, 47–77.

'A gold stater from Pensford, Somerset'. *Proc. Somerset Archaeol. Natur. Hist. Soc.* **109,** 108.

'Primitive currency in a provincial museum'. *Cunobelin* II (Year Book of Brit. Assoc. Numismatic Societies), 55–7.

'Belas Knap long barrow'. *Archaeol. J.* **122**, 194–5.

A Survey and Policy concerning the Archaeology of the Bristol Region, Part II. Part author of chapters 4, 6 and 9 (architecture; mines and quarries; facilities for research).

1966   *Belas Knap long barrow, Gloucestershire*. HMSO.

'A bronze torc from Winscombe, Somerset'. *Notes Queries Somerset Dorset* **28**, 259–60.

Prehistoric Sites in the Mendip, Cotswold and Bristol Region. (Bristol Archaeol. Res. Group Field Guide no. 1).

The Preparation of Archaeological Reports (with P.A. Rahtz and Alan Warhurst). John Baker.

A Survey and Policy . . . (Part I). Second edition of 1964.

'A palaeolithic implement from Poole Keynes'. *Trans. Bristol Gloucestershire Archaeol. Soc.* **85**, 207 –8.

'The Royce collection: supplement' (with D. Janes). *Trans. Bristol Gloucestershire Archaeol. Soc.* **85**, 209–13.

1967   'Barrow treasure in fact, folklore and legislation'. *Folklore* **78**, 1–38.

'The Bath Mint'. *Spink's Numis. Circular* **75**, no. 11, 299.

'A small medieval coin hoard from Maesbury' (with M.M. Archibald). *Notes Queries Somerset Dorset* **28,** 344.

'Silver coins of the Dobunni from Naunton'. *Trans. Bristol Gloucestershire Archaeol. Soc.* **86**, 193–4.

1968   *Guide Catalogue to the South Western British Prehistoric Collections*. Bristol City Museum.

'Opening of mounds near Arundel Castle'. *Sussex Notes & Queries.* 17 (2), 38–40.

1968   *Roman Sites in the Mendip, Cotswold, Wye Valley and Bristol Region* (with Max Hebditch). (Bristol Archaeol. Research Gp. Field Guide no. 2).

1969   *Prehistoric Bristol* (Bristol branch of the Historical Assoc.)

'A visit to William Cunnington's Museum at Heytesbury in 1807'. *Antiquity* **43**, 62 (reprinted in *Wiltshire Archaeol. Natur. Hist. Mag.* **64**, 118–20).

The Cheddar Caves Museum: a Brief Guide, summary catalogue and bibliography (Cheddar Caves Museum).

'Somerset Barrows. Part I: West and South'. *Somerset Archaeol. Natur. Hist.* **113**, Supplement, 1–43.

'North Devon Barrows'. *Proc. Devon Archaeol. Soc.* **28**, 95–129.

'A note on the Rillaton barrow'. *Cornish Archaeol.* **8**, 126–7.

'Copper mining on Alderley Edge'. *Industrial Archaeology*, May.

1970 *The Archaeology of Exmoor.* David & Charles.

'Introduction to the Prehistoric Remains', in *Gloucestershire* (The Buildings of England), by David Verey, 69–76.

South-Western England. Discovering Regional Archaeology; Shire Publications.

The Mendip Hills in Prehistoric and Roman Times. Part author. Bristol Archaeol. Research Group Special Publication no. 1.

'Archaeological distribution maps'. *Actes du VII Congrés Internationale des Sciences Préhistoriques et Protohistoriques, Prague 1966*, (1970). I, 64.

1971 *Wessex.* Discovering Regional Archaeology; Shire Publications (with James Dyer).

'Somerset Barrows. Part II: North and East. *Somerset Archaeol. Natur. Hist.* **115**, Supplement, 44–137.

'The past and future of archaeology in Somerset'. *Somerset Archaeol. Natur. Hist.* **115**, 29–38.

1972 'Archaeological distribution maps', in *Prehistoric Man in Wales and the West.* Essays in honour of Lily F. Chitty, ed. Frances Lynch and Colin Burgess, pp. 5–18.

'Witchcraft at barrows and other prehistoric sites'. *Antiquity* **46**, 58–9.

The Bristol Mint: an Historical Outline. Bristol branch of the Historical Association.

Guide Catalogue to the Collections from Ancient Egypt. Bristol City Museum.

'The Individual Fieldworker', in *Field Survey in British Archaeology*, ed. Elizabeth Fowler, pp. 10–13. Council for British Archaeology.

'Perambulations of the bounds of Mendip parishes'. *Notes Queries Somerset Dorset* March 1972, 212–13.

1973 'Ancient British Coins and Coins of the Bristol Mint', in *Sylloge of Coins of the British Isles*, vol. **19**.

'Prehistoric skeletons from Tormarton, Glos' (with Charles Browne and R.W. Knight). *Trans. Bristol Gloucestershire Archaeol. Soc.* **91**, 14–17.

The Folklore of Stanton Drew. Toucan Press, Guernsey, C.I.

The Bath Mint. Spink, London.

'Witchcraft at Prehistoric Sites', in *The Witch Figure*: K.M. Briggs *Festschrift*, ed. Venetia Newall, 72–9.

1974 *The Preparation of Archaeological Reports* (with Philip Rahtz and David Price Williams). John Baker.

'A Viking burial in a stone coffin in Bath'. *Notes Queries Somerset Dorset* **30**, 67.

'A Bath penny of Aethelred II, Benediction Hand type'. Spink's *Numismatic Circular*, Sept., 1974, 339.

'Disc-barrows'. *Proc. Prehistoric Society* **40**, 79–112.

1975 *Barrow Pyramid and Tomb.* Thames & Hudson.

Ancient Burial-Mounds of England. (Fresh introduction and bibliography). Greenwood Inc., Westport, Conn.

1976   *Legendary History and Folklore of Stonehenge.* Toucan Press. Guernsey C.I.
'Legendary history and folklore of Stonehenge'. *Folklore* **87**, 5–20.
Folklore of Prehistoric Sites in Britain. David & Charles.
'Folklore of prehistoric sites in Britain'. IX UISPP Congress, Nice. **I**, 12.
Prehistoric Sites in the Quantock Country. Somerset Archaeol. Nat. Hist. Society.
1977   'Notes on some medieval moneyers in Bath and Bristol' (with Frances Neale).
Spink's Numismatic Circular. May.
Cut in the Chalk (with Owen Legg). Folio volume privately printed.
Barrow Pyramid and Tomb. Paperback edn.
1978   *The Rollright Stones and their Folklore.* Toucan Press. Guernsey C.I.
The Druids and Stonehenge: The Story of a Myth. Toucan Press, Guernsey, C.I.
The Stonehenge Barrow Groups. Salisbury Museum.
Piramidi, Necropoli e Mondi Sepolti. Rome, Newton Compton Editore. Italian
translation, updated, of *Barrow, Pyramid and Tomb* (1975).
1979   *Barrows in England and Wales.* Shire Archaeologies.
'Dartmoor Barrows'. *Proc. Devon Archaeol. Soc.*, no **36**, 85–180.
'Notes on the folklore of prehistoric sites in Britain'. *Folklore* **90**, 66–70.
Letter, 'Bevis's Thumb'. *Country Life*, 5 July, 32–3.
1980   'The Cerne Abbas Giant: 1764–1980'. *Antiquity* **54**, 29–33.
'The Druid Stoke megalithic monument'. *Trans. Bristol Gloucestershire Archaeol. Soc.*
97, 119–21.
'A century of the folklore of archaeological sites'. *Folklore Studies in the Twentieth
Century*, ed. Venetia Newall, 213–16.
'Thomas Hardy and the Giant of Cerne Abbas'. *Notes Queries Somerset Dorset*,
March, 38.
'The Saxon period', in *Early Medieval Sites (410–1066) in and around Bristol . . .*, ed.
Elizabeth Fowler (B.A.R.G. Field Guide) 3a, 16–21.
1981   'Exploring prehistoric Minorca'. *Popular Archaeology*, June.
'The Naveta of Els Tudons'. *Antiquity* **55**, 196–9.
'Stone rows of Dartmoor' (letter). *Current Archaeology* no 76, 158.
'Exmoor', in Prehistoric Society *Excursions Guide*, Exeter Meeting.
1982   *Dorset Barrows Supplement.* Dorset Natur. Hist. & Archaeol. Soc.
Mitchell's Fold Stone Circle and its Folklore. Toucan Press, Guernsey, C.I.
Exmoor's Archaeology: Early Man. Exmoor National Park Department.
Belas Knap long barrow. (revised edn.) D. of E.
Stoney Littleton Long Barrow (revised edn.) D. of E.
'The stone at Snivelling Corner, Ashbury'. *Trans. Newbury Dist. Field Club* **12**(6),
54–5.
'The later history of Ty Illtud long barrow'. *Archaeol. Cambrensis* **130**, 131–9.
'Folklore of archaeological sites in Corsica' (with Dorothy Carrington). *Folklore* **93**,
61–9.
1982   'Wessex round barrows since 1930: a progress report'. *Current Archaeology.*
March, 313–14.
Prehistoric Sites on Mendip. Folder Guide, Bristol Archaeol. Research Group.
1983   'Priddy Nine Barrows: a "Correction" corrected'. *Somerset Archaeol. Natur.
Hist.* **126**, 103–4.

'A nineteenth century Devon antiquary. *Antiquity* **57**, 126–7.

'Peter Orlando Hutchinson: his advice on barrow-digging'. *The Devon Historian*, no. **26**, 23.

Discovering Roman Britain (Part author). Ed. David E. Johnston. Shire Publications.

1984   *Barrows in England and Wales*. 2nd edn. Shire Archaeologies.

'The barrows of South and East Devon'. *Proc. Devon Archaeol. Soc.* **41**, 5–46.

'The popular names and folklore of prehistoric sites in Menorca.' *Folklore* **95**(i), 90–99.

1985   'Hangman's Stones and their traditions'. *Folklore* **96** (ii), 217–22.

'Out with the prehistorians'. *Current Archaeology* no 95, 362–5.

'Making a local barrow study', in *Archaeology and Death*, ed. James Dyer, 11–13. Council for British Archaeology.

The Stanton Drew Stone Circles and Associated Monuments. Folder Guide. Bristol & Avon Archaeological Research Group.

1986   *The Bristol Mint*. City of Bristol Museum and Art Gallery.

'Bronze Age artifacts in Avon'. *Bristol and Avon Archaeology*, **4**, for 1985, 2–5.

'Wiltshire prehistoric sites in recent fiction'. *Wiltshire Archaeol. Natur. Hist. Mag.* **80**, 234–7.

'Carrying flint cores to Mendip'. *Lithics*, no **6** for 1985, 15–17.

'Rainbarrows and Thomas Hardy'. *Thomas Hardy Journal*, II(2), 59–61.

1987   'John Jarmain and *Priddy Barrows*'(1944). *Notes Queries Somerset Dorset* **32**, 594–5.

'A beaker from a cairn at Thornworthy, Chagford'. *Trans. & Proc. Torquay Nat. Hist. Soc.* **19** (iv), 180–1.

'Bronze Age settlement and Burial Ritual' (pp. 29–39) and 'The Mints of Bath and Bristol' (pp. 173–5) in *The Archaeology of Avon*, ed. by M.A. Aston and Rob Iles.

'The Christianization of prehistoric and pagan sites'. *Landscape History*, **8** for 1986, 27–37.

'The Lower Bristol Avon as a thoroughfare from prehistoric times to the Norman conquest'. *Bristol and Avon Archaeology*, **5** for 1986, 2–4.

1988   'Address on the 25th Anniversary of B.A.(A).R.G.' *Bristol & Avon Archaeology*. **6**, 1–2.

'Surrey Barrows 1934–1986: a reappraisal'. *Surrey Archaeol. Collect.* **78**, 1–41.

'Somerset Barrows: Supplement'. *Somerset Archaeol. Natur. Hist.* **131** for 1987, 13–25.

In the press

'Alfred Watkins and *The Old Straight Track*' (*Trans Woolhope Naturalists' Field Club*)

'Gloucestershire Barrows: Supplement' (with Tim Darvill). *Trans. Bristol Gloucestershire Archaeol. Soc.*

Barrows in England and Wales. 3rd edn. Shire Archaeologies.

'The U.B.S.S. and the scheduling of Mendip barrows'. *Proc. Univ. Bristol Spelaeol. Soc.* **18**(iii).

ii.   *Reviews* (See also under *Ephemera*)

1936   Saintyves, P. *Corpus du Folklore Préhistorique en France et dans les Colonies Francaises*. 3 vols 1934–6. *Antiquity* **11**, 117.

1937 *Op. cit. Folk-lore* **48**, 105–7.

1942 Bachatly, C. *Bibliographie de la Préhistoire Egyptienne. Antiquity* **16**, 288.

1943 Jequier, G. *Douze Ans de Fouilles dans la Necropole Memphite. Antiquity* **17**, 108–9.

1944 Hassan, Selim. *Excavations at Giza.* I–IV. 1936–43. *Antiquity* **18**, 104–5.

1946 Steinmann, A. *The Ship of the Dead in Textile Art.* (CIBA Review no 52). *Folklore* **57**, 199–200.

1949 Edwards, I.E.S. *The Pyramids of Egypt.* (1947). *Antiquity* **23**, 225.
Marples, M. *White Horses and Other Hill-Figures. R.I.B.A. Journal.*

1950 Emery, W.B. *Nubian Treasure. Archaeol. J.* **105**, 95.
Winlock, H.E. *Rise and Fall of the Middle Kingdom at Thebes. Archaeol. J.* **105**, 94–5.

1954 Noel-Hume, I. *Archaeology in Britain. Folk-lore* **65**, 119.
Curwen, E.C. *Archaeology of Sussex. Proc. Prehist. Soc.* **19**, 232.

1956 Head, J.F. *Early Man in Buckinghamshire. Bedfordshire Archaeol. J.*

1957 Goneim, Z. *The Buried Pyramid* (1956). *Antiq. J.* **37**, 75.

1958 Radomersky, P. *The Dead Obolus of the Slavs in Bohemia and Moravia.* (English summary of text in Czech). *Folklore* **69**, 209–10.

1961 Ashbee, Paul. *The Bronze Age Round Barrow in Britain. Man,* **61**, 94–5.
Daniel, G.E. *Prehistoric Chamber Tombs of France. Man,* **61**, 212.

1962 Clark, J.B. *Cornish Fogous. Museums J.* 62, 364

1962 Piggott, S. *The West Kennet Long Barrow. Man.* **62**, 175.

1966 Tongue, Ruth. *Somerset Folklore. Proc. Somerset Archaeol. Natur. Hist. Soc.* **110**, 116.

1977 *Iron Age and Romano–British Monuments in the Gloucestershire Cotswolds.* R.C.H.M. *Museums J.* **77**, 80–81.

1980 *Long Barrows in Hampshire and the Isle of Wight.* R.C.H.M. *Antiquity,* **54**, 78.
Stonehenge and its Environs. R.C.H.M. *Current Archaeology* 7(i), 22.

1980 Aubrey, John. *Monumenta Britannica.* I. *Bristol Archaeol. Res. Gp Review.* I, 59.

1980 De Garis, M. *Folklore of Guernsey* (1975); Stevens Cox, J. *Prehistoric Monuments of Guernsey and Associated Folklore* (1976). *Folklore,* **91**, 247.

1981 Evans, Jane. *Worlebury. Bristol Archaeol. Res. Gp Review* 2.

1982 Gray, Irvine, E. *Antiquaries of Gloucestershire and Bristol. Antiquaries J.* 61, 405–6.

1982 Aubrey, John. *Monumenta Britannica.* II. *Bristol and Avon Archaeology* I, 60.

1983 Boon, G.C. *Cardiganshire Silver and the Aberystwyth Mint.* 1981. Nat. Museum of Wales. *Welsh History Review* 11, 415–16.
Darvill, Tim. *Megalithic Chamber Tombs of The Cotswold–Severn Region* (1982). *Bristol and Avon Archaeology* 2, 60–1.
Proceedings of the International Congress of Cultures of the Western Mediterranean. Internat. Folklore Review.
Wilson, D.R. *Air Photo Interpretation for Archaeologists.* (1982). *Bristol and Avon Archaeology* 2, 60.

1984 Lambrick, G. *The Rollright Stones* (1983). *Folklore,* 95, 267.
Sabrafin, G. *Leyends . . . Menorca y Mallorca. Folklore* 95, 134.
Veny Melia, C. *La Necropolis protohistorica de Cales Coves, Menorca. Antiquity* 58, 162–3.

1986 Orfila Pons, M; Sintes Espasa, G; and Taltavull, E. *An Archaeological Guide to Menorca* (1984). *Popular Archaeology*, Dec 1985/Jan 1986.
1987 Bord, J & C. *Sacred Waters. Landscape History* 8, 100.
Kinnes, I.A. and Longworth, I.H. *Catalogue of the excavated prehistoric and Romano–British material in the Greenwell Collection* (1985). British Museum. *Trans. Bristol Gloucestershire Archaeol. Soc.* 105, 251–2.
1988 Darvill, Timothy. *Prehistoric Gloucestershire. Bristol and Avon Archaeology* 6, 74.
Greeves, Tom. *The Archaeology of Dartmoor from the Air.* CBA XIII Newsletter.

iii. *Obituaries*
1968 Dr. D.P. Dobson-Hinton. *Proc. Somerset Archaeol. Natur. Hist. Soc.* 112, 114–15.
1978 Charles Whybrow. *Devon Archaeol. Soc. Newsletter*, October.
1980 Dr E.K. Tratman. *Somerset Archaeol. Natur. Hist.* 123, 145.

iv. *Ephemera*
1929 'Sussex in the Old Stone Age' *Brighton Herald* 9 Nov 1929.
1930 'Prehistoric Falmer'. *Brighton Herald*, 19 April 1930.
1930 'Sussex in the Bronze Age'. *Sussex County Magazine* Nov 1930.
1931 'Barrows and their folklore'. *Sussex County Herald* 23 Jan 1931.
1931 'Barrows of the South Downs'. *Sussex County Magazine* June 1931.
1932 'Regional objects for regional museums'. *Museums Journal* June 1932.
1934 'Downland tumuli'. *Sussex County Magazine* Feb 1934.
1936 'Legend of Wayland the Smith'. *The Open Road*, Dec 1936.
1936 Letter to *The Listener*, 12 August, in reply to review of *The Ancient Burial-Mounds of England*.
1937 Review, 'Arbor Low and Birchover', by J.C. and J.P. Heathcote. *The Open Road*, February.
Review, *The Archaeology of Sussex,* by E.C. Curwen. *The Open Road*, April.
'Barrows and the fairies'. *The Open Road*, April.
1937 'The Coronation Stone'. *The Open Road*, May.
'Druids, Danes and Romans'. *The Open Road*, June.
Review, 'Sixpenny books on prehistory'. *The Open Road*, Aug.
'Stones of Stonehenge'. *The Open Road*, October.
1938 'Dean Hill'. *Antiquarian Journal,** January.
'Field archaeology'. *Antiquarian Journal,** Feb., March & April.
'Antiquary's diary'. *Antiquarian Journal,** May and July.
'Preserving the Ridgeway'. *The Times*, 9 June.
'The Ridgeway and the Icknield Way'. *The Autocar*, 1 July.
Review, *The Dawn of the Human Mind*, by [?] . *Antiquarian Journal,** July.
'The study of prehistory'. *The Spread Eagle* (Barclays Bank magazine), August.
1939 Review, Ancient Monuments guides. *Antiquarian Journal,** January.
'Purbeck prehistory'. *Antiquarian Journal*.
'Avebury'. *The Spread Eagle*, June.
1940 'The country of Richard Jefferies'. *The Spread Eagle*.

1946   'Wiltshire barrows. *Wiltshire Life*, October.
1947   Review, *Field Archaeology* by R.J.C. Atkinson. *Discovery*.
       Review, *Plough and Pasture*, by E.C. Curwen. *Discovery*.
1949   Review, *Ancient Egyptian Materials and Industries*, by A. Lucas. *Discovery*.
1949   Review, *Roman Ways in the Weald*, by Ivan Margary. *Discovery*.
1956   'Field archaeology in Gloucestershire, Somerset and Exmoor'. *Y.H.A. Guide*.
1960   'Exmoor barrows'. *The Exmoor Review*.
1961   'Barrows of the Cotswolds'. *Gloucestershire Countryside*, Sept.
1962   Review, 'The Axbridge Mint' by F. Elmore Jones. *Axbridge Caving and Archaeological Bulletin*, February.
       'Axbridge trade tokens'. *Axbridge Caving and Archaeological Bulletin*, March.
       'Reading the past'. *The Farmer and Stockbreeder*, July, August and September.
1964   'Numismatics in Bristol City Museum'. *Coins and Medals* (Nov).
1967   'The Bath Mint'. Spink's *Numismatic Circular* 75, no 11, 299.
1968   'Barrows as repositories for coin hoards and other treasures'. *Seaby's Coin and Medal Bulletin*, no. 3, 90–91.
1970   'Prehistoric and Roman monuments on Exmoor', in *Exmoor National Park Guide*.
1973   Review, *The Celtic Church in Somerset*, by H.M. Porter. *BARG Bulletin*.
1976   'Later History of some prehistoric sites in Avon'. *Avon Archaeol. Council Newsletter*, May.
       'Burial chambers and stone cists on Dartmoor'. *BARG Bulletin*, Spring.
       Review, *Prehistoric Britain*, K. Branigan, *BARG Bulletin*, Sept.
1977   'Archaeology and Bishop Browne of Bristol'. *Avon Archaeol. Council Newsletter*, Spring.
1978   'The county of Avon and the Druids'. *Avon Archaeol. Council Newsletter*, May.
       Review, *General Pitt-Rivers*. M.W. Thompson, *BARG Bulletin*, June.
       'Development of local archaeology in Bristol City Museum until 1952'. *BARG Bulletin*, October.
       'The continuing need for B.A.R.G.' *BARG Bulletin*, December.
1979   'Exmoor antiquities in popular tradition'. *Exmoor Review*.   Review, *Stonehenge*, by L.E. Stover and B. Kraig. *BARG Bulletin*, April.
1980   Letter, 'The course of the Ridgeway and Icknield Way west of R. Thames'. *Popular Archaeology*, January 1980.
       Review, *Monumenta Britannica*, I, by John Aubrey. *BARG Review*, no. 1.
1980   'Archaeological tourism in Menorca'. *Roqueta*, July.
       'Barrows in the county of Avon'. *Avon Past*, Autumn.
1981   Review, *Worlebury*, by Jane Evans. *BARG Review*, no. 2.
       'The barrow of "The man in the tumulus" of Richard Jefferies'. *Wiltshire Archaeol. Society Newsletter*, March.
       'An archaeological visit to Menorca'. *Roqueta*, September.
       'The naveta of Els Tudons'. *Roqueta*, October.
       Revisions to *The Bath Mint*, by L.V. Grinsell. *Bath & Bristol Numismatic Society Newsletter*, October.
1983   'Stanton Drew: from folk tradition to the New Archaeology'. *Avon Past*, no. 8, pp. 4–8.

'Mitchell's Fold'. *Earthlines*, no. 2.

1984　'Cales Coves: dwellings, tombs, or both ?' *Roqueta*, October.

1985　'The past in West Country Literature'. *West Country Writers' Association Newsletter*.

Review, *The Archaeology of Dartmoor from the Air*, by Tom Greeves. C.B.A. Group *XIII Newsletter*, Autumn. p. 15.

'Death and the after life: the Bristol theme 1955 in Retrospect'. *British Association for the Advancement of Science*, Norwich, Section H. 1985.

1987　'The Hangman's Stone, St Weonards'. *Excursion Guide*, Cambrian Archaeological Association, Hereford Meeting.

1989　Review, *First Light*, by Peter Ackroyd. [A novel dealing with the excavation of a chambered tomb in S.W. England.] C.B.A. XIII *Newsletter*, September.

INDEXES

Archaeological Sites

Abbreviations
clb   chambered long barrow
crb   chambered round barrow
ct   chambered tomb
hf   hillfort
lb   long barrow
rb   round barrow
rsc   recumbent stone circle
sc   stone circle

BRITISH ISLES

ENGLAND
Avon
Banwell caves 67
Dolebury hf 68
Maes Knoll hf 68
Stanton Drew sc 58, 60, 67, 76, 106
Stoney Littleton clb 27, 68
Wansdyke 68
Worlebury hf 67

Berkshire
Lambourn 7 barrows 10
Lambourn lb 10
Sparsholt rb 10

Cheshire
Bridestones clb 66

Cornwall & Scilly
Bant's Carn 92
Innisidgen cairns 92
Porth Hellick cairns 92
Rillaton rb 73
Stripple stones sc 58

Cumbria
Castlerigg sc 61
Hardknott hf 66
Keswick sc 60
King Arthur's Round Table 60, 66
Little Meg 66
Long Meg sc 66
Mayburgh henge 60, 66

Derbyshire
Arbor Low 62
Bee Low 62
Buxton, Lismore Fields 62
Creswell Crags 62
Five Wells crb 62
Green Low crb 62
Minning Low crb 62
Nine Ladies sc 62
Stanton Moor rbs 57, 62

Devon
Broad Down rbs 49
Chudleigh rb 49
Dornafield mounds 49
Farway rbs 56
Hembury hf 73
Kent's Cavern 61
Shaugh Moor 61
Upton Pyne rbs 49

Dorset
Ackling Dyke 40, 62
Cerne giant 94
Deverel barrow rb 110
Dorset cursus 62
Hambledon hill hf 62
Hod Hill hf 62
Knowlton circles 40
Maiden Castle hf 40, 62
Martin's Down barrows 40, 62
Maumbury Rings 40, 62

Oakley Down rbs 39–40, 62
Poor Lot rbs 62
Poundbury hf 62
Sturminster rb 109
Thickthorn lbs 57, 62
Woodyates rbs 57
Wor Barrow lb 57, 62

Essex
Bartlow Hills Roman barrows 58

Gloucestershire
Bagendon 40
Belas Knap clb 33, 40, 61
Bulwarks 58
Chedworth R. villa 40
Corinium 40
Hetty Pegler's Tump clb 58
Hull Plantations rbs 61
Jack Barrow clb 40
Marshfield rbs 26, 27
Nympsfield clb 58
Salmonsbury 40
Sodbury hf 60, 61
Uleybury hf 58, 61

Hampshire
Butser Hill farm project 62, 66
Danebury hf 53, 62, 66
Meare beorg rb 7
Silchester 66

Herefordshire
Arthur's Stone ct 68
Hangman's Stone 68
Sutton Walls hf 93
Treago Castle 68

Hertfordshire
Six Hills Roman barrows 37

Lancashire
Bleasdale timber circle 52

Norfolk
Arminghall 'henge' 57

Oxfordshire
Blowing Stone 10, 12–13, 59
Kingston Lisle rb 13
Rollright Stones 61, 76
Uffington Castle hf 12, 59
Wayland's Smithy clb 10, 11, 12, 59, 77
White Horse 12

Shropshire
Mitchell's Fold sc 41, 76, 97
Offa's Dyke 41

Somerset
Almsworthy Common rb 61
Bat's Castle hf 41
Bury Castle hf 41
Charterhouse-on-Mendip Roman settlement 68
Dead Woman's Ditch 41
Dolebury hf 68
Dowsborough hf 41, 73
Furzebury Brake enclosure 41
Nunney Castle 68
Pool Farm cist 27, 47
Priddy barrows 68, 95
Priddy circles 47, 68
Tynings Farm rbs 27
Wallmead rbs 27
Wookey Hole 67

Sussex
Bevis's Thumb lb 5
Boxgrove palaeolithic site 62
Bow Hill rbs 5, 93
Devil's Jumps rbs 5
Fishbourne Roman palace 62
Hove rb 8
Wolstonbury 2

Wiltshire
Avebury 60, 62
Bokerley Dyke 61–2
Budbury 96–7
Durrington Walls 62
Jug's Grave rb 27
Kennet Avenue 62
Manton clb 38
Manton rb 38
Mere rb 25
Robin Hood's Ball 62
Silbury Hill 62
Snail Down rbs 6, 70, 93
Stonehenge sc 24, 53, 62, 76
Stonehenge rbs 48, 66
Tilshead lb 57
Wansdyke 38
West Kennet clb 62
Whitesheet Hill 25
Woodhenge 62

Yorkshire (North Riding)
Hutton Moor henges 93
Thornborough Rings henges 93

IRISH REPUBLIC
Athgreany sc 69
Castledermot holed stone 69
Four Knocks crb 56, 69
Knowth crb 69
Monasterboice 69
New Grange crb 69
Slieve na Calligh crbs 69
Tara 56

ISLE OF MAN
Ballakelly 60
Braaid sc 60
Cashtal-yn-ard clb 60
King Orrey's grave 60
South Barrule hf 60
Tynwald 60

SCOTLAND
Balnuaran of Clava crbs 62
Broomend of Crichie henge 62
Burghead fort 62
Cairnpapple henge 57, 60
Cullerlie sc 62
Dunadd 57, 60
Dunideer hf 62
Glassel rsc 63
Kilmartin barrows, 57, 60
Loanhead of Daviot rsc 62
Nine Stanes sc 63
Rhynie Man 63
Sueno's Stone 62
Tomnaverie rsc 63
Tormore cairn 60
Woods of Finzean lb 63

ULSTER
Beaghmore 60
Lyles Hill 60
Tievebulliagh stone axe site 60

WALES
Dyfed
Carreg Coetan Arthur ct 59

Cerrig y Gof crb 59
Gors Fawr sc 59
Maen Lwyd 67
Pentre Ifan clb 59
Twlc y Filiast ct 67

Glamorgan
Arthur's Stone crb 59, 60
Carn Bugail rb 60
Castle Ditches hf 60
Cilifor Top hf 66
Parc Cwm clb 59, 60
Penmaen Burrows clb 59
St Lythans clb 59, 60
Samson's Jack 66
Thurba hf 66
Tinkinswood clb 59, 60

Gwent
Caerleon 66
Grey Hill sc 60, 66
Harold's Stones 66
Heston Brake clb 60, 66
Y Garn Lwyd ct 60

Gwynedd
Barclodiad y Gawres crb 58, 67
Bryn Celli Ddu crb 58
Bryn yr Hen Bobl crb 67
Bwrdd Arthur hf 67
Carnarvon Castle 67
Conway Castle 67
Lligwy ct 67
Mynydd Rhiw stone axe site 58
Plas Newydd crb 67
Ty Isaf clb 60
Ty Mawr huts 67
Ty Newydd ct 67

Powys
Pen-y-Wyrlod clb 65
Pipton clb 65
Ty Illtud clb 95

OTHER COUNTRIES

BALEARIC ISLANDS
Ibiza
Puig des Molins Carthaginian cemetery 84

Majorca
Alcudia Roman theatre 84
Almaluttx monolith 85
Cala San Vicente cts 85
Capocorb Vey village 84

Punta de sa Dent quarries 85
Sa Canova talayot 84
Sa Figuera 85
Ses Paisses village 84
Son Boquer (Bocchoris) 85
Son Boscana tomb 85
Son Caulelles tomb 85
Son Oms talayotic site 84

Son Sunyer rock tomb 85
Son Toni Amer rock tomb 85

Minorca
Alcaidus tomb 86
Argentina naveta 85
Biniac naveta 85
Cales Coves rock tombs 85, 86
La Cova naveta 86
Montplé tomb 86
Naveta dels Tudons 86
Rafal Rubi navetas 85
Sa Torreta naveta 86
Ses Roques Llises 86
Son Bou basilica 85
Trepuco village 63

CHANNEL ISLANDS
Guernsey
Dehus crb 58
Les Fouillages 61

Herm
Le Petit Monceau cairns 61

Jersey
Cotte de St Brelade 58
Le Couperon 58
Faldouet 58
La Hougue Bie crb 58, 61
Le Pinacle 58
La Sergenté 58
Mont Ubé 58
Ville es Nouaux 58

CORSICA
Cucuruzzu fort 84
Filitosa 83
Fontanaccia dolmen 83–4
Palaggiu alignment 84
Renaggiu alignment 84
Settiva crb 84
Stantare alignment 84

CRETE
Arkhanes 88
Hagia Triadha 88
Knossos 88
Phaestos 88

CYPRUS
Ayios Agapetikos cave 90
Ayios Lambrianus cave 90
Ayia Solomoni cave 90
Curium 80
Enkomi, tomb 81

Karmi/Palaeolona tombs 80
Khirokitia 80
Kition 90
Myrtou Pighades 80
Nicocreon, tomb of 81
Paphos
    Amphitheatre 89
    House of Aion 90
    House of Dionysos 89, 90
    House of Theseus 90
    Saranda Colones 90
    Tombs of the Kings 80, 89
Salamis 81
Vasilia 80
Vouni palace 80

DENMARK
Fyrkat Viking area 59
Grønhoge 59
Jellinge royal tombs 59
Knebel ct 59
Ladby Viking ship grave 59
Lindholm Hoge Viking cemetery 59
Maglehoge rb 59
Trelleborg Viking site 59
Troldkirchen ct 59
Tustrun ct 59

EGYPT
Abbassieh, granite quarry 18
Abu Gurob, sun temple 15
Abu Roash, pyramid 16
Abusir, pyramids 15
Aswan, tombs of the nobles 30
Beni Hasan, tombs 18
Giza
    pyramids 15, 18
    tomb of Debehen 19–20
    tomb of Seshemnefer 19
Lisht, tomb of Senusret-ankh 20
Saqqara North
    Step pyramid of Zoser 17, 19, 30
    Tombs of Ankhmahor, Mera and Ptah-hotep 20
Saqqara South, pyramids and private tombs 18
Seheil island, rock inscriptions 20
Thebes, temple of Nebhepet-Re Mentuhotep 30
Valley of the Kings
    Tomb of Sety I, 31
    Tomb of Tutankhamun 32

FRANCE
Finistère
Barnenez 91

Ille et Vilaine
Essé passage grave 91
Dol menhir 91, 92

Morbihan
Carnac stone rows 91
Gavrinis 91
Kermario passage grave 92

GREECE
Athens
  Kerameikos cemetery 84
  Menidi tholos tomb 84
Marathon tombs 84
Messinia, tholos tombs 84
Mycenae, tholos tombs 81
Pylos
  tholos tombs 84
  palace of Nestor 84
Tiryns
  citadel 81
  tholos tomb 81

ITALY
Cerveteri tombs 82
Pietrera tomb 82
Populonia tombs 82
Tarquinia painted tombs 82

LEBANON
Byblos 79
Dog River 80
Sidon 80
Tyre 80

MALTESE ISLANDS
Borg en Nadur track 87
Gigantija temples (Gozo) 87
Skorba 86–7
Tarxien 87

NETHERLANDS
Bergeyk 58
Eext hunebed 58
Nordse Veld rbs 58
Papeloze Kerk hunebed 58
Rolde hunebeds 58
Toterfout Halvemijl rbs 58

PORTUGAL
Alapraia rock tombs 91
Alcobertas dolmen 91

RHODES
Kamiros 88, 89
Lindos 88, 89
Monte Smith 89
Yalysos 88

SARDINIA
Anghelu Ruju cts 83
Elephant Rock, tombs 83
Imbertighe giant's tomb 83
Molafá rock tomb 83
Santa Gavino giant's tomb 83

SICILY
Agrigento, Temple of Concord 81
Gela, Archaeol. Museum 81
Palermo, Archaeol. Museum 81–2
Pantalica necropolis 81
Piazza Armerina Roman mosaic 81
Segesta temple 81
Selinunte temple 81
Syracuse 81
  catacombs 82
Taormina theatre 81

SPAIN
Cueva de Menga 63
Cueva de Romeral 63
Cueva de Viera 63
Los Millares 63
Montefrio 63

SWEDEN
Kivik, cairn 93–4

TUNISIA
Carthage 90
Dougga 90
Kairouan 90

Personal Names

Aboudi, M. 17
Addyman, P.V. 60
Allen, G.W.G. 7
Almgren, Bertil 37
  Oscar 37
Anderson, J.R.L. 94
ApSimon, A.M. 105
Armstrong, A.L. 57
Arnold, Dieter 30
Ashbee, Paul 23
Atkinson, Donald 40
  R.J.C. 12, 47–8, 57, 59, 62, 93

Babington-Smith, C. 14
Badawy, Iskander 17
Bailey, Donald 36
Baines, John 53
Balch, H.E. 31
Barton, Ken 29
Bernabo Brea, L. 81
Bishop, C.A.N. 13
Blunt, C.E. 29
Boon, G.C. 66
Bosch-Gimpera, P. 41
Bowden, Mark 61
Bowen, H.C. 66
Bradford, J.S.P. 103
Bradley, Richard 37, 61
Brailsford, J.W. 23, 58
Branigan, Keith 44
Brentnall, H.C. 25
Browne, Charles 71
Bull, J. Mollie 35, 64
Burdo, Father C. 52, 58
Burgess, Colin 44
Burl, Aubrey 62, 63, 97
Burnett, D. 94
Burstow, G.P. 56
Bush, P. 27
Bushell, W. Done 64
Bushell, W.F. 64
Butler, J.J. 59
Butler, M. 12

Calverley, Amice 19
Campbell, John 106
Carnarvon, Countess of 32
Carrington, D. 77, 83

Carter, G.E.L. 56
Case, Humphrey 10
Castaldi, Editta 76, 83
Cerny, J. 74
Cesare, Jean 83
Chapman, Gillian 40
  R.W. 63
Chehab, Maurice 79
Childe, V.G. 5, 52, 57, 63
Chippindale, C. 53, 76
Chitty, Lily 51, 52, 64, 96
Clare, Tom 66
Clark, Grahame 14, 42, 44, 55, 58, 103
Clarke, R.R. 74
Clifford, E.M. 40, 43, 72
Cogbill, Stephen 95
Colbert de Beaulieu, J. 58
Cole, Mavis de Vere 7
Coles, John 50
Cook, J.M. 71, 107
Cossons, N. 106
Cowen, J.D. 30, 60
Crawford, O.G.S. 42, 52, 56, 97
Creswell, K.A.C. 17
Cross, John 103
Cubbon, A.M. 60
Cumming, A.A. 105
Cunliffe, Barry 45, 62, 66
Cunnington, B.H. 24, 25, 26
  M.E. 26, 52
  R.H. 63
Curwen, Eliot 4, 5
  Eliot Cecil 4, 5, 52, 56, 93

Daniel, G.E. 31, 41, 74, 97
Darvill, T.C. 72
Davies, Ellis 58
Delargy, J.H. 77
Dennison, Ed. 68, 105
De Valera, R. 56
Devonshire, Duke of 62
Devonshire, Mrs R.L. 17
Digby, Adrian 33
Diskul, Prince S. 93
Dobson-Hinton, Mrs D.P. 18, 42, 57
Donovan, D. 67
Douch, H.L. 58
Drew, C.D. 8

132

Drioton, Etienne 17
Dunham, Dows 19

Edwards, I.E.S. 14, 19
Eliades, G. 90
Elkington, D. 106
Engelbach, Rex 17
Eogan, George 56, 69
Evans, Sir Arthur 81
    George Eyre 67
    J.G. 60
    Jane 67
    Dr Joan 72

Fairman, H.W. 17, 19
Fell, Clare 61, 66
Filip, Jan 52
Fleure, H.J. 51
Fowler, Elizabeth 105
    Mrs M. 57, 71
    Peter 45, 60, 106
Fox, Sir Cyril 12, 28, 51
    Lady Aileen 49, 56, 73
    James 23

Gardiner, Sir Alan 18, 35
Gardner, Dr Eric 5
    G.B. 12, 75
    J.W. 42
Gaster, Moses 75
Gaster, Theodor 75
Gelling, Peter 60
Gerloff, S. 52
Gettins, G.L. 26
Giffen, A.E. Van 52, 58, 93
Gilchrist, J.S. 103
Giot, P-R. 51
Gjerstad, E. 80
Glanville, S.R.K. 19
Glasbergen, W. 58
Golding, F. 53
Gomme, Lady Alice 74
    Sir Laurence 74
Gracie, H.S. 46, 72
Gray, H. St. G. 47, 52, 58, 104
Grdseloff, B. 16
Green, H.S. 38, 66
    Martin 62
Grimes, W.F. 66
Grinsell family 1
Grosjean, R. 83
Grundy, G.B. 7
Guest, Edith 74
Gulland, Ian 36

Habachi, Labib 30

Hague, Douglas 66
Hamlin, Ann 38
Hancock, J.E. 43, 108
Harris, John R. 31, 35
Hart, Clive 62
Hartland, E.S. 33
Hawkes, C.F.C. 22, 23, 40, 56–7, 66, 75
    C.J. 67
    Nicholas 40
Haynes, J.S. 61
Heathcote, J.P. 57
Hebditch, Max 29, 105
Helbaek, Hans 27
Hemp, W.J. 67, 85
Henshall, Audrey 60
Herity, M. 69
Hernandes Mora, J. 86
Hill, Sir N. Gray 103
Hoare, Sir R.C. 24
Holland Martin, R.M. 12
Holleyman, G.A. 56
Hooke, Della 50
Hooper, Dr W. 5
Howell, Roger 84
Hughes, Thomas 11
Huntingford, G.W.B. 12, 33
Hurst, John 41
Hutchinson, P.O. 49
Hyndman, H.M. 95

Iles, Rob 106
Inglis, J.A. 64

James, E.O. 75
Jarmain, John 95
Jessup, R.F. 50
John, Mary 94
Jones, Barri 106
    T. Herbert 19
Joyce, Major & Mrs 40

Keiller, A. 52
Keimer, L. 16
Kempson, E.G.H. 25, 42
Kendrick, Sir T.D. 23, 27
Kenyon, K.M. 55, 93
Kersting, A.F. 19
King, D.J.C. 68, 69
Kinnes, Ian 61, 91

Lacaille, A.D. 74
Lake, H. Coote 74
Lake-Barnett, H.A. 77
Langmaid, Nancy 38
Lauer, J-P. 19
Lawson, Andrew 61

Leeds, E.T. 11
Legg, Owen 94
Leibovitch, J. 16
Le Rouzic, Z. 92
Liddell, Dorothy 73
Lively, Penelope 94–5
Lucas, A. 17, 19
Luke, Sir Harry 80
Lynch, Frances 66, 67, 69

McBurney, Charles 15
McGrail, Sean 53
Mapp, C.R. 30
Mascaro Pasarius, J. 85, 86
Martin-Atkins, E. 10, 11
Maryon, H. 28
Mayes, Stanley 31
Megaw, Basil 60
Mekhitarien, A. 16
Mercer, Roger 62
Merrieson, Sir A. 107
Meyrick, O. 25
Minns, Sir Ellis 41
Moberg, A.C.A. 94
Modderman, P.J.R. 58
Moore, Donald 67
Morey, June 35
Mullard, J. 97
Murray, K.C. 33
   Margaret 36, 77, 86
   W. 11
Mynors, Sir Humphrey 68
   Sir Roger 68

Nankivell, Florence 64
Neale, Frances 105
Newall, Venetia 77
Noble, Frank 41, 65

Oakley, K.P. 75
O'Farrell, R. 69
O'Neil, Bryan 35, 47
   Helen 35, 40, 43, 47, 72
Opie, Peter 77
Organ, R.M. 28
O'Riordain, S.P. 56
Orme, Bryony 61
O'Sullivan, S. 77

Passmore, A.D. 24
Patchett, F. 35
Peake, H.J.E. 10, 11, 43
Peers, Sir Charles 24
   Roger 40
Peretti, G. 83–4
Petch, Dennis 66

Petrie, Sir Flinders 15
   Lady 104
Phillips, C.W. 11, 23, 103
Piggott, C.M. 93
   Stuart 10, 11, 12, 22, 23, 25, 57, 60, 62
Pitts, M. 48
Powys-Lybbe, U. 14
Preston, F.L. 57
Proctor, G.L. 37
Pugh, C.W. 23, 70
   R.B. 23
Pull, J.H. 43

Quinnell, H. 73

Radford, C.A.R. 25, 67
Raglan, Lord 75
Rahtz, P.A. 67, 68, 96, 105
Reece, Richard 40
Renfrew, Colin 44
Richards, C. 68
Richardson, Sir Albert 36
Richmond Brown, R. 15, 18, 104
Ritchie, Graham 62, 63
Rynne, Etienne 56, 69

Salzman, L.F. 8
Sanderson, S.F. 8, 97
Saville, Alan 61, 72
Savory, H.N. 65, 66, 67
Scott, Sir Lindsay 52, 55, 57, 103
Seaby, W.A. 6
Seavill, E.W. 106
Selkirk, Wendy 108
Senogles, H. 104
Serra, M.L. 85
Sewell, Barbara 35
Shaw, Thurstan 73
Shefton, Brian 32
Sheppard, Ian 62, 63
Sherwin, G.A. 8
Shortt, H. de S. 25, 57
Skelton, R.A. 42
Smith, Dr Isobel 106
   Ken 62
Stanford, S.C. 68
Storrs, Sir R. 19
Straw, Allan 49, 61
Stylianou, A. 80
Sumner, Heywood 45, 48

Taylor, Arnold 67
   Christopher 47
   Herbert 26, 27
   Michael 46
Thomas, Nicholas 25, 39, 40, 93, 107, 108

Thomson, T.R. 25
Tonkin, J.W. 68
Tratman, E.K. 27, 47, 60
Trump, David 86
Tucker, J.H. 67
Turner, J.R. 49
Tyler, F.C. 96
Tymms, Simon 73

Underhill, F.M. 6, 10
Underwood, Guy 27, 96

Varley, W.J. 52
Vatcher, Major 66
Vince, Alan 38

Wace, A.J.B. 17, 81
Wainwright, G. 97
Waldren, W. 63
Wallace, Patrick 69
Wallis, F.S. 27, 31, 71, 104
Warhurst, Alan 33, 72, 96, 104
Warren, Prof. P. 15, 84, 108

Waterbolk, H.T. 58
Watkins, Alfred 68, 97
Wedlake, A.L. 40, 41
  W.J. 27, 68
Wheeler, Debby 69
  Sir R.E.M. 7, 67
Whittle, Alasdair 37
Whybrow, Charles 47
Wickham, Prof. Glynne 107
Williams, David Price 96
  Cdr E.H.D. 68
  J. Gwyn 68
Williams Freeman, J.P. 7
Wills, Sir E. Chaning 49
  Jan 72
Wilson, Sir David 42
Woods, Gertrude 73
  Roland 73
Woolley, Sir Leonard 27
Woolner, Diana 12
Worth, R. Hansford 49, 56
Wymer, John 13

Zammit, Charles 86